Too Much is Never Enough

Too Much is Never Enough

Morris Lapidus

RIZZOLI
NEW YORK

Contents

1. A Pyramid in Brooklyn   9

2. Russian Roots and New York Ghetto Life   15

3. Uncle Harry   31

4. Hospitals   39

5. Acting   51

6. Architecture School   59

7. First Jobs   71

8. Marriage   79

9. New Theories in Store Design   87

10. The 1939 World's Fair and Independence at Last   115

11. A Protégé, Charlie, and the Sans Souci   135

12. The Fontainebleau   157

13. The Hotels and the Critics   183

14. More Commissions and a Book   225

15. Two Exhibits   249

16. A Most Unusual Building and a Return to the Theater   261

17. Africa, Another Exhibit and a Last Hotel   275

18. Life After Architecture   289

Epilogue   295

Bibliography   298

List of Works   300

Index   302

To the memory of Bea

First published in the United States of America in 1996 by
Rizzoli International Publications, Inc.
300 Park Avenue South, New York NY 10010

Library of Congress Cataloging-in-Publication Data

Lapidus, Morris.
    Too much is never enough : an autobiography / by Morris Lapidus.
        p.   cm.
    Includes bibliographical references and index.
    ISBN 0-8478-1978-7 (HC)
    1. Lapidus, Morris.   2. Architects—United States—Biography.
I. Title.
NA737.L32A2   1996
720'.92—dc20   96-13259
[B]   CIP

Designed by Hahn Smith Design, Toronto

Printed and bound in Hong Kong

Front jacket illustration: Morris Lapidus in front of the Aruba Caribbean Hotel, Aruba, 1957.

Frontispiece: Entrance, Eden Roc Hotel, Miami Beach, 1955
p. 4: Lobby, Fontainebleau Hotel, Miami Beach, 1954
p. 7: Lobby, Eden Roc Hotel, Miami Beach, 1955

" **The Free Spirit is the spirit of Joy.** "

Louis Sullivan, *The Autobiography of an Idea*

Public park and swimming pool on Kosciusko Street, Bedford-Stuyvesant, Brooklyn, designed by Lapidus, 1958–60.
Children can jump off the concrete pyramid at lower right to a strong cargo net at the bottom.

1 A Pyramid in Brooklyn

On a bright summer day in 1969 I found myself on a concrete platform fifteen feet above the sweltering pavement of Kosciusko Street in Brooklyn. The small platform crowned the top of a three-sided, stepped, concrete pyramid that contained the bath houses of a large swimming-pool park I had designed in Bedford-Stuyvesant, a black ghetto then as it is now. On a sudden impulse, I decided to visit the park I had designed ten years before. As I stood there, sixty-five years old at the time, I was surrounded by gleeful, shouting black young-sters who had scrambled up to the top of the pyramid. Once at the top, they had the choice of climbing down again or jumping off the fourth side — a sheer per-pendicular wall. Knowing the unrestrained daring and energy of these young-sters, my son Alan and I had designed this sheer wall with a stout cargo net at the bottom as a challenge. To these youngsters it was a challenge they could not resist, a challenge of fear and bravado as they hurtled to the net below. They stood at the edge of the platform to wait their turn to jump — and jump they did.

In 1958 the newly appointed Commissioner of Parks for New York City was Thomas Hoving, the son of Walter Hoving, chairman of Tiffany's. Hoving, a member of New York's elite, had the novel idea that the architect who designed luxury hotels for the wealthy should design a park for the people living in Bedford-Stuyvesant, the poorest area of Brooklyn. Commissioner Hoving (later the director of the Metropolitan Museum of Art) invited me to have lunch with him at The Inn on the Park, a restaurant in Manhattan's Central Park, and asked if I would design a swimming-pool park in Bedford-Stuyvesant. He wanted me to use the same approach for this park that I had used for the Fontainebleau Hotel in Miami Beach and other opulent hotels I had designed. Although taken aback by this odd proposal (I had never designed a park), I read-ily agreed to accept the commission. I did so for two reasons: first, the challenge of a project for which I had no previous experience, and second — unknown to Hoving and more important to me — a good part of my youth was spent grow-ing up in this very neighborhood before it became a ghetto.

The commissioner told me that he wanted a park built of concrete without a single blade of grass or a single tree. Keenly aware of the rough, destructive nature of youths at play, he made many suggestions for facilities that could become outlets for their boundless and occasionally violent energy. In addition to an Olympic-sized pool—which would become a huge outdoor ice-skating rink in winter—and a smaller diving pool, he wanted to create an open neighborhood meeting place suitable for many and varied activities. He wanted structures the children could climb on and hang from, even seemingly dangerous structures; enclaves where street gangs could congregate and stay off the streets; places where neighborhood clubs could gather, as well as large bleachers for watching swimming and diving meets. In short, it was to be a most unusual, and at the same time a most attractive, park. It was to be all out in the open, a Roman forum for adults, teenagers, and children.

When my preliminary plans and full-color perspective presentations were ready, Commissioner Hoving arranged a meeting with the leaders of the black community. After my presentation, which met with grateful acceptance and praise, Hoving rose to address the group. He said he wanted to give the people of Bedford-Stuyvesant the amenities that were usually enjoyed only by the wealthy. All he asked of the black leaders was their cooperation to control the sometimes destructive nature of the youngsters in the neighborhood. All those present pledged their support and gave us their assurance that everyone, young and old, would be not only cooperative but also enthusiastically helpful. We left the meeting with high hopes of creating a unique park, which would be Hoving's first completed project as commissioner.

When the plans were ready, the contract awarded, and the work finally started, everything that could go wrong did! On three successive occasions during the early stages of construction, night watchmen, all black men, were attacked and had to be hospitalized. One almost died. The contractor, then unable to secure the services of watchmen, decided to get fierce watchdogs to keep people away from the job site during the night. Each dog was poisoned, but somehow the work went forward despite the constant vandalism.

One night just after the excavation for the large pool had been completed, the towering crane used for digging toppled into the hole. Was this the cooperation that we had been promised? Only a large gang of powerful men, pushing and shoving, or perhaps somehow starting the motor, could have overturned the crane. Instead of completing the project in the year called for by the contract, we took more than two years. But our troubles were not yet over. Once the project was practically finished, the plumbing contractor began installing the nickel-plated shower heads and faucets, locking the toilet and shower rooms each night to prevent pilferage. In the morning the plumbers found that the doors had been forced open and all the shower heads and faucets removed. A platoon of police then guarded the project around the clock until the park was opened with much fanfare and a neighborhood celebration.

Ten years later, I went back and climbed the pyramid to watch adults and children enjoying the park and the swimming and diving pools. As I stood there, I looked to my right, where I could easily see Brooklyn Boys High School, my alma mater. This venerable structure of learning for countless generations of Brooklyn boys had been built in the middle of the nineteenth century. To my left, I could clearly see the streets of the old Williamsburg section, where I had first entered P. S. 2 in 1909 to begin the process of turning an immigrant youngster from Russia who spoke no English into an American. For a moment I forgot the shouting children who surrounded me, and once again I found myself, in my mind, entering the school on that humiliating, awful day, my first day in strange and frightening surroundings, my first day at school.

"Memory," wrote Cicero, "is the treasure and guardian of all things." For almost sixty years I had buried this awful memory in my subconscious. I dreaded that January morning in 1909 when for the first time I was thrust into the maw of the New York City public school system and the unfriendly arms of my young peers. My apprehension and excitement produced the natural result: I just had to go to the toilet. My Uncle Harry had instructed me that all I had to do was raise my hand and get the teacher's attention. But then the whole class would know of my predicament. I debated going up to the teacher and whispering to her — but whisper what? And how? I knew no English; she understood no Yiddish or Russian. So I just sat there, striving with every fiber of my will to overcome my urge. I failed and was sent home, clothes soiled and reeking, disgraced! I cried all the way home.

Once again I became conscious of the black kids surrounding me on the platform. As I climbed down from my perch on the pyramid, my mind raced back to long-forgotten memories.

Many years have passed since that day of pilgrimage to the park in Bedford-Stuyvesant, and the harder I have tried to push back my early memories, the more they have haunted me, demanding to be relived. But what are these memories that keep insisting on being remembered? They are the memories of the immigrant child whose roots go back to the Russian pale, who dreamed and believed in the American dream. They are the dreams of a growing boy who hoped against hope that he would find success and happiness when he grew up. There are also the memories of the young man, an American trying to overcome his adolescent feelings of inferiority and timidity, seeking fulfillment in his chosen profession. Finally, there are the memories of a seemingly mature man, now an architect, striving for recognition and even acclaim through his buildings — structures in which he tried to convey a feeling of joy.

In 1970 it seemed that I had achieved my goal when the Architectural League of New York, a prestigious group that included architects, artists, and related professionals, voted to give me a one-man show. It was to be an exhibit of all my work — architecture, interiors, and paintings. Entitled "An Architecture of Joy,"

"*I readily agreed to accept the commission for two reasons: first, the challenge of a project for which I had no experience, and second, a good part of my youth was spent growing up in this very neighborhood before it became a ghetto.*"

the show included photographs, photo murals, and multicolored and multi-screened projections of every phase of my work through the years. A few years later, I was the only American architect invited to have his own installation, among dozens of architects from around the world, in an international exhibit in Linz, Austria. These events allowed me to believe that I had succeeded in my hopes and dreams of creating a fine body of architecture. But the old memories still persist, and the harder I try to push them into oblivion, the more they demand to be relived. "We are the real you, do not forget us. We formed you, we fashioned the man you are today. Remember us." If I am to find the puzzle and the paradox of my life and career, I must permit these memories to resurface in order to set down what took place so many years ago. The memories are of a boy who went further than his wildest and most impossible hopes and of a man who went as far as he dreamed he would in an American Dream.

Lapidus's father, who had the rank of the highest non-commissioned officer in the Russian army, and his mother, a seamstress, in a wedding photograph, 1901.

The first memories of my childhood come floating back like the lifting wisps of a morning mist. I was a toddler, insecure in my newfound ability to walk, looking for something to play with. Toys were still unheard of. I toppled over and fell with a crash, trying to reach for whatever it was. Mama, hearing me fall, came running to see if I had hurt myself. "What were you looking for, *mine hertsala*?" (Yiddish for "my little heart"). I looked up at her with solemn eyes and said, "I found a place to sit." This childish wisdom convinced Mama that I was destined to become a brilliant man. This is my first and earliest recollection, remembered or repeated by Mama so often that I really thought I remembered it.

An earlier memory, and perhaps truly my first, is of sitting on the steps of a stoop leading up to the tenement house where we lived. (Stoop is probably derived from *Stoep*, the Dutch word for the broad flight of steps leading up to the veranda at the front of houses in Holland.) I sat there, knees hugged to my chest, beset with real or imagined fears, dreaming of escaping the noise, confusion, and strangeness of my squalid surroundings. Sitting on those steps, I developed an intense dislike of the world in which I found myself.

I sat there trying to recall the stories I had heard about a faraway place I had come from, the story of my beginnings. My father's father and my father were born in a small town in what is now Kurland. The language they spoke was German, even though Kurland was part of Russia. My paternal grandfather started life as a farmer but went on to become a saloon keeper. In those days, Jews were not allowed to operate taverns, so, in effect, my grandfather was running an illegal grog shop. It must have been a rough, wild existence. My father remembered that his father had had an eye gouged out in a drunken brawl. My father, though, at an early age, learned to read and write Russian. But at the age of nine, his formal education ended when he became an apprentice to a coppersmith.

My mother's parents came from Lublin, a town in Poland. While still a child, my mother was taught to sew, and she became an accomplished seamstress. Her father was a tailor who sewed costumes for the theaters in Poland and Russia. He died of throat cancer. From my mother's stories, I have a vivid picture of this stoical old man sitting at a table sewing whenever the pain would let up. The spreading throat cancer made it impossible for him to lie down. Night after night, he would sit at the table dozing as he rested his head in his hands with his elbows propped up on the table. He never went to a doctor. If it was God's will that the agony of the spreading growth in his throat would eventually choke out his life, then that was the way it had to be. One morning his family found him dead, still sitting upright, his head in his hands and his elbows still on the table. His wife, my mother's mother, had died long before. When I was born, I was given his name.

As I was growing up, my father often told me of his early days as an apprentice. Once he had been turned over to the coppersmith, he became a member of that man's household. At first, he was able to see his parents each Sabbath. But soon his saloon-keeping father moved to another town, too far away for a one-day visit. He heard of his father's death from a traveler who happened to recognize the name. When my parents married, my father's mother came to live with them, but she died before I was born.

The status of an apprentice in the latter part of the nineteenth century was not much better than that of a slave. My father, the youngest apprentice, slept on a bench in the coppersmith's shop. In the morning he was required to fetch water and wood for the coppersmith's wife. Then he would sweep the shop and start the charcoal fires in the small stoves used for heating the soldering irons. This work had to be finished by the time the master and the older apprentices finished their breakfast. Then he was allowed to go to the kitchen and eat what porridge and black bread was left. There never seemed to be enough to eat. My father grew only to a height of five feet two inches, but he became an expert in the craft of coppersmithing. When he reached the age of fourteen, he was given a salary of a few kopecks a week. Military conscription finally took him away from his master and his hard lot of incessant toil.

Most Jews in Russia dreaded being conscripted into the czar's army. Some saved as much as they could so they could be smuggled across the border and out of Russia. Many made it, but some were caught and a few were shot. Others chopped off their right forefingers or their toes, making them useless for the army. My father, however, looked forward to being conscripted. For him it would be like a vacation. Young Jews usually hated the army, not only because of the unaccustomed hardships they endured but also because they were forced to eat non-kosher food. For the Orthodox Jew, this was a fate worse than death. As far as my father was concerned, whether he ate pork or other ritually forbidden food was of little consequence. What mattered was that there would be food — plenty of it. And so my little father donned the too-large, ill-fitting uniform of a soldier in the Royal Army of the Holy Czar. Life in the army was hard, but there was food and a bed and a warm stove in the winter. Papa often spoke of his military service as one of the most wonderful times of his life. He even achieved the rank of the highest non-commissioned officer — an unheard-of event in those times for a Jewish person.

After leaving the army, my father settled in Odessa. He set up his own coppersmith shop and, eventually, married his sweetheart, my mother. In 1902, less than a year later, I was born.

The first years of the twentieth century were hard for Jews in Russia. To placate the Russian peasants in their miserable existence, the czar allowed pogroms in which Cossacks with lead-tipped whips rode into Jewish communities, slashing and whipping any unfortunate Jew who happened to be in the streets. Peasants followed — robbing, burning, pillaging — thus having something to take their minds off their hunger and poverty. Even killing was legal in the ghettos. But many Christians hated the unjust treatment of their Jewish neighbors and often warned the Jews of an impending pogrom. They also loaned Jewish families crosses to nail to their doors so that their houses appeared to be occupied by Christians.

My mother, ecstatically happy with her firstborn child, heard of the pogroms and atrocities in the small towns and hamlets. She wondered what would happen if the Christians of Odessa were to rise up against their Jewish neighbors. And then came the pogrom in the city of Keshinov, one of the bloodiest and most horrible. Jews were slaughtered by the hundreds. My mother, fearful for the future of her child, pleaded with my father to emigrate to America.

My father objected, saying he did not know anyone in that strange land, and that since his shop was doing so well, why should they leave home? He told her the trip would be fraught with danger and uncertainty; he also reminded her that they had little money. He tried to reassure my mother by predicting that the czar would soon stop the terrible pogroms. He reminded her that he had been an officer in the Russian army.

There was no placating my mother. She had made up her mind that her son was not to grow up in a land where Jews were beaten and killed. She had heard that in America no one asks if you are a Jew; everyone is equal. She insisted that my father sell his shop, sell everything we owned. She told him to borrow money from friends and family that we would pay back once we got our start in the New World.

My mother prevailed. Everything was sold. Train tickets were bought to take us to Antwerp, the port from which the ship sailed. Passage in steerage was paid for. We needed only a few clothes, but we had to take enough food for the entire trip. We were Orthodox Jews, and my mother would eat only kosher food; she had halted her husband's dietary indiscretions. Baskets were loaded with loaves of rye bread, herring, and kosher salamis. Fruit could be bought on the way. Then came the tearful farewells. My parents were the first of their families to leave for the New World. Brothers, sisters, aunts and uncles — all were left behind. My father promised to work hard so that he could make

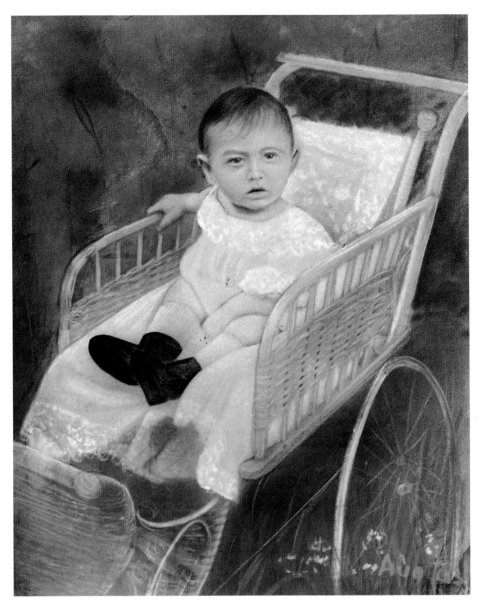

Morris Lapidus, 9 months old, 1903.

"A week after we arrived in America, my mother, so proud and happy, had a street photographer take this picture of me at nine months of age, seated in my Russian carriage. The photographer used pastel to suggest a bucolic setting even though I was on the sidewalk of an East Side ghetto."

money to repay his debts; then he would start saving so that he could send money for passage to America for the rest of the families.

For endless days we traveled by train through Russia, then Germany, and finally through Belgium to Antwerp. In July 1903, we boarded the *Kronberg*. Crowded like cattle in the steerage quarters below decks, my parents endured the misery of ten days at sea. They refused the food which they were entitled to; only boiled potatoes were considered kosher. These, along with the herrings, salamis, and the stale bread dipped in free tea, made up their daily fare, washed down by an unlimited number of glasses of tea with free sugar.

At the end of the trip came the confusion of disembarking and the bewildering process of being admitted to the shores of the land where they said everyone was equal. This process, my parents told me, took place in "Kesselgarten." For years, I heard the term Kesselgarten used to denote a place of clamor and confusion where immigrants disembarked and were finally admitted to America. Years later I learned that the place they were referring to was called Castle Garden, located at the tip of Manhattan in New York harbor. Not only was their pronunciation wrong, but they had actually disembarked at Ellis Island, not Castle Garden.

My family was met by some friends from Odessa who had emigrated the year before. And so began our lives in the new country, the land of golden opportunity. There was a saying in Russia that the streets in America were paved with gold, but my parents found no gold. There was crowding, noise, dirt, hard work, and little money. But my mother was happy. Her son would grow up in a country with no pogroms, no Cossacks with lead-tipped whips, in a land where everyone had a chance, the land of the free.

We stayed at the home of the family from Odessa until my father found a job. The first week in New York he was hired as a coppersmith, and we were able to move into an apartment of our own — our first home in this new land — in the ghetto of the Lower East Side. The shop where my father worked made oil carriage lamps that were in demand for the new automobile industry. He worked for a Jewish immigrant named Becker who had come to America a number of years before. After a few years carbide gas was substituted for oil, and the Becker company grew as the demand for carbide headlights increased. Eventually my father became the foreman. Within ten years the storage battery was invented, and a few years later electric light was used for the new headlamps in the growing auto industry. My father was made a partner in the new firm, the B & L Auto Lamp Company.

Outside our apartment building on the Lower East Side was the pungent smell of herring and fish. But an even stronger smell was the ever-present odor of horse droppings. The streets were always crowded with horse-drawn trucks and carts in endless procession. Every morning, white-clad street cleaners wearing white helmets would trundle their cans and brushes on wheeled carts along the streets, which would remain clean until the next horse came along.

Fruit and vegetables piled on pushcarts were always a show. The women, with their inevitable shawls over their heads, would study the prices and the merchandise on display. Looking was not enough. Each piece had to be smelled, pinched, and poked. No pushcart peddler was going to palm off any rotting fruits or vegetables on them. Rising above the hubbub were the strident, hoarse voices of the peddlers shouting, "Don't touch! Don't squeeze! You are ruining me!" The high nasal voices of the women were no match for them. "You *gonif* (thief), trying to sell me rotten tomatoes, wormy apples, moldy potatoes for my good money. You should be ashamed of yourself."

Between the rows of pushcarts that lined both sides of the street came an endless stream of horse-drawn wagons. The "whoa" and "giddyap" of the drivers, the cloppety-clop of the horses' hooves, and the raspy grinding of the steel-bound wagons wheels on the cobbled streets almost drowned out the shouting of the pushcart peddlers. As if this eternal din were not enough, there were the ice trucks, with the endless cry of icemen shouting, "Ice, who wants ice? Ice, I got ice," and in winter, his shouts of "Coal, coal, nice black coal for your stoves." Then there were the secondhand clothes dealers wandering down the streets and carrying shoulder packs, whining their own sales pitch, "I cash. I cash clo's: I cash." Syrian immigrants, with trays of sesame candy carried on their heads, added their plaintive cry "Turkish candy. Turkish candy." In the summer, cold drink vendors with copper tank dispensers strapped to their backs called, "Col' drinks, col' drinks." In the winter, enterprising merchants had sheet-metal ovens mounted on wheels with several drawers or trays. In the bottom tray glowed a bed of charcoal with a flue coming up through the top of the tin stove. Above the charcoal, drawers pulled out to display the wares: baked, hot sweet potatoes and hot knishes. These merchants had their own special call: "Hot knishes, hot knishes — I got 'em all. I got potato, I got kasha. I got knishes — delicious knishes — knishes like Mama bakes."

How much more pleasant it was to stay upstairs with Mama in our own flat, a haven of peace and quiet. I always preferred to stay with her rather than go downstairs to play. I loved every moment of my mother's cooking and baking, which she did on a black iron stove heated with a coal fire. During the winter, I loved to stay near the stove while pots cooked, boiled, and bubbled, while the *challah* (a double-braided loaf of bread) and cakes slowly browned. In the summer, it was insufferable.

On Fridays the final preparation for the Sabbath took place. Mama would ask me to leave the kitchen so she could wash the floor. After she scrubbed it on her knees, using a scrubbing brush and Octagon soap, she spread newspapers to make sure that the floor remained spotless until Papa came home and we sat down to the Sabbath meal.

When this chore was finished, Mama filled a large tin tub with hot water in order to take her weekly bath and wash her hair. During this operation, I was banished to the bedroom. When she was done, it was my turn to be scrubbed and combed. If there was any question in Mama's mind, she added a little kerosene to the water when she washed my hair to make sure that there were no lice. After Mama washed my hair, she would comb it with an exceedingly fine comb to make absolutely certain. Lice were a common affliction in tenements. If she found one—and find them she did—she crushed it with a fingernail.

Sometimes I was permitted to polish the heavy brass candlesticks that Mama had brought as a part of her dowry. Then the Sabbath cloth was spread. During the week, we used an oilcloth table cover, but on Friday night, a fine linen cloth was placed on the table. The places were set, the candles prepared for lighting, a bottle of sweet red wine was put out for the blessing of the "fruit of the vine," and the freshly baked *challah* was put in the center of the table and covered with an embroidered cloth. And the drip pan under the icebox was emptied.

Every other day, the iceman brought up a cake of ice to our flat, carrying it on his shoulder on which he had placed a burlap bag to absorb the water from the melting ice. The icebox was a four-foot-high wood chest with a hinged cover on top. The pan under it had to be emptied every morning and evening; forgetting this meant a flooded kitchen. The flypaper, with its week's catch of flies (no one had invented screens for the windows) was discarded and fresh flypaper set out. More than once, however, I forgot that it was on the dining-room sideboard—getting stuck on it was a messy operation. But finally everything was ready to usher in the holy Sabbath.

After Papa came home, he washed and combed, and when he came to the table, we were ready to celebrate the Sabbath. Mama lit the Sabbath candles, covered her head with a small shawl and, holding her hands before her face, closed her eyes and uttered her own special prayer. On this important occasion, I thought she could speak directly to God. She never told us what she was murmuring, but she must have told God about her trials and tribulations in this new land and asked for His help, asked Him to bless us all, to keep us well. I am sure that the last thing she did was to thank God for those blessings that were hers— her husband, her children, and her home in America. On Fridays, I simply refused to go downstairs to sit on the stoop.

Sunday was the day that Papa usually stayed at home; sometimes he had to go to work in the morning, but Sunday afternoons were his time to go to his *traktier* (a Russian tea house). The *traktiers* where Russian Jewish immigrants gathered were the equivalent of English pubs. Unlike a pub, however, the strongest drink available was Russian tea, *Russki-Tchai*. On one particular autumn Sunday afternoon, Papa took me by the hand, and we walked several blocks to his favorite *traktier*, leaving my pregnant mother and my baby brother, Ben, at home. *Traktiers* were an exclusively male domain.

"My painting shows the East Side streets where I grew up.
I used Bettmann Archive photos to create the atmosphere of those ghetto streets.
I am the little boy in the lower right-hand corner."

My World at Five. Painting of the Lower East Side by Lapidus, 1973.

Many Russian Jewish immigrants were homesick and found a little touch of the old country at a *traktier*. During afternoons and evenings, they would gather around charcoal-heated samovars to drink glass after glass of strong, scalding Russian tea. A contest of sorts would take place to see who, in a group, could drink the most tea. Letting the glass stand while the tea cooled was an admission of weakness. Foot-high loaves of sugar (cubes were still in the future) were broken into bits. Each tea drinker would hold a morsel of sugar between his upper and lower teeth and sip the steaming tea, passing it through the sugar to sweeten it. This was known as *porusski*, the Russian way of drinking tea.

As glass followed glass, the men would reminisce about life in the old country and their own particular *shtetels*, or small towns. Forgetting the poverty and the cruel anti-Semitic restrictions of the czar, they often asked themselves why they had left their old homes and their close communal life where everyone knew everyone else, where everyone was ready to help a neighbor in times of trouble. Why had they left behind the holidays with their special foods, the wonder of Passover, and the holy atmosphere of the Sabbath, the weddings with plenty of food and drink and dancing until dawn? Here in this strange, crude, noisy America, it was all gone. There were no cool forests to walk in, no green fields. In winter the snow was dirty and gray. They talked of the open countryside where you could see the sun sink behind the dark green forest. In New York, the tall buildings hid the sun. They talked of how they would walk through the village streets at night with soft candlelight illuminating the windows, the bright moon lighting their way.

One man talked of his years in the synagogue studying the Talmud and the Bible. He would start his studies by candlelight early in the morning before sunrise and continue until the candles were lit once again when the sun set. His life was filled with philosophical discussions and holy thoughts, not this bitter life of toil and struggle. There was no time now to think of God while working in a sweatshop sewing clothes, making paper boxes, operating machines. The bosses here were no better than the Cossacks in Russia.

Another man spoke of his farm, his cows, and his chickens. You worked hard, but there was always bread and milk and eggs. You could see trees and sky. Here there were only tenements and crowded streets.

No matter how often I heard them, my father's stories of life in the Russian army were the most fascinating of all. Papa would start talking about his experiences as a Russian soldier. The colonel of the regiment needed a new bathtub, he would begin, and as he told the story I practically stopped breathing. The officers were instructed to seek out a competent coppersmith in their ranks to make it. As luck would have it, Papa was the only coppersmith in the regiment. He was warned that if the tub had any seams or scratchy surfaces, the colonel would order him off to Siberia. With this admonition still in his ears, my father started his task. He had learned his trade well. He hammered and soldered, creating the finest bathtub he had ever made. When it was finished, the entire regiment waited for the verdict while the colonel took his first bath. The colonel bellowed for "that Jew." The sergeant booted my father out of the ranks, remarking that Papa would soon be with the bears in Siberia.

But my father did not go to Siberia. The colonel was delighted with his bathtub, and soon my father was making tubs for the generals. From then on the Russian peasants and *mujiks* that made up most of his regiment showed him more respect. At meals he was among the first, along with the biggest and brawniest members of the regiment, to dip his tin cup into the huge pot of borscht. Those who dipped their cups first got most of the *khrochunkos*, or meat; the others had to be satisfied with the cabbage and potatoes that were left. To this day, I remember the taste of Russian soldier borscht (our name for it). My father taught my mother how to make it. And she, in turn, gave the recipe to my wife. Made with meat, cabbage, potatoes, and plenty of mouth-burning spices, it can bring tears to the eyes of strong men.

When my father's reputation as a master craftsman and coppersmith came to the attention of the officers in charge of the Russian munitions factories, he was reassigned to the division that fabricated field kitchens for the Russian army; soon he was in command of the entire mobile field-kitchen operation.

The Russian army at that time was in a deplorable state. The Russians asked the French army to send experts and officers to help reorganize and modernize the Russian forces. When a group of these French specialists and officers arrived for an inspection of the munitions shop where my father had become shop foreman, the head of each department was asked to accompany the group on their tour. When they came to the field-kitchen plant, my father, a buck private, was ordered to accompany the inspecting party. The French officers, thinking that a mistake had been made, asked why the officer in charge of the kitchen plant was not present. They were told that the head of this special division was a private. The Frenchmen were aghast—an army private could not be in charge of a department. They were told that he was the best man available.

The logical French insisted that he be made an officer because no modern army could, or should, allow a private to take charge of a division; in order to command respect, they reasoned, a division head must be an officer. Even though a Jew was not allowed to hold any office in the czar's army, the French argued that a modern army must have an officer in charge. Since my father could not be replaced by an officer, there was no choice but to make him one, probably the first Jew in the entire Russian army to be raised above the rank of private. Because it was impossible to give him a commission, they raised him to the highest non-commissioned rank, equivalent to sergeant major in the U.S. Army.

Besides the three gold-braid stripes on his epaulets and the special cap, he was issued a sword and a horse; most important for my father, he was issued rations of the strong black tea leaves reserved for officers. The small leaves, and the tea dust from the bottom of the tin boxes in which the tea was shipped to Russia from China, were issued to the enlisted men. My father never mounted his horse. He fed the animal and curried him but never rode him. He did wear the sword, however, when he went on leave. He wanted to impress his friends and especially the girl he hoped to marry — my mother.

My father and his cronies would sit in the *traktier* stroking their mustaches, drinking tea, telling stories. So the hours would pass as I inhaled the pungent odor of smoldering charcoal, lulled by the murmur of voices speaking of strange places and creating beautiful pictures in my imagination.

Mama, too, had her dreams of the good life that she had left, the old country, the old ways. Often she was jealous that Papa had a retreat away from the crowded noisy tenement, a place where he could escape the reality of their lives in America.

My mother had two sisters and two brothers living in New York, all of them recently arrived from Russia. Another sister had moved to a faraway place called Cleveland. She died many years later without my ever having known her. My mother had yet another sister, but I was a young man before I learned about her. When the Bolsheviks overthrew the czar and took over Russia in 1917, my mother mentioned this sister for the first time as she wondered about her well-being. "What sister?" I wanted to know. And then I was told the story of a sister who was dead but still alive.

Marcia, my mother's oldest and prettiest sister, was a highly talented seamstress. Her services were in demand by the wealthy Russian women in Odessa who lived in the upper city, the elegant, Paris-like part of Odessa. Mama's family lived in the lower city near the waterfront, in an area known as "unter de Treppe" (Yiddish for "below the steps"). Marcia was asked often to come to the homes of the wealthy, where she learned to enjoy the life of the Russian upper class. The elegant homes, the fine food, and the servants were things that did not exist in the life of an ordinary Russian Jew. She was especially welcome in the home of a family with a fine young son, an officer in the czar's army. This dashing young man, with his blond mustache and his brightly colored and gold-braided uniform, fell in love with the black-haired, dark-eyed Jewish seamstress. At first, Marcia was too timid even to speak to the handsome scion of this wealthy family who had fallen in love with her. But she, too, found herself deeply in love. The parents of the love-smitten lad urged the young couple to get married. There was, however, the problem of religion. Marcia would have to convert to the Catholic faith of the Eastern Orthodox Church. Conversion in the latter part of the nineteenth century for an Orthodox Jew was literally a fate worse than death. It meant not only that Marcia must renounce her religion, but also that she would have to forsake her mother, her father, and all of her family. For them, she would be as one who had died.

Marcia loved her family dearly. To stay with them meant poverty and the isolation of the pale, the Jewish subworld. Marrying her young Russian officer would open doors to luxury, a gay social life, and, above all, the acceptance to the wonderful opulent life that was *Bella Russeya* (Beautiful Russia).

My Orthodox grandfather, proud of his Judaism, spoke of the wonders of the God of Moses, who had sustained and preserved the Jews through thousands of years of torture and persecution. He talked to her of the peace that would be hers in the bosom of her faith. He made her understand that much as he loved her, his firstborn, once she married a gentile, she would never be allowed to return home. All her brothers and sisters and her mother would be forbidden to see her, to talk to her, or even to mention her name ever again.

Wealth, position, acceptance, and, above all, love won out. The sad day Marcia bade her family farewell forever, my grandfather, in the tradition of the Jewish faith, picked up a knife and cut the hem of his coat, a symbolic act in the tradition of the biblical "he rent his garments." He then cut a part of the garments worn by each member of the family.

The entire family observed a week of mourning, "sitting *shivah*" (seven). All mirrors in the house were covered. Ashes were strewn across the floor, and the entire family ate and slept on the floor. No one was permitted to sit on a chair. Neighbors brought food to the bereaved family; no cooking was permitted. Each morning and evening, at sunrise and sunset, a group of ten men (the minion) would come to the house of mourning to recite the *kaddish*, the prayer of faith offered in honor of the dead.

Thirty years later, my mother could not help worrying and wondering how her sister would fare under the harsh revolutionaries in Russia. The stories of the brutal treatment of the Russian aristocracy by the Bolsheviks filled my mother and her siblings with a desire to do something for their long-lost sister who might now be in dire need. But there was nothing they could do. They had lost her forever.

At home, Papa would read the *Jewish Daily Forward* aloud to Mama while she prepared breakfast. Mama had not been taught to read, and Papa dutifully read the paper to her every Sunday morning. Along with most of the Russian Jewish community in America, my mother followed closely the story of Mendel Bayliss, a poor, uneducated Jew in Russia who was accused of the ritual slaughter of a Christian child. His imprisonment was a severe setback for the starving Russian peasants and an excuse for pogroms. Many years later Mendel Bayliss was given a retrial and released.

The janitor of our tenement was a bitter Pole whose only pleasure was getting roaring drunk on Saturday nights and beating up his wife. He was a sour individual whom we children hated and feared. "Stop running around the yard you Jew brats!" he would scream. "No make noise. Shaddup!" To escape him, we raced around the building. I was the youngest and the smallest, and though I tried to keep up with the rest, I always ended up at the end of the line. One day, the janitor had just finished scrubbing down the hallways. He stood with his pail of soapy slop water at the top of the stairs leading from the side entrance to the side-yard alley below.

"I teach you rotten Jew kids to stop yelling," he shouted, and with that he hurled the contents of his pail at us. Being the last one to pass, I got hit with the whole pail of filthy water. For a moment I was too stunned to move. The liquid not only drenched me from head to foot but also filled my ears, my eyes, and my open mouth. I thought I would drown. I fought for breath. Then I screamed. All the mothers came running. It took a little time for my mother to realize that the drenched youngster was her own child. She was furious. So were all the other mothers. "Go get a policeman," Mama shouted. "Make him arrest that Jew-hating, wife-beating Pole. Run, somebody, and find the policeman on the corner."

While I stood there dripping wet and crying, the policeman appeared. It took him some time to understand the half-Yiddish, half-English demands that he arrest the janitor. Soon the entire procession moved toward the police station a block away. We stood in front of the desk sergeant, who was trying hard to understand in the midst of the uproar. One of the mothers acted as interpreter. He finally explained that it was necessary for my mother to fill out a complaint, and then the police would issue a summons for the janitor to appear in court. The complicated procedure did not take into account that my mother could not write. In the end, the janitor, by now completely subdued and fearful of the police, swore by his holiest saint that he would never do it again.

A year or so later we moved. On our new block, as in all ghetto neighborhoods, the children had no playground except the sidewalks in front of the tenements and the empty lots. The empty lots, which were dumping grounds for the neighborhood, were sources of unexpected treasures. A discarded broom handle would be pressed into service as a bat. A short piece of stick became our ball. One day six of us, all boys, found a real treasure — a roller skate. We took turns riding with the one skate on one foot while propelling ourselves with the other.

We soon moved again, this time to the Bronx. Papa had a good steady job, but the hours were long and the pay just enough to live above the poverty level. Feeding, housing, and clothing three children and two adults meant careful budgeting. The summer was ending, and Mama began to worry about outfitting us for the High Holy Days. For my brother and me there were new knickers and new shoes and stockings to be bought. Mama sewed all our white cotton blouses.

One Sunday morning before the holidays, Mama decided to dress my younger brother, Ben, and me in our new outfits. She wanted to see how nice we looked, and she probably also wanted the neighbors to see how well dressed her children would be when they went off to synagogue with Papa.

It was a lovely fall day. Mama told us to go out to the park but to make sure that we did not soil our clothes or scrape our new high-buttoned brown shoes.

Ben and I walked along the paths of St. Ann's Park, kicking the brightly colored autumn leaves along the way. We came upon a grassy hillside with a large outcropping of shiny black rock which extended from the top of the hill down to the grass bordering the path where we stood. The surface of the black rock was as smooth as glass. Children were climbing to the top of the hill, squatting on the rock's shiny surface, and sliding down at incredible speed. At the bottom they jumped, just as they reached the lower grass area. They were having a wonderful time, shrieking as they hurtled down this natural slide.

At first Ben and I just watched. Mama had warned us to stay out of mischief and to keep our new clothes clean. But the temptation was more than we could bear. We climbed to the top of the hill and waited our turn to slide down the rock. When my turn came, half afraid and half excited by the prospect of this beautiful ride down to the grass below, I sat down and started the descent. Never had I experienced such a thrill. I could hardly wait my turn when once again I climbed to the top of the hill. Soon Ben and I were experts, shrieking with wild abandon as we sped down the wonderful shiny black rock over and over again. Finally, the sun began to sink and the air became chilly. We left St. Ann's Park and hurried home, happy as any two little boys could be.

At first I could not understand the horror Mama's face showed as she saw us come through the door. I felt that something was terribly wrong, but what could it be? "Look at your clothes! My God, what have you done? Where have you been? How could this happen? What will I do now? Where will I get money for new clothes?"

She burst into tears. What had we done? I looked at Ben and myself. The seats of our new knickerbockers were worn through so that our underdrawers showed. The backs of the black stockings no longer existed. The soles of our cheap high-buttoned shoes were completely worn through. And the backs of our new blouses were in shreds. Mama stood wringing her hands. Then she became furious. "Into the bedroom, you offspring of Satan. I'll show you what it means to break your mother's heart."

We scurried into our bedroom, trembling with fear, waiting for something terrible to happen. Mama came in with the strap. She began beating us with a fury I had never seen before and have never seen since. The strap caught us on our backs, our arms, our shoulders, our faces. Sobbing hysterically, she just kept repeating "Why God, why?" and hitting us again and again. At last she was spent. We had welts all over our bodies. The strap had caught me across one eye. It was puffy and black and blue. Sobbing with pain and the injustice of how we had been punished, I found myself repeating over and over again, "I hate her, I hate her. I hope she dies. I hate her."

My brother kept saying through his sobs, "You mustn't say that. God will punish you."

"I don't care what God does. She has no right to hit us like that. I hate her."

Soon all was quiet. I had no more tears. In the kitchen, we heard Mama preparing the evening meal. Soon Papa would be coming home. He had worked all day this Sunday. The door to our bedroom opened. Mama had dried her tears. She had washed her face and combed her hair. She looked at us with a face filled with pain and remorse. "Oh, my poor little children. What have I done to you? You know Mama loves you."

Coney Island, New York, c. 1907

*"Before I could close my gaping mouth and get my eyes accustomed to these wonders,
we were in a new world of wonders and miracles: Coney Island."*

3 Uncle Harry

Uncle Elya, my mother's youngest brother, was the first relative my father brought over from Europe. He must have been eighteen, although to me he was a mature man. Young and aggressive, he learned to speak English almost immediately. By this time we had moved to South Fourth Street in the Williamsburg section of Brooklyn, just a few blocks from the East River. Uncle Elya lived with us in our flat. He was the first of an endless line of boarders who shared our cramped tenement quarters, but he spent most of his time outside our ghetto.

One quiet Sunday morning after breakfast, Uncle Elya announced that he was going to show me the world. Although he told Mama that we were going to the river to see ships from all over the world, we did not stop there. The nearly completed Williamsburg Bridge, which connected Brooklyn to Manhattan, was Uncle Elya's destination. I wanted to stop and rest and look around, but Uncle Elya kept urging me on.

After a while I was too tired to walk any more. So Uncle Elya took me in his arms and hurried along the wide walkway until we reached the very center of the awesome span. And it was wonderful. Overhead was a cloud-flecked sky. The summer sun had turned the river into a glistening mirror reflecting the blue of the sky. Strung along the wharves on both shores were ships from faraway places. Masts and spars and riggings of the cargo schooners created an intricate, patterned, lace-like border along the docks and quays. Cargo was piled high on the docks and in front of the warehouses. Summer sun and Sunday's quiet, the high-vaulted heavens and the placid river formed a huge mural of breathtaking beauty. Standing between the sky and the river, I felt like a soaring bird. Far below me were the river, the docks, the peaceful streets of Brooklyn, and the empty streets of Manhattan. Now and then, a trolley rumbled by, disturbing the delicious silence of our airy perch. Standing out like a totem towering over the skyline was the Singer building, the tallest building in the world, twenty-five stories high. For the first time I heard the phrase *himmel kratzer* — Yiddish for skyscraper. Uncle Elya put the idea in my head that I too could build a skyscraper — maybe even higher than the Singer Building, because in his view anything was possible here in America.

Uncle Elya's inquisitive mind made him curious about every facet of life in America. He enrolled in night school for immigrant adults. He read everything he could find about his new country, its people, its history, its traditions. He seemed to know about everything. Everything was a source of merriment for him. America was his first love, and it was a love affair that lasted throughout his life.

"So look at him," my mother would say, "a real Yankee Doodle Dandy."

"That's me, my darling sister, I am a Yankee, and from now on, no more calling me Elya. From now on my name is Harry."

So, he became Harry. My own Uncle Harry.

Uncle Harry died years ago, but he will forever be my fairy godfather. He eventually married and had children of his own, but the young Uncle Harry never grew up, he never died. He remains in my memory as a teller of tales and a maker of miracles.

Uncle Harry introduced me to the world of cowboys and Indians and the Wild West. He told tales of the early West, the intrepid settlers, and those romantic heroes, the cowboys. Then would come the stories about the American Indians, wild, naked red men with fierce eyes and deadly tomahawks. It took a whole evening of explaining just to make me understand the word *tomahawk*. All these stories were told in Yiddish, the only language I used.

To explain the word *tomahawk*, he took me down to our tenement's cellar. There he found the ax the janitor used to chop the wood that started the coal stoves in our flats. Uncle Harry picked up the ax and began splitting wood. By this time, I had developed a healthy respect for the cleaving power of a hatchet. Then he playfully swung the ax in my direction. I was terrified. Now I realized what a deadly weapon a hatchet could be, and a tomahawk was like a hatchet. He then told me about scalping, how Indian braves would take the top of the head and hair of the defenseless settlers they killed, including little boys.

But there was always a reason for Uncle Harry's stories. He knew that in Coney Island that summer there was going to be a presentation of Buffalo Bill and his Wild West Show. One fine Sunday that summer, he took me for my first elevated train ride from Williamsburg to Coney Island. This would be a day of miracles. High above the street, riding over the low rooftops at what seemed to me an incredible speed, I was struck by a delightful terror that the rushing train would leave the tracks and hurtle to the streets below.

Before I could close my gaping mouth and get my eyes accustomed to these wonders, we were in a new world of wonders and miracles: Coney Island. I had my first sight of a merry-go-round and a roller coaster. I knew what a horse looked like, the heavy plodding animals pulling wagons on our street, but the glorious merry-go-round horses, with their jeweled trappings, their flashing eyes, and their flowing tails, were nothing like the horses I knew. Other creatures whirled by—lions and swans—and the beautiful animals seemed to come alive as the merry-go-round turned faster and faster.

I was trembling with fear and expectation as Uncle Harry strapped me firmly to the jeweled saddle of a beautiful white horse. I do not think that I breathed during the entire ride. My legs trembled as I stepped down from the magic carpet when the ride was over. I felt that I could spend the rest of my life riding that glamorous horse as it raced through space, seeming to dance in perfect rhythm to the glorious cacophony of the music from the merry-go-round calliope. I had seen myself reflected in the twinkling facets of the mirror that formed the center of the merry-go-round. It was another me riding a fiery steed through a world of dreams.

On the roller coaster people rode in little wagons. I watched as they went higher and higher on tracks supported by gossamer trestles, until they nearly touched the sky. Then there was that breathless moment when they hung poised between heaven and earth before taking that horrible plunge to earth and, I was sure, to instant destruction. But this was the land of wonders. They rose again unharmed. Uncle Harry wanted to take me for a ride on the roller coaster, but I was terrified. What if the little wagon never came down but kept going up and up until it disappeared into the sky? What if it crashed as it hurtled to the ground?

Uncle Harry then hurried me to a place high up on a sort of grandstand. In front of us was an arena. Off to one side was a house of cloth. I was mystified. How could it stand? I had never seen a tent before. A flourish of bugles sounded, and before my startled eyes came a wagon train, horses, women, children, and—cowboys.

Out of nowhere came a bloodcurdling sound, the Indian war whoop. I watched breathlessly as the wagons were maneuvered into a circle and the few brave cowboys, long guns ready, crouched behind the wagons. Then they came, naked Indians riding wild horses, swinging their tomahawks. The scene in the cellar with the hatchet flashed through my mind. I clung to Uncle Harry, afraid to look and yet unable to keep my eyes off the action below us. Although the little band of brave cowboys did their best, they were outnumbered. Soon would come a terrible massacre. Why did all the people watching just sit there? Couldn't they help do something? Just when everything seemed lost, there was a great shout, and before our bulging eyes a posse of cowboys came dashing out on their beautiful horses. Leading them was Buffalo Bill himself. He was dressed from head to toe in white, fringed buckskin, riding a pure white charger. The Indians were all killed; the settlers were saved. The great Buffalo Bill, hero of story and legend, rode toward the grandstand. He doffed his tall white hat and bowed. He had shoulder-length white hair, a flowing white mustache, and a full white goatee. It was scores of years later that I learned that the beautiful man, Buffalo Bill (William Cody) was a habitual drunkard and had to be tied to his saddle to keep him from falling off his horse. Like the real trouper he was, he would go through his derringdo, take his bows, and then ride back to

Coney Island, New York, c. 1907

*"Luna Park was like an earthly paradise for me.... For the first time in my life,
I experienced the excitement of electric light. A million glittering lamps outlined towers,
minarets, domes, arches, the weird twisting roller coasters, the revolving ferris wheels,
all the fantastic structures on this island of marvels."*

the tent, where he would be lifted off the horse and promptly pass out until he was roused again for his next appearance.

After the Buffalo Bill Wild West Show was over, Uncle Harry took me on a tour of Coney Island. Luna Park was like an earthly paradise for me, with flowers and trees and fairy-tale castles of pastel hues and all the colors of the rainbow. Gondolas propelled by gondoliers floated on an artificial lake. Steeple-chase, with the face of a grinning clown as big as a house over the entrance, was a wonderland of whirling, tumbling, speeding, and spinning fantasies. A street called the Bowery promised wonders, freaks of nature, dancing girls, mysteries, and laughter. Signs strung between buildings announced German food, Chinese food, photos, and moving pictures. For a penny I was able to look through a peephole and see a camel crossing a desert. Surf Avenue was a street of delicious smells: the sweet smell of spun candy being made before my unbelieving eyes, popcorn with its bursting fragrance, hot ears of sweet corn cooking in huge vats, and the palate-teasing fragrance of frying frankfurters.

By now the sun was setting. Uncle Harry and I walked along the sand, watching the white-topped waves chasing each other as they hurried to tumble on the beach. He stretched out his arm toward the ocean and told me that beyond it were Europe and Russia and Odessa, where I was born and where Mama and he had grown up. Then it was time to eat before starting home.

He took me to a place called Feltman's. It was huge, with countless tables and chairs and mirrored walls and columns. Mustached waiters in white aprons were scurrying everywhere, trays raised high, carrying platters of food and mugs of foaming beer. Uncle Harry had a pork sandwich and a mug of beer. I ate a frankfurter and drank lemonade.

When we were ready to get on the elevated train for our ride home, we stood on the platform waiting as the lights of Coney Island were turned on. For the first time in my life, I experienced the excitement of electric light. A million glittering lamps outlined towers, minarets, domes, arches, the weird twisting roller coasters, the revolving ferris wheels, all the fantastic structures on this island of marvels. Here, instead of the flickering gas lights like those that lit the streets where we lived, were brilliant lamps brighter than the moon and the stars in the heavens.

Many years later, where Luna Park once glittered, high-rise apartments I designed were built. By an implausible twist of fate, I planned a large housing complex where Steeplechase had stood. Little did I dream, as I stood on the train platform that evening with Uncle Harry, that all this wonder would vanish and that I would be the architect to replace much of the glittering splendor with mundane housing for thousands of people. The development is called Trump Village, built by Fred Trump, father of Donald Trump.

I never consciously tried to create a version of Coney Island in my architecture, but its wonders and beauties, as seen through the eyes of a child, are echoed in a good deal of my work. Consciously or unconsciously, I try to recapture the glamor and joyous wonder I experienced as a child.

I had been attending school for more than a year when I first heard the word Christmas. Being Jewish, and living in an insulated ghetto, I knew nothing of Christian ways and Christian holidays. Little by little, the story of Christmas and Santa Claus began to produce a picture in my childish mind. It was Uncle Harry who filled my ears with the miraculous doings of Santa Claus. He made the old gentleman with the ruddy cheeks, the red nose, and the white whiskers as real as the fat mustached policeman on the corner. What miracles he performed! He brought toys to children! Toys, those wondrous things I stared at in store windows but never owned. Red, cast-iron fire engines, little fur-covered horses with wagons, jumping jacks in their brightly colored boxes. I had seen these, and I had asked my parents for them, but I learned that shoes and stockings were more important. Toys were for the rich, and we were really poor. As Christmas approached, Uncle Harry told us more and more wondrous stories about the patron saint of all Christian children, Santa Claus. How we wished that the miracle of Christmas could occur in our house. Then came the most unbelievable part of Uncle Harry's stories. Santa Claus loved all children and, if we were good, Santa would visit us on Christmas Eve. Santa, he told us, would come down the chimney and leave toys and candies for us. How could he possibly do that? The chimney in our cramped tenement flat was connected to the only heat we had, the kitchen stove. How well I remember that black monster and my mother's constant ministrations with the stove polish until it shone in all its ebony splendor. Certainly Santa could not squeeze through that small chimney in the stove and enter our kitchen.

Then came the day before Christmas, a cold raw day with a thin snow sifting down from leaden skies to hide the ugliness that was everywhere. And now it was evening, and we all sat around the kitchen table. When Uncle Harry told us to hang up our stockings, we had the same disbelief. Santa Claus might come to the homes of Christian children but not to us. Urged on by Uncle Harry, and now even by our parents, we finally hung our stockings on chairs placed as close as we dared to the hot stove. Of course, I knew that they would be hanging there limp and empty the next morning. Wonders like this never happened. I knew of miracles but none like this.

Our parents finally got us to bed, but I was too excited to fall asleep. Away from the kitchen stove, our bedroom was bitterly cold, but that did not stop me from crawling out of bed to stare up at the black sky with its sparse falling snow. Could there really be a Santa Claus with his tiny reindeer racing through the sky, leaving presents for children?

I could think of only one thing as I wakened that Christmas morning: those long black stockings hanging so empty and forlorn in the kitchen. I just could not make myself get out of bed; the disappointment would be too hard to bear. Why had Uncle Harry filled our heads with such nonsense, Santa Claus, toys, candy? On the other hand, my Uncle Harry had shown me such wonderful new things — the circus, Coney Island — perhaps there really was a Santa Claus. Hardly breathing, I crept out of bed and tiptoed into the kitchen. Till all my Christmases have run their course, I shall never forget the wondrous sight I saw. The stockings were bulging with toys and candy, and a small Christmas tree gleamed with tinsel and snow! Garlands of popcorn and striped candy canes had made a fairyland of our little kitchen. There was a cast-iron, red fire engine for me, a little wagon for my brother, and a doll for my baby sister — toys and treasures beyond belief. My shout of joy awakened the entire family. There never was such a Christmas. Though the years soon disillusioned me about Santa Claus, they never robbed me of my belief in wonders. Life has brought its joys and its sorrows, but always there are new experiences, new joyful things that come to all of us who believe in miracles. What a fortunate child I was to have had an Uncle Harry who taught me to believe and to find joy and wonder in so many ways.

Lapidus family photograph, 1910.

"To celebrate my recovery from my accident and the arrival of my new relatives, we went to a photographer's studio for this picture. Top row, from left: my mother, my cousin Bernardo, my Bolshevik uncle [Harry] (a friend of Lenin), my Brazilian aunt. Second row: My father and my Brazilian uncle, a gaucho. Bottom row: me, my baby brother Sol, my sister Lily, and my brother Ben."

4 Hospitals

I was eight years old when we moved again to the Bronx to East 138th Street. Once again we found ourselves in a low-rent tenement. One of the first boys that I met on our block was Mikey, who told me about the railroad tracks and trains several blocks away from our house near Brooks Avenue. Mama absolutely forbade me to go with Mikey to see the tracks. Each time Mikey spoke about the trains, my resolve to disobey my mother grew. The final story that Mikey told me broke down my resistance and won me over. Beyond the tracks were fields of flowers.

The only flowers I had ever seen were geraniums growing in pots on fire escapes during the summer. I had also seen beautiful flower wreaths at funerals and weddings. A few times I had had the opportunity to smell their perfume but I had never held a flower in my hand.

The day Mikey was going to take me to the tracks, I found him waiting for me downstairs, and with a sense of high adventure we began to walk to the forbidden land. We finally came to a stone wall that separated the end of the street from the embankment that led down to the gully where the tracks ran. At last, there they were, those shining ribbons of steel, stretching as far as my eyes could see. I stood with a wildly beating heart, my eyes fairly popping out of their sockets. The tracks seemed to start out wide, but as I looked off into the distance they kept getting closer and closer, until finally they converged to a dot way out on the horizon as the tracks seemed to meet. Marching along the side of the tracks was a parade of telegraph poles moving toward the point where the tracks came to a dot and disappeared. They stood like soldiers with their arms stretched out high in the air. On each arm there were glistening glass buttons shining in the sun. To these buttons were fastened gossamer thin wires that ran from pole to pole until they, too, like the tracks, came to a mysterious dot way off on the horizon. Everything seemed to join together at that mysterious point —the railroad tracks, the poles, the wires, the roadbed with its black wooden ties that looked like a ladder laid down under the tracks. I stood there trying to figure out why everything came together at that little dot way out there on the edge of the world. I wondered whether I would get smaller and smaller if I were to walk along the tracks until I became just a dot at the end of the line. Years later I would understand, when I learned the secrets of perspective and that mysterious vanishing point to which all lines lead.

It was a peaceful summer day. Overhead, clouds like baby sheep drifted slowly toward the same little dot on the horizon as if they, too, wanted to join the parade of the telegraph poles and the tracks. Big fat horseflies buzzed around us with a lazy curiosity. There were no noisy horses or wagons on the street. A warm sun and a gentle breeze made the newfound world of the railroad tracks a place of peace and awe for me. Mikey and I sat on the stone wall, our eyes and ears straining to see the first train go by. Finally, way off in the distance a whistle sounded — my first train whistle — an unforgettable sound. Since I heard that first whistle I have traveled extensively by train; still, whenever I hear a train whistle I get a feeling of exhilaration. A train whistle has many voices. There is the mournful tone of the whistle heard in the dead of night as the train hurtles through a sleeping, snowbound town. Then there is a joyous sound as the train approaches a crossing in an open field and the commanding tone, telling passengers to get aboard after the train has stopped at a station.

Finally, the train hurtled into view. I saw the huge black monster of a steam engine, with its great wheels, its powerful driving pistons, the steam, the smoke, and the wondrous sound of a speeding locomotive. All too soon it rushed by, followed by the mail car, the baggage cars, and, at the end, the passenger cars. It was all there, just as Mikey said it would be. The locomotive steam engine seemed all whirling wheels and black steel, more terrifying than the fire-breathing dragons in the fairy tales I had read. Behind it came the cars with all the people sitting and reading and talking — even eating. Finally, with a rush of sound the train was gone, hurtling down the shining tracks, getting smaller and smaller until it too disappeared into the little dot where the tracks and the telegraph poles and the wires ended. I sat there wondering where they went when they came to that little point way off there. Did the train and all those people become so tiny that they vanished, just like when the evil witches in my fairy tales made people disappear? This mystery puzzled me and was the cause of recurring dreams for years.

Mikey wanted to go, but I wanted to wait for another train, so we sat there in the warm sunshine, kicking our heels against the wall. After a while we got tired of just sitting so we got up and walked along the top of the narrow coping of the wall, balancing ourselves with outstretched arms. I felt like a tightrope walker in the circus. Far below me on one side were the tracks, and on the other side was the street. When we tired of this sport we resumed our waiting, sitting on the wall, looking to the left and to the right, waiting for the next train to come by. Time lost all meaning for me; how long we sat there I do not remember. It must have been several hours. Eventually another train came by and then another. When the wonder wore off, I suddenly remembered the flowers. Mikey told me we had to cross the tracks, so off we went on the other side of the tracks, and there they were — flowers, millions of them. There were white ones that looked like small, white lace doilies and yellow ones that looked like little dabs of butter climbing up a green stem. There were blue ones and some bright red ones. As the breeze blew over them they seemed to wave toward me, inviting me to come and look at them and smell them. I stood and stared. It was like a dream. Could there really be so many flowers in the world?

Feverishly I began to pick those beautiful wild flowers. At first I picked those nearest me. When I had an armful I became more discriminating. I wanted to make sure that I had some of each color. I began to discard some and to select more carefully. I wanted to bring home a bouquet that was varied and beautiful. I wanted the most beautiful bouquet of flowers in the world for Mama.

At last my final selection was made. It was huge bouquet. I could hardly see over it as I followed Mikey back over the tracks and scrambled up the embankment. Mikey held my bouquet as I climbed over the wall. And now I wanted to get home as fast as I could to show Mama all these beautiful flowers. At last I was approaching the corner across the street from my own block. By now I was running, running breathlessly with my precious armful of beauty. Just across the street, then into the house, and up the stairs to my mother.

My eyes were still closed, but I knew that I was awake. I heard a murmur of voices, strange voices. And what were those oddly disturbing smells? Slowly I realized that I was not in my own bed at home. I tried to remember when I had gone to sleep. I wanted to get up, but I could not move. I felt a warm liquid slowly trickling out of my ear. Finally I opened my eyes. I was lying on a floor. It was a cold, white tile floor. There were many people standing around me. I began to cry. Why were all those people staring at me? Why was I here?

A man in a white uniform was speaking. I looked around and saw my mother. Why was Mama kneeling beside me and crying? Then I saw a policeman. And now I recognized those strange smells. I was lying on the floor in a drugstore. Then I remembered the train tracks and the field of flowers. Where were my flowers? What was I doing lying there on the floor? Who had brought me here? Who are all these people? Why was the big policeman standing there bending over me? Who was the man in white with those black tubes in his ears? How had I gotten here, and why were they all staring at me? What was the warm trickle of something running out of my ear? I tried to speak. I wanted to know what was happening — why was I there — but no words came out. I could only lie there and look and wonder.

Everything blacked out again. I have no recollection of the ride to Lincoln Hospital. I vaguely recall being put on a stretcher as they took me out of the ambulance. Then I was wheeled from one awesome room to another. Men in white looked at me, touched me, and finally put a big black object over my head for a few minutes. Then I was wheeled through long corridors, and at last I was put into a bed. For a while I remembered nothing, but when I opened my eyes my mother was sitting beside me. I tried to speak. I wanted to tell her about the flowers — those beautiful flowers.

Later I found out what had happened. I was running across the street with my precious armload of flowers. This was in 1910 and brakes on the new automobiles were a sometime thing. The driver could not stop. I was struck down, and there I lay, unconscious, flowers strewn all around me. People came running. I was carried into the corner drugstore. Mikey ran to get my mother. By the time she reached to the drugstore, the police and the doctor and the ambulance had come. There followed the ride in the ambulance and I finally arrived at the hospital. Diagnosis: a fractured skull, bleeding from one ear. Condition: extremely critical.

The days in the hospital ward seemed endless. I was in a large room with about twenty beds backed against the two long walls. A pair of doors was at one end of the room. A nurse in white sat in front of them. Everything else in the ward seemed to be green: the floor was dark green, highly waxed linoleum; the walls were pale green; the ceiling was a lighter shade of green; even the beds were green. Attached to the foot of each bed was a board with papers clipped to it. At night when the lights were turned off, the green world disappeared. Only a red glow was visible at the end of the ward where the doors were.

Little by little I became conscious of the people in the ward. On one side of me was a man who remained in a coma during my entire stay in the hospital. Now and then a nurse would place a white painted screen around this man. A young doctor in white and a nurse would bring in pans and trays, and I would hear the man groan as they did things to him. I was afraid to look. Only once did I manage to open my eyes and look behind the screen. It was a horrifying experience. The doctor was inserting a tube into the man's erect penis. It was the first time I had seen a male organ in full erection. The unconscious man groaned in agony as the tube was inserted. I closed my eyes and looked no more. On the other side of me was a young Italian boy of my own age. He had a broken leg, but he was allowed to hobble around the ward.

When my food trays came I could not eat, which was just fine with the Italian boy, who ate everything on his own tray and then everything on mine except the bread. In the hospital, I discovered a new kind of bread. At home we ate cornbread and rye bread and crusty rolls that were baked fresh every night in the neighborhood Jewish bakery. The only other bread was the Sabbath *challah* that Mama baked. Here in the hospital we were served Ward's Tip Top bread; it was the first factory-baked bread I had ever eaten. I thought that it was delicious. It was the only food I ate during the six days I remained in the hospital. My infatuation with this soft, white, tasteless bread did not last long after I left the hospital.

Sick, frightened, lonely, afraid, most of the time I lay in my hospital bed staring at the green ceiling in my green world. I felt as if I were suspended in a plate of pea soup. When Mama was not there sitting beside me, I would cry. My Italian friend tried to cheer me up, but all I wanted to do was to go home and be with my Mama and Papa. The only comfort I had during my first few days in the hospital was the fact that my parents could come and visit me at any time during the day or night. Mama would come as early as she could after finishing her daily chores and arranging to leave my two brothers and sister with neighbors. She sat by my bedside for hours. We did not talk much. I was happy to have her near me. At night Papa would come. We had little to say to each other, but Papa's nearness was all that I needed. Tony, my Italian friend teased me about the fact that I must be a privileged character. All the other patients in the large ward could have visitors only at specified hours but my mother and father could come any time they wanted to. It made me feel happy to know that I was so privileged.

One day I waited and waited for Mama, but the hours dragged by and she did not come. I lay there crying, wondering if Mama had forgotten about me. Tony tried to console me, but I was inconsolable in my loneliness and grief.

Late that afternoon during the normal visiting hours, Mama came into the ward with the rest of the visitors. She had come to the hospital earlier, but they told her that she could visit only during the regular hours. Mama imagined that something terrible had happened to me. It was only years later that I learned that the unlimited visiting privileges were for patients who were on the critical list and were not expected to live. When I was no longer in danger — the fracture in my skull was knitting well — I was taken off the critical list. Doctors tell me that mine was a most unusual case. A fractured skull accompanied by bleeding from an ear is almost always fatal. I was one of the lucky ones.

The next evening Papa and Uncle Harry came to the hospital with a bundle of my clothes. The lights had been turned off, and the nurse who was sitting in the red glow at the doorway came to my bed with Papa and Uncle Harry. She simply said, "You can take him home now." Papa helped me to get dressed as I sat there in my bed. I was deliriously happy at the thought of getting dressed and getting out of bed, out of the hospital, away from all these things that were alien to me, away from this frightening atmosphere of doctors and nurses and sick people. I had not been out of bed for six long days. As soon as I had my clothes on, I slipped off the bed ready to run home. My legs failed me, and I found myself in a heap on the floor. Papa bent down and took me up in his arms.

At last I found myself back at home, the most wonderful place in the world. It was a memorable evening. While I had been in the hospital, a newfound uncle and aunt and cousin had arrived from South America. It was all so exhilarating and exciting — home at last with Mama and Papa, my brother Ben, my little sister Lily, my baby brother Sol, my wonderful Uncle Harry, and the new relatives. Papa laid me down on the sofa, and Mama fussed over me to make sure that I was comfortable. I was the center of attention. I was introduced to my new uncle and *tante* and my cousin, Bernardo. Only Bernardo could speak English. Uncle Victor and Tante Etta spoke in Yiddish. No one in the family understood their Spanish. Mama insisted that I eat her delicious chicken soup with noodles. I had to get my strength back again.

Soon after my return from the hospital, a lawyer visited Papa in the factory where he worked. The lawyer said that Papa could collect a great deal of money from the man who had hit me with his automobile. Papa had no idea that it was possible to collect money for this injury. The hospital had made no charges. Papa did not earn enough, so I was a charity patient. The lawyer explained that Papa could sue the man who had hit me, and the court would force the automobile driver to pay for the terrible thing that had happened to me. The lawyer took out a long legal document from his briefcase and told my father to sign at the bottom. He assured Papa that as soon as the paper was signed, he, the lawyer, would go to court and start suing the driver.

One evening a few days later another lawyer, who was a friend of the doctor who had taken care of me, came to see us. Papa was confused. He told this second lawyer that another lawyer had already come to see him about the accident. Our visitor seemed perplexed and asked Papa if he had signed any papers.

Papa told him that he had. The young lawyer looked worried and said that he would look into the matter. A few days later the second attorney told Papa that he had been duped and that the entire affair was ended. The first lawyer represented the driver, and the paper that my father had signed was a complete release for the driver of the automobile. Papa, of course, had never read the paper, and I am sure that if he had, he would not have understood it. As he said to us later, "Such long words and such small type, who could understand it? He seemed to be such a nice honest man."

Soon I was well enough to go back to school, but I never forgot those flowers and their glorious colors. That was my first contact with beauty, the beauty of color and form. It marked the beginning of a lifelong quest, seeking the reason for that overpowering surge of emotion that people experience when confronted with a thing of beauty. But I could not help thinking that again I had suffered disaster after experiencing so much joy — the joy of seeing my first train and the soul-stirring joy of that beautiful field of glorious wild flowers. Was this the way that life was going to be? Was there no possibility of pure joy, joy with no pain or suffering? Perhaps someday I would find the answer in my never-ending quest for joy. But try as I might, I seemed to live in a pattern of joy and pain.

Years later I realized that my love of color came from the beautiful field of colorful wild flowers that had been absorbed in my subconscious and that the green hospital room has kept me from ever using green.

When I was twelve years old we moved to a house in East New York. I had not met any of the kids on our block. I was shy and I blushed when someone spoke to me. Adults frightened me. More than once, people would ask my parents if I could speak at all. One evening a teacher from P.S. 158 came to visit my parents. He was trying to supplement his meager income as a teacher by selling a library of books called *The Book of Knowledge*. After showing us sample books, he explained that we could have the full set of twenty on an installment payment plan, just a few dollars a week. I had never owned a book of my own, let alone a set of twenty books. Papa said he would think it over. When the teacher left, I pleaded with him to buy the twenty beautiful books. I promised that I would read them and study harder for my hated school work. Mama liked the idea, and finally Papa agreed to sign the contract and make the first down payment. When all the twenty volumes were delivered, I was deliriously happy — twenty books that were my very own. I could keep them forever. No more returning my fascinating books to the library. And they were, indeed, a wonderful source of information. Most of all, I fell in love with the poetry in those books. I spent hours memorizing my favorite poems. There was the chillingly dramatic "Wreck of the Hesperus," as well as "The Wonderful One Horse Shay," "Darius Green and His Flying Machine," "Whispering Jim," and one that was very special, perhaps because it spoke of things so close to the lives we led, "The Song of the Shirt," by Thomas Hood, who wrote most of his poetry in the early days of the industrial revolution in England during the middle of the nineteenth century.

One evening, Uncle Harry asked me to read a poem aloud. Standing in front of my family and my aunts and uncles, I recited "The Song of the Shirt." When I finally came to the last stanza my voice must have conveyed the pathos I felt. Then, suddenly, there was applause. For one heady moment, I stood there, the center of attention. I, who always tried to hide in a corner whenever we had company at home, was the most important person in the room. It was a new sensation, something that had never happened to me before. And I liked it. I had found a new place in our family life. Every time relatives and friends dropped in, and this happened quite often, I was asked to recite a poem.

One day in school, our teacher suggested that we memorize a poem, which we would then recite in front of the class. Although every pupil had memorized a poem, when it came time to recite, most of them stumbled and mumbled, trying to get through it as quickly as possible and back to the security of their desks. When my turn came, I felt a surge of confidence, and even pride in my mastery of reciting before an audience. From that moment on, my reputation as a speaker — an actor, if you will — was established. I was even sent to other schools to recite poems and stories. I had made a remarkable discovery. Shy, introverted, and withdrawn when with people, I found that I possessed a confidence and sureness of self when confronted by an audience. I was convinced that I had the makings of an actor.

At fourteen years of age I was a graduate of P.S. 158. My best friend was named Harold. He had a high forehead topped with curly brown hair, and he knew that he would someday be a great man. He would go to college and become a prominent attorney. He was sure of it. My other good friend was Manny Lepofsky. We spent many long hours together going to and from Boys High School talking about our future aims in life. I still thought only of the stage. Manny wanted to be a writer.

All of us lived in the same type of house. Our parents owned their own homes, and each had a tenant who lived upstairs. Most important was the fact that this was truly their home, their own piece of property. There was a backyard where they could grow a few vegetables in the summer. Our home, like the others, had a cellar where Papa could press grapes in the fall and make his own sweet wine, which was kept in large barrels. Mama pickled barrels of sauerkraut with apples and stored jars of homemade jellies and homemade catsup and large crocks of preserved fruits in season. It was almost like the old days in Russia, with fruits and vegetables of summer stored against the long hard winter.

It was in a cellar such as ours that I first met Archie, another friend who forms a separate chapter in my life. He had turned his cellar into a sculptor's studio. Archie's family shared their two-family house with relatives. One night our friend Harry, the arranger, had arranged a party at a girl's house. The girl was Archie's cousin. While we were there, I saw an interesting piece of sculpture and asked the girl where she had found it. She explained that her cousin had made it and offered to introduce me. We went down to the cellar, and there I met Archie. He was just about my own age. When we were introduced we did not shake hands. He glanced over his shoulder and grunted. The girl wanted to go back to the party upstairs, but I wanted to stay and watch her cousin Archie work.

"Well, if you would rather stay down here in this messy cellar instead of having fun upstairs, that's fine with me, but you had better ask my cousin, the genius, if he will let you stay." This was said with all the sarcasm that a pretty young girl could muster. "He hates to have people watch him. Can he stay down here with you, genius?"

Archie grunted and nodded his head almost imperceptibly, so I stayed and watched Archie at work. I forgot all about the party. Archie was working in plastacine. He had a picture of an intricate piece of sculptural relief next to his table. It was a difficult subject—nymphs and cupids in a leafy bower. Some of the figures were in full relief. I watched with rapt admiration as he skillfully modeled each delicate leaf and flower. The little figurines came alive under his fingers and his modeling tools. After almost two hours of work during which neither of us said a word, he put down his tools and threw a piece of cotton gauze over the almost completed work. Then and only then, he turned and spoke to me for the first time.

Lapidus (right) and friend Harold, 1918.

"My closest friend Harold and I discovered an abandoned railroad track and put on an act as hobos."

"If you want, you can come back tomorrow. I'm going to make a waste mold."

I did not know then what a waste mold was, but I knew that I would be back in Archie's cellar the next day, Sunday.

So began my friendship with Archie. He had quit high school after the first year. He spent his evenings and often his days at the Cooper Union studying sculpture. I would find him in his cellar either staring at a soft wet clay figure that he was working on or furiously slapping lumps of clay on a metal armature as he started a new piece of sculpture. I would walk down the wooden stairs and say, "Hi, Archie." Sometimes he would grunt hello, but more often he would go on working without any sign of recognition. I knew better than to start a conversation. Once, when I had asked him what he was working on, he told me to "Get the hell outa here." I would find a box to sit on and watch silently. When he grew tired he would stop modeling and start talking to himself about his work. Soon, without stopping, he would include me in his conversation.

"Someday I'm gonna be a great artist. I'm gonna have a studio in Paris, and I'll be rich and famous. I know that I'm great. My teacher tells me already I'm better than he is. You just wait. Someday you'll say, 'I knew Archie, the great sculptor. He was my friend.' I know that I'm a genius."

I had decided that I was going to be an actor, but I had always loved to draw. I sometimes dreamed of being a famous painter, but I never talked about it with a single soul. Soon I found myself confiding my dream to Archie. He began to feel a kinship with me. Archie, the eccentric, the loner, seemed to feel that he had found a friend, a friend in his own neighborhood.

My first two years in high school were deplorable. My poor beginning in public school was a poor preparation for high school. Boys High School in the Bedford-Stuyvesant area of Brooklyn had a reputation for the highest scholastic standing in New York City. Latin was a disaster, and after two years, my total knowledge seem to be "All Gaul is divided into three parts." Algebra was a nightmare. And I wasn't doing too well in my other subjects. At the end of my second year, I was informed that I could leave of my own accord or be expelled.

My parents had hoped that their firstborn son in this new land of opportunity would go on to become a doctor or a lawyer. But this was not to be. So I began my search for a job, any job. I finally was hired as a file clerk in the X-ray department of Bellevue Hospital in Manhattan. The personnel office thought that a young man with two years of high school education should certainly have the capacity to see that the X-ray plates of names beginning with A went into the A file and those beginning with B went into the B file, and so on. At fifteen dollars a week, with lunches included, I became a member of the working class. I was given a white jacket and assigned a little office all my own. I was encouraged to observe and to learn. Perhaps if I applied myself, then someday I might even become an X-ray technician — not a brilliant future, but a future nonetheless. Gone were my dreams of becoming an actor or a painter.

During the time I worked at Bellevue, the head of the X-ray department was Dr. I. Seth Hirsch, a specialist in what was then a comparatively new field in medicine. He was of slight build with a baby pink complexion. He had piercing blue eyes and a shock of white curly hair. There was a quiet dignity about him. He spoke with precise diction in a low but rich voice that commanded the respect of his listeners. Since the X-ray was something new in the medical profession, doctors came from all parts of the United States to take courses with Dr. Hirsch to learn how to interpret the photographs of the internal organs, bones, and tissues of their patients at home. Whenever I could, I would listen with rapt attention to the sonorous voice of Dr. Hirsch as he expounded the intricacies of the various ailments that were revealed on the X-ray plates. To me, he was a great man.

I worked in the X-ray department of Bellevue for eight months. During that period I experienced a growing resolve to go back to school, to try to improve my studies and eventually enter college. I visited my school and pleaded with the principal to be readmitted. He showed me my record with the red markings of my failures, but I finally persuaded him to let me come back for one term on probation. I was determined to exert every effort to somehow get through high school and then go on to college where I wanted to study drama.

The day finally came for me to give my notice of departure from the hospital. I sought out Dr. Hirsch and formally announced that I was returning to school to continue my education. To my chagrin Dr. Hirsch was delighted to see me go. He wished me luck in school and then said, "I hope you do better in school than you did here, although I doubt it. With luck we should get our files straightened out in a year or so."

I knew that I had spent a great deal of time daydreaming instead of watching my filing, but I never thought that Dr. Hirsch was aware that I had been misfiling the X-ray plates. My pride was shattered. One day, I swore to myself, I would finish college and get an important role as an actor. I was determined to go back to Bellevue Hospital, seek out Dr. Hirsch, and tell him that in spite of his low opinion of me, I had succeeded.

Whether it was the devastating valedictory of Dr. Hirsch or whether I just woke up intellectually, I do not know, but I found myself making excellent grades. I even made the high school Honor Society for Scholarship and Service. I graduated and went on to college. I selected Washington Square College of New York University because it had an excellent drama department. Reading the college catalogue, I learned that there was a little theater group known as the Washington Square College Players. Papa's new business, the auto lamp company in which he was a partner, was doing nicely, and he was able to pay my tuition and give me a reasonable allowance so that I could earn a college degree. So, at long last, I started what I hoped would be the foundation for my career as an actor.

The Washington Square College Players, a New York University theater group, in a scene from
At the Sign of the Greedy Pig, 1923. Lapidus is second from right.

"In the early 1920s, small experimental theaters flourished in Greenwich Village…
My first taste of accomplishment came when Theater Magazine *published a story and pictures
of [this] play… I was credited twice, once as an actor and again as the costume designer.*"

5 Acting

Professor Randolph Somerville was the head of the drama department at New York University in Washington Square. He was a tall, handsome man with a shock of bright red hair, green eyes, and a rich baritone voice that rolled out the sonorous soliloquies of Shakespeare to illustrate parts of his lectures. As a freshman I had little hope of becoming a member of the school's Washington Square College Players, but that did not keep me from haunting the small experimental playhouse where the players rehearsed.

One night, I asked a young woman painting sets if I could help. She was delighted, and I went to work and painted a soft blue sky, shading from palest blue at the bottom to a deep indigo at the top of the drop. Across the sky I painted gossamer-thin fleecy clouds. I was not aware that the redoubtable Professor Somerville had come in and was watching. I was enjoying myself tremendously and was completely immersed in the scene painting. I heard someone applauding from the back of the darkened theater. Then Dr. Somerville walked up onto the stage and asked if I would like to be the scene painter for the company. The young woman I had helped was graduating that term. I accepted gratefully. He appointed me to be the scenic artist and eventually the costume designer for the Players.

But this was only part of the goal that I was reaching for. I wanted to act. One day, fortified with a courage I did not really feel, I refused to do any more sets unless I was given a part in a play that was being cast. Professor Somerville needed the scenery, and I got a small part in the production.

In the early 1920s, small experimental theaters flourished in Greenwich Village. One of Somerville's favorite playwrights was Stewart Walker. Walker had developed his own group, which he called the Portmanteau Players, and he had written a whole series of one-act plays for them. These simple playlets were specially written for small acting companies that could produce fascinating but uncomplicated plays with a minimum of scenery and a great deal of imagination. The first play in which I was given a part was Walker's *Six Who Pass While the Lentils Boil.*

Not only did I paint scenery, design costumes, and act, but I also became the official makeup man for the group. The smell of grease paint was sweeter than any perfume. There was no doubt in my mind that the theater would be my life from then on. My first taste of accomplishment came when *Theater Magazine* published a story and pictures of a play called A*t the Sign of the Greedy Pig*, by Charles Brooks, which the Washington Square College Players had produced. I was credited twice, once as an actor and again as the costume designer.

After I had been with the College Players for two years, Professor Somerville was asked to recommend two young men to become a part of the permanent company of the young Theater Guild group. He recommended me and another young man who had started at the same time as I, and whose ambition was also to become an actor. Rehearsals for a play called *He Who Gets Slapped*, by the Russian playwright Leonid Andreyev, were to start that summer.

During the two previous summers I had been a counselor at Camp Kiowa in Pennsylvania. That summer I was offered the post of drama counselor with a fantastic salary of five hundred dollars for the season. My dilemma was whether to accept the appointment to the Theater Guild, which would mean spending most of the summer rehearsing with no pay at all, or going off to camp and earning five hundred dollars while spending June, July, and August in the Poconos. I finally decided to take a chance that there would still be an opening for me with the Theater Guild at the end of the summer.

When I returned to New York, *He Who Gets Slapped* was a successful play on Broadway. My friend from the Washington Square College Players had a one-line part, but he was about to get a more important role, and I was offered his part. My first night backstage was a thrilling experience — the actors arriving, going to their dressing rooms, getting into costume, putting on makeup, and waiting for the curtain call. Then came the breathless moment when the stage manager announced, "Places please. Curtain going up." Where the back of the front curtain had been, there was now a dark void, and beyond it the hushed audience. Backstage the actors waited for their cues to go on stage.

On stage everything was beautifully bright and colorful, bathed in the light from a hundred spotlights and floodlights, all with their lovely pastel-colored gelatin filters. Overhead was the vast space of the fly gallery with its intricate pattern of grids, weights, ropes, pulleys, and catwalks. On one side of the stage behind the wings was a huge electrical panel with its switches, dimmers, and controls. The red brick side walls were lined with a pattern of vertical ropes that stretched high up into the dark reaches of the fly gallery. Backstage all was dark, quiet, and breathless with the anticipated excitement of entering on cue. Between the acts there was the pleasant banter of the actors while waiting for the next act to begin. At the end of the last act the actors took their bows as the enthusiastic audience applauded. Finally it was over, my first night back-stage in a Broadway theater. Each evening I reported in time to see the play start. I watched the action, especially the part played by my young friend whose place I would soon take. The instructions were simple: wait for the offstage shot and then run into the scene, entering stage right, and breathlessly speak the line, "The baron has shot himself." The very instructions were spine-tingling: "Enter stage right."

During each performance I became more conscious of the life in the wings. The excitement of watching the action on stage was wearing off. What the actors did while waiting to go on absorbed me. Little by little I became aware of the fact that acting was just another job. What was exciting for me was simply a way of life for these people in their costumes and makeup. They began to seem tired and bored. They were earning a living waiting for their cues. Was this the life that I really wanted? Sitting around backstage waiting for my cue to "enter stage right"?

This real theater was not the same as the experimental Little Theater I loved so much. There everything was action. Building and painting scenery now seemed to be more of a challenge than learning lines and appearing on stage. And the rest of the time? Sitting in the wings waiting for a cue? No, this was not what I wanted. Yes, I loved the theater but not the long waits in the dark backstage. At last I came to a decision. The stage was what I wanted but not acting. I loved the stage; it was a world of illusions, of dreams, a mirror of all human emotions. As a ghetto loner, I had found refuge in a world of dreams, of romance, of love and hate, a world that had nothing in common with the everyday world I lived in — a world I wanted to get away from. If I was not able to live in a world of illusions created by an actor, then I wanted to create a world of illusion by designing the settings against which these emotions were portrayed. I resolved to become a scenic designer. In this field I could maintain my contact with the theater and do what I knew I could do well — draw and paint and design. I visited several scenic artists to see if I could become an apprentice. Each one asked if I had had architectural training. I was advised to study architecture and go on from there to become a scenic artist. So I left New York University and the Washington Square College Players and entered the School of Architecture of Columbia University. I gave up my dream of becoming an actor. This time I was sure that my future would be that of becoming a scenic designer for the stage.

During my two years at New York University, I had tried to keep up my friendship with Archie and my other friends. Archie was always interested in what I was doing. Once he suggested that I bring home a costume that I had designed for a play set in medieval times, in which I had played one of the parts. This started a new phase in our friendship. I became Archie's model. I was happy to pose in various costumes that I borrowed from the Players while he modeled in clay. He taught me how to make plaster-of-paris casts of these figures.

Archie's father was a big, powerful man who worked as a tailor. He was a hardworking, devout Jew whose heart was broken because his only son, his *kad-*

dishal, was like a stranger to him. A good Jew prays that he may have a son who, after the father's death, would help him gain entry into *Gahn*, the Hebrew paradise, by reciting the *kaddish* (the prayer for the dead). *Kaddish* is said twice a day for a full year by a son after his father's death. Archie's father had long ago given up the hope that his only son would ever say *kaddish* for him after he died. In fact, Archie laughed at his father and his old-fashioned belief that reciting a meaningless Hebrew rigmarole would help his father gain entrance to paradise. I recall Archie's father as he was then, a large, square-jawed man with a granite-like face, deep lines etched into it by toil and sorrow. His iron gray hair was cropped close, further heightening his rugged features. But his sad, resigned, deep-sunken eyes told of his heartbreak.

"Tough luck," Archie would say of his father's hopes and expectations for his son. "This is my life. I'm gonna live it in my way. To hell with the old man. I didn't ask to be born. He doesn't mean anything to me. When I get to be a great sculptor he's gonna be proud of me." Archie's father did not live to be proud of his son. His death came like a hammer blow to my friend. One night soon after his father's death, I found him in his cellar crying like a baby. He had smashed all his work.

Not long after, Archie dragged me back to his cellar. A huge block of granite sat in the middle of the room. It was about five feet square by five feet in height. He told me that he had to rip out a section of the wall to get the stone into the cellar. Archie had decided that the only way he could reach his father and show him what a genius he had for a son was to carve a tombstone for his grave. But not just an ordinary tombstone. It was going to be a gigantic head of his father carved in gray granite. It took a whole year. I would find him stripped to the waist in sweltering summer heat, with mallet and chisel, furiously carving the emerging head. In freezing weather he kept chiseling away, his hands chapped and bleeding. Slowly the head emerged from the block of granite. The square jaw, the close-cropped hair, and finally the eyes. Somehow, perhaps because of his guilt, he had achieved such a look of sorrow and compassion in the eyes that it almost broke your heart to look at them. Archie had created a masterpiece. To this day I believe that this one piece of sculpture would have established Archie as an artist. But then this was not a piece for a gallery; it was to be the headstone for the grave of Archie's father.

He arranged to have a cement base prepared at the cemetery. One spring day he hired a truck with a winch to come to his house to load the gigantic head and deliver it to the cemetery. I was there when he knocked out a part of the cellar wall so that the sculpted head could be taken out. For the first time in a year, my friend Archie's face was radiant with happiness. At last he was going to atone for the heartbreak he had caused his father. He was going to make amends in the only way that he knew how.

That evening I walked over to Archie's house. The dinner dishes were set on the dining-room table. His mother was waiting for Archie to come back from the cemetery. She knew that it would be heartbreaking, backbreaking work to set the carved granite head on its base and that Archie would want to do this all by himself. She wanted Archie to have a hot meal when he returned. It was getting dark and growing late, but his mother and I waited. By eleven o'clock there was still no Archie. His mother's face was drawn with worry. I too was worried about my erratic friend, but I had to leave because I had school the next morning. I told Archie's mother not to worry, that he was probably being thoughtless, which was his way, and had gone someplace to celebrate. The next day I hurried over to Archie's house as soon as school was over. No Archie. His mother had not slept that night. The poor woman sat huddled in a chair in the kitchen, waiting. I joined her in the long vigil, neither of us speaking.

Just as I was about to give up and go home to have supper with my family, Archie walked in. What a change from the radiantly happy Archie of the morning before! His clothes were covered with dust and chips of granite. His hands were bruised and bleeding. But it was his face that held my eyes and the eyes of his mother. It was haggard and gray. He had grown old overnight. His eyes were sunken, glazed. Neither of us dared to ask what had happened. We sat and waited for him to tell us.

"Go wash your face and hands, Archie. Supper is waiting. Maybe your friend will stay and eat with you."

Without a word, Archie went into the bathroom. When he came out his hands and face were clean. He had soaked his hair and removed the granite dust, and he had combed it. We sat down to eat, but not a word was said. The meal was over. Finally, Archie spoke.

"The bastards—the dirty filthy bastards—those lousy Jews—to hell with them and their goddam religion!" Little by little the story came out. He was crying, sobbing, when he finished telling us what had happened. He had arrived at the cemetery gates and asked the guard to open the gates so that he could take the granite head of his father to the grave and set it in place. The guard looked puzzled, but told him to wait while he went in to talk to the cemetery superintendent. After a long wait, the superintendent, a tall man wearing a *yarmulke* (skullcap) came out and asked who Archie was and what the carved head was for. Archie outlined his mission: that his father had died a year ago, and he, the only son, had carved a portrait head for his father's tombstone. The superintendent admired the work but told Archie that he could not bring the sculpture into the cemetery. They argued back and forth, the older man explaining the restrictions on images in a Jewish cemetery, the younger man becoming increasingly angry and frustrated.

The argument went on and on. Archie had a furious temper, and he swore and raged, shouting that he would "bust the goddamn gates down." By this time the trucker who had waited to see what would happen told Archie that he could not stay any longer; Archie either could have the piece of sculpture unloaded in the front of the cemetery gates or the truckman would take it back to Archie's house and unload it there. Archie told him to unload it in front of the cemetery entrance together with his tools. The head was finally set in front of the gates, and the trucker left. Archie just sat there waiting.

Hours passed and Archie just sat there. The staff came out one by one and pleaded with Archie to go home. He had come to set his father's tombstone, and he had made up his mind to sit there until they finally gave him permission. Eventually a bearded patriarch — the kind who stayed at Jewish cemeteries to say prayers for the departed when asked to do so by relatives who visited the graves of their loved ones — came out to talk to Archie. Gently, the old man quoted passages from Exodus and explained to Archie again that no graven images were allowed in a Jewish cemetery. He told him that a pious Jew was not allowed to make a statue nor was it permitted to have any statues that were graven images in a place of worship or in a still holier place, the cemetery. Archie could not understand what something that happened thousands of years ago had to do with a granite headstone that he had just carved for his father. He knew only that he wanted to be there and remember his father, to look at his face and to assure him that his son loved him. The patriarch implored Archie to go home, saying that his father, as well as God, would understand.

But Archie did not go. The cemetery staff left as night fell, but Archie still sat there. All through the night he stayed and prayed in his own fashion, asking God to let him be able to set the carved granite head on his father's grave.

The next morning the cemetery staff came back. With aching hearts they saw the haggard-eyed young man sitting next to his work of art. He had not moved or eaten since the morning of the day before. They knew better than to try to talk to him. Slowly, but finally, a furious rage boiled up in my friend. He had come to a decision. Seizing his mallet and a chisel, he started hacking at the beautifully carved head of his father. All day long he kept smashing the granite head until he had reduced it to a pile of granite rubble. The beautiful carving, that labor of love and devotion that had taken a year of toil and sweat and dedication, was destroyed. Only when there was not a vestige of the carving left did Archie leave the cemetery gates. And so he came home.

When he finished telling his story, he buried his head in his arms on the dining room table and cried with sobs torn from his innermost being. His mother sat rocking and moaning. There were no tears left for her. I quietly rose and tiptoed out of the room and went home.

Archie later went to Paris. When he came home, he had fantastic stories to tell of his adventures and his battles with artists and teachers in Paris. The Frenchmen called him "the crazy American," and from the stories he told me, the title was well earned. To me he looked like a wild-eyed lunatic — long hair, dirty, unkempt. I promised to keep in touch, but I knew that Archie and I could never again be friends. He was too wild. I never heard from him again, although years later I learned from one of his relatives that he had been committed to an asylum. Through the years I followed news of artists, sculptors, and exhibits in the hope that someday I would see his name mentioned as one of the exhibiting artists. Perhaps, I thought, some day my untamed friend Archie would finally show the world the promising talent that he had. What I did not realize then was that one day my fiercely unyielding friend Archie would have a profound influence on my life and my career.

Lapidus in his favorite corner in the atelier at Columbia University's
School of Architecture, 1923.

6 Architecture School

On my first day at Columbia University's School of Architecture I took the uptown I.R.T. and got off at the 116th Street station. Autumn leaves were drifting across the campus and up a broad flight of monumental steps, at the top of which sat a statue of Alma Mater gazing serenely at the new crop of students hurrying to their first classes. Charles Follen McKim's stately library acted as an imposing backdrop for the students climbing the steps to reach their various schools — engineering, law, or architecture. I hurried past the library and St. Paul's Chapel to Avery Hall where the School of Architecture was housed. My first class, An Introduction to the History of Architecture, was on the fourth floor. There were thirteen of us in the class. I slipped quietly into my seat. I wanted to look around and see who my classmates would be for the next four years, but I thought it best to keep my eyes on the empty lecture podium. The classroom door opened, and a short elderly gentleman entered the room. He walked quickly to the desk and stood there looking over the class. He was a perfect example of what I thought an architecture professor should look like. Professor A.D.F. Hamlin must have been in his seventies. He had unruly white hair, which looked as if he had been running his fingers, rather than a comb, through it. His mustache and carefully trimmed goatee framed a pair of pursed quizzical lips — half smile, half frown. His cheeks were ruddy, a pair of piercing blue eyes looked through steel-framed spectacles, which sat perkily on his small button nose. His tie was, in fact, a knotted black scarf flowing over a well-worn tweed jacket.

He stood there examining each of us. His eyes went from one to another. His expression seemed to say, "So this is what architecture has come to." Finally he spoke:

> Gentlemen, I see before me thirteen young men who have decided that they want to become architects. I presume that, since I am the senior professor, it is my prerogative and duty to welcome you to Avery Hall and to start you on the road to becoming members of an ancient and honorable profession. Now gentlemen, there must be some specific reason why each of you has decided to follow in the footpaths of such men as Vitruvius and Christopher Wren.

Vitruvius, that ancient Roman architect, summed up the profession by saying that buildings should be designed to embody three principles: firmness, commodity, and delight. I might as well start my lecture by explaining these three esoteric words.

By firmness, he meant the building would have to be strong enough to stand there without collapsing. By commodity, he meant that the building would function properly. And by delight, he meant that a building should be designed to be something pleasant to look at, something to be enjoyed, a thing of joy.

Professor Hamlin welcomed us to the profession, in a manner of speaking. He emphasized that architecture had been, and continued to be, a gentlemen's profession, and that no one would ever become rich practicing architecture. He recommended that any of us who might be entering the profession as a means of achieving wealth should choose another profession; for those of us who might remain, he asserted that the study and practice of architecture would be highly rewarding in every way but financially. He then left the room for ten minutes to give us time to think about what he had just said.

I really had no visions of ever becoming wealthy. I had assured my father, when I decided to study architecture, that I could "make a living" at it. I stayed. I do not know what the other twelve thought, but they all remained.

The other men were graduates of Ivy League colleges — Princeton, Harvard, and Yale. I had had only two years of liberal arts, most of which was devoted to studying drama at Washington Square. All of my classmates were what Professor Hamlin called "gentlemen" who were entering a gentleman's profession. I was the outsider, a prisoner of my own deep-rooted sense of inferiority.

There was only one classmate with whom I seemed to have any rapport. He was an Austrian named André who had decided to come to the United States to study architecture. He was as Germanic as a young man could be, not only in his speech and his manners, but also in the way he thought. Since we were two outsiders, we found time to discuss many differences between Americans and Europeans. One of the earliest courses required in the study of architecture was the copying of the classical orders: the Doric, the Ionic, the Corinthian, and the Composite. The first step was the preparation of a precise pencil drawing with all the crispness of a steel engraving. At this type of work, André was perfection itself. My pencil lines could never achieve the precision and the uniformity of André's, but when it came to rendering these orders, it was another matter.

Rendering is the term used to indicate the coloring or toning of a drawing which gives it a third dimension by the use of shades and shadows. A five-month course was devoted to that one subject, the study of shades and shadows using Chinese ink. Chinese ink is made by taking a stick of hard Chinese ink, which looks like a stick of sealing wax, and grinding it with water in a slate mortar. The result is a gray or black liquid, depending on how much ink was ground into the water. This liquid could be applied to appear almost black or, by thinning it down with water, it could be applied to create an almost imperceptible gray transparent tone. The column, the capital, the cornice, the frieze, and the entablature were rendered, or painted, with the Chinese ink to give them a third dimension to show the delicate modeling and to create crisp shadows.

I loved every phase of my studies in architecture except the courses in engineering. To begin with, I was never much good at mathematics; in fact, I hated the entire subject. I knew that I would never receive my degree in architecture unless I passed them so I gritted my teeth and studied those ridiculous formulas, saying to myself, "Just get through it and get a passing mark. After all, I will never have to figure the strength of a column or a beam or a footing. Who needs it? I am going to design theater settings."

Our curriculum was largely based on our professors' own early studies in Paris or Rome. Our courses included perspective, watercolor, drawing in charcoal of classic plaster casts, and life drawing. The most important texts we used were written by A.D.F. Hamlin: *The History of Architecture* and *The History of Ornament* in two volumes.

And, of course, a major part of our work was design. We took elementary design the first year, then intermediate, and finally senior design. Three design presentations were required of us each semester. We were to present the plans for a building, as well as a picture of the building, in any medium — Chinese ink, watercolor, or tinted pencil. As we worked on our projects, a critic (usually a practicing architect) was designated to oversee and make suggestions as the problem advanced from rough sketches and studies to the final presentation. Some of the finest architects came to the drafting room two or three afternoons a week. They went from table to table and spent about a half hour talking with the students and often sketched their ideas on what the student should do. The final presentation was judged and marked by a group of practicing architects together with some of our critics. If the design did not meet with their approval, the design was X'd — meaning no credit points. If the design was accepted, it was given a "passed," which meant three credit points. If the design was above average it was given a "first mention," which earned the student four points. If the design was exceptional, it received a "first mention placed," which earned the student five points.

Our first project was the design of a garden dome used as a small shelter. All the students used classical ornament and designs. Some were in the Greek style, some in the Roman style with classical columns and entablatures around the bottom of the dome. I searched for something different — the beginning of my rebel phase. I noticed that the subway stations all had peculiarly shaped domes for a roof. I decided to adapt the odd domelike structure as my design concept. My critic was not sure he liked it, but he let me have my way.

In the end, my presentation was given a "first mention placed" for my originality and the colorful presentation. I wondered if any of the jury even noticed the subway domes that I had copied. I was beginning to earn a reputation as a innovative designer.

I remember another elementary project in which we were asked to design a "Cemetery Gateway." Most of the students who were studying Greek and Roman architecture designed a Greek or Roman section of a wall with a classical arch, complete with flanking columns, crowning the walls with a classical cornice. My design was not a classical expression of a cemetery gateway. I started with a large circular fountain around which arriving cars circled to the cemetery entrance. In the center of the fountain I placed a figure which to me symbolized Grief. It was a tall figure dressed in a monk's robe and hood. The shoulders were bent, the hands covered a bowed face. This tall figure was rendered in almost black Chinese ink. At the cemetery gateway, I used two flanking walls of marble with no adornment. In the central space between the two walls which curved with the driveway, I used a tall, wrought-iron grill which I copied from a cathedral screen. At least a hundred marble blocks formed the walls. I rendered each block separately with Chinese ink in varying tones. Using a principle I had learned in my watercolor class, I left a white paper hair line at the left and the top of each stone. It was a tedious chore, each block taking a long time to render.

One day, while absorbed with my task, I felt as if somebody was behind me. I put down my brush and turned around. About forty students were watching me. One of them, noticing my embarrassment, spoke up and told me that Dean Williams Boring had been watching my work and had gone through the drafting room telling the entire school about a first-year student so devoted to his tedious work he never looked up. He suggested they come to my table and watch what a dedicated student was doing. I was truly embarrassed, but I was given a "first mention placed" in the final judgment.

During the years that I studied architecture at Columbia, a great revolution was beginning to take place in the profession. I was actually living through the death throes of an era. As far as architecture was concerned, the nineteenth century did not end until the 1920s were over.

The period is known as the eclectic era — an era in which architects copied what had been done before. Architects throughout the world were copying everything in sight. The École des Beaux-Arts in Paris was doing its damnedest to keep the seventeenth- and eighteenth-century styles alive. Victorian Gothic was simply a copy of the true thirteenth-century Gothic with a great deal of meaningless ornamentation added. The great American architect Henry Hobson Richardson was finding his inspiration in the Romanesque style of the twelfth century. Banks were designed to look like Greek or Roman temples of the time of Pericles or Caesar and colleges to look like fourteenth-century cathedral towns. Smart suburban mansions masqueraded as thatch-roofed, half-timber English country homes of the time of Shakespeare, or as French chateaux, or Italian Renaissance villas. Addison Mizner was convincing his millionaire friends that a castle from Castile was what they should live in — down in Palm Beach. Millionaires in Newport had their mansions designed like tremendously magnified shingled cottages, which one associated with the stories of Hansel and Gretel. Here and there, small, still voices were heard, like the Greene brothers in California, who were trying to create a contemporary regional style. Frank Lloyd Wright was designing houses in the Midwest that are now recognized as great monuments of architecture but were then most unacceptable to the American public. At the time Americans were much happier with a reproduction of a Cape Cod saltbox or an ante-bellum mansion from the deep South.

As architecture students, we studied all the great styles of the past. One of the design problems we were given to work out was a ten-room house in the suburbs. Our design critic for this project was a Mr. Hirons, a graduate of the École des Beaux-Arts. As our mentor, what was the suggestion he made to his class? "Look at the magazines and copy a house! There is nothing new, gentlemen, so copy a good one." Some of us timidly asked about the houses being designed by the German architects or by Frank Lloyd Wright. "That crackpot!" Hirons said. "Don't be misled. The poor chap is doing weird things. Steer clear of him."

We studied the classic styles so assiduously that we could recognize a thousand famous buildings at a glance. If we had been taken to any city in Europe blindfolded, we could have told you where we were by simply looking at a cathedral or a palace or a mansion. I recall questioning our senior design critic, Harvey Wiley Corbett, about the modern skyscrapers. These after all, were a product of the twentieth century. Why, I wanted to know, were they being clothed in Renaissance or Gothic styles? Our curiosity had been aroused by the International Competition for the Chicago Tribune Building. The first prize and the commission had been won by Raymond Hood. The winning design still stands next to the Chicago River, a stretched-out, attenuated version of a Gothic cathedral. The second prize was the one that fascinated us. It was designed in the new *modern* style. The architect was Eliel Saarinen. If a building like a skyscraper is modern architecture, why use a classic style? Why not develop a modern idiom? Corbett's answer to us was: "If you dress a Chinese in Western clothes, he is still an Oriental. So what difference does it make if we dress a building like the Woolworth Building in Gothic clothes? It is still a modern skyscraper." But the seeds of discontent had been sown.

We saw pictures of the Paris World's Fair of 1925 — L'Exposition Internationale des Arts Décoratifs et Industriels Modernes — and were excited by this new architecture, which eventually gave birth to the term *art deco*. We looked at designs of Mies van der Rohe's German Pavilion for the Barcelona World's Fair. Erich Mendelsohn was creating buildings with free-flowing lines in Germany;

Le Corbusier, the Swiss, was making sketches of wild-looking buildings that we thought no one would ever build. The Dutch architect Willem Dudok was creating a new school of design. The group of German architects who had founded the Bauhaus were advocating stripping buildings of all adornment to produce what they called an honest structure. All of this was forbidden territory for us. But eventually Professor Boring decided to give seniors one lecture on the modern movement. During this speech, the dean appeared actually embarrassed to talk about the new architecture, as if it were a lewd subject.

I wanted to experiment with these new modern styles. I wanted to get into the twentieth century. I wanted excitement and resolved that if ever I got a chance to design a building, I would kick over the traces and take off in this new medium. All of that, however, would have to wait, and who knew if I would ever be an architect and be trusted to design a building? I was still determined to be a set designer.

In my third year, a new critic was assigned to our class. His name was Wallace Harrison, and he had recently returned from Rome, where he had been studying at the American Academy. He came to my drawing table and told me that he had decided to make me his assistant critic. I was pleased and astonished by this offer, but I told Mr. Harrison that I had my own projects to work on. He said, "You can design and render your project in two weeks — so do that and become my assistant critic." He had been studying my work and was sure that I could handle my own projects and still make the rounds with him as his assistant critic.

During my four years in Avery, I was especially proficient in presentation drawings. These drawings were perspective views of our designs. Using watercolor or pencil, I made a picture of how my proposed building would look. I often wondered whether my designs were as good as they should be, but my renderings were about the best that anyone in my class could produce. I sometimes think that the jury of architects was more influenced by my skill in presentation than my skill in designing, because I had more grades of "first mention placed" than any of the others in my class. I was able to finish my major work in design in the School of Architecture in three years, thus finding myself with only two courses in engineering to take during my fourth year. I decided to go to work during that fourth year in the office of an architect and finish the two engineering courses at night.

I took some examples of my school work and went from one architect's office to another, looking for a job. When I was asked if I had had any experience, I answered truthfully that I was just starting. No one seemed to want a beginner. Jobs were scarce in 1926 because the bubble of the Miami Boom — the South Florida land speculation of the early 1920s when plots in new cities such as Miami Beach and Coral Gables sold out almost as quickly as they appeared in the market — had just burst. Hundreds of architects and draftsmen who had flocked to Florida for the high salaries that were being offered there were now back in New York. There were more men than there were jobs. My professor in watercolor, who thought very highly of my design ability, finally was kind enough to recommend me to the firm of Warren and Wetmore. I was completely awed by the busy drafting room of this large firm which was responsible for the designs of such buildings as New York's Grand Central Terminal and the New York Central Building behind it on Park Avenue. They were also the architects of many mansions in New York and Newport and elegant apartment houses along Park Avenue. When Mr. Holland, the chief draftsman, asked what salary I expected, I told him that I had no idea what I was worth. Therefore, he started me at the lowest salary which was given to drafting-room boys with no experience: twenty-five dollars a week. I was turned over to one of the job captains, who was informed that I was a brilliant young designer and was to be given some type of work in which my design ability could be used. Despite this glowing recommendation, my first assignment was drawing up the toilet rooms for the Atlantic City Convention Hall, which was on the firm's drawing boards at that time. For two weeks I did nothing but draw toilets.

At the end of two weeks, I felt that I could not take any more and sought out Mr. Holland one day at lunch. With a very serious mien, I tendered my resignation from the firm. To begin with, Mr. Holland had no idea who I was. With two hundred men working for him, he had forgotten all about me, and the formality of my resignation startled him. As a rule, draftsmen would simply walk up and say, "I'll take my paycheck because I am leaving the firm." Mr. Holland must have been thoroughly amused although he did not show it. It so happened that, right then, one of the partners of the firm, Ronald Pearce, a nephew of that grand old man, Whitney Warren, walked by, and Holland, feeling that the joke was too good to keep to himself, called to Mr. Pearce.

Of course, Mr. Pearce had no idea what was going on, except that the whole thing seemed to be rather amusing. Holland told Mr. Pearce that Professor Armstrong at Columbia had recommended me, but that I was leaving because my abilities had been immersed in toilets, and, because of this oversight, the firm of Warren and Wetmore was going to lose a bright young talent.

Pearce joined in the fun and said, "Our firm cannot afford to lose a talent such as yours, Mr. Lapidus. You must stay on with us. Why don't you come to my office tomorrow morning and we'll discuss how we can put your talents to use."

I did not resign. Instead, I spent a sleepless night wondering what great new project I would be given when I saw Mr. Pearce the next morning.

Promptly at nine o'clock, I was waiting in his office, anxious to meet the man who was going to start me on my design career. He arrived there at about ten o'clock and asked who I was and what I wanted. He had apparently forgotten all about me. I reminded him of our meeting at Mr. Holland's office the day before. For the moment he did not know what do with me, but turning to his reference table, he noticed the finished set of plans for the residence for William K. Vanderbilt.

"Why don't you take the plans for the William K. Vanderbilt residence," he said, "which is being built in Northport, Long Island, and look them over and tell us where you would improve the design."

I did not realize that the building, in a Spanish style, was almost completed and that Mr. Pearce was simply trying to get rid of me.

I took the set of plans back to my own drafting table and went through them. A carving over the garage doors struck me as an anachronism. The drawings showed a large wagon wheel with a fine, carved horse's head growing out of the wheel. A symbol such as this had been used over stables and carriage houses for more than a hundred years, but I felt it was the wrong emblem to put over a garage that housed motor cars. I finally found the opportunity to bring the plans back to Mr. Pearce and tell him my opinion. He suggested that I make some drawings and present them to him whenever I was through. Anything to get rid of me. I did not know at that time that a sculptor was already working in his New York studio on this very piece of carved ornament. By the end of the day, I had at least a dozen sketches of how I thought the ornament over the garage doors should look. My next problem was to catch Mr. Pearce. He was a busy man and hard to get to. Finally, at the end of the second day, I simply remained in the drafting room after everyone had left, hoping that Mr. Pearce, who usually stayed late, would come by so that I could catch him and have him look at my sketches.

When he did come by on his way home, I said, "Mr. Pearce, I've got those sketches for the Vanderbilt garage." For a moment I could see that once again he had forgotten all about me. He finally remembered and casually glanced at my first sketch and flipped the sheet and looked at my second sketch. He became quite interested, pulled up a stool, sat down at my board, and really began to examine the sketches. He turned to me and said words that have seemed to echo for me through all the years since then: "My God, man, you can design!"

Mr. Pearce actually became quite excited with the sketches and had some difficulty in selecting the one that he liked best. Finally, he chose one that showed the radiator front of a Packard automobile. In 1926 Packard was *the* car. Packard Motor Company had coined one of the first status advertising slogans — "Ask the Man Who Owns One." I reinterpreted the radiator grille as Spanish plateresque, since the Vanderbilt mansion was being designed in traditional eighteenth-century classic Spanish style.

At that time we were going through the Spanish rediscovery period. Addison Mizner was creating Spanish houses in Florida for the wealthy, and the symbol of influence for the moment was a Spanish palace or villa. It made no difference whether it was for Florida or, as in this case for Mr. Vanderbilt, on Long Island.

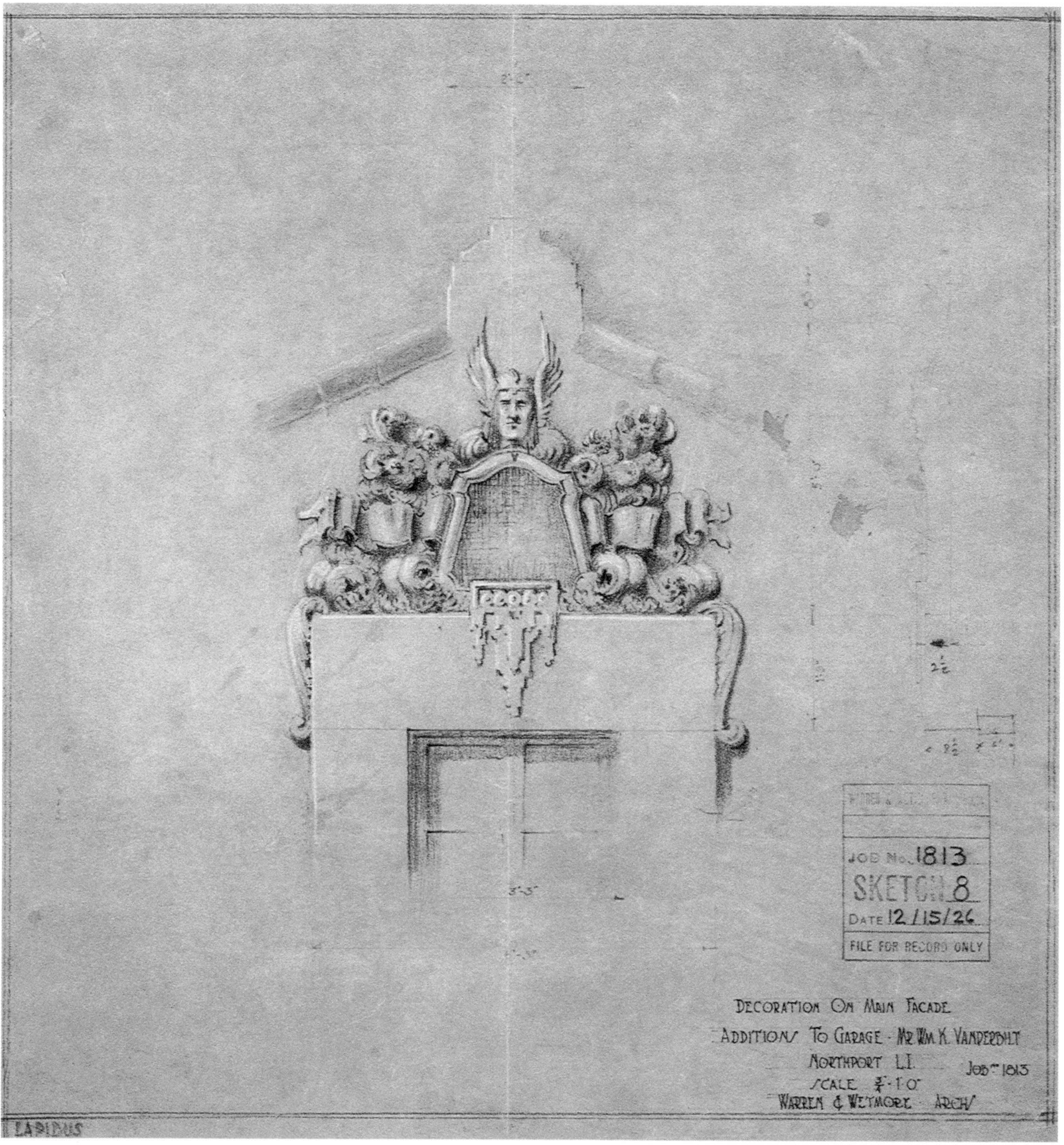
JOB No. 1813
SKETCH 8
DATE 12/15/26
FILE FOR RECORD ONLY
DECORATION ON MAIN FACADE
ADDITIONS TO GARAGE - MR WM K. VANDERBILT
NORTHPORT L.I.
JOB 1813
SCALE ¾"-1'0"
WARREN & WETMORE ARCHS
LAPIDUS

Lapidus's first professional sketch, of a carved garage ornament for the William K. Vanderbilt mansion on Long Island, adapted the radiator grille of a Packard automobile in a plateresque Spanish style, 1926.

At the top of the radiator I had indicated a strong-featured face of Mercury with his winged cap. Instead of the fenders, I had designed curly-cued acanthus leaves. The license plate frame was designed in a plateresque Spanish style dripping with ornaments. This was the sketch that Ronald Pearce selected. Then and there, he picked up the telephone and called the sculptor, Rene Chambalin, at his studio. "Rene," he said, "scrap the horse's head and wheel over the garage. I've got a wonderful new design. I'll have the young man who designed it stop by your studio tomorrow morning. I think you will love it. Let's get it done as quickly as possible to replace the horse head."

And so I had my first architectural design actually going into a building. At least I would no longer be drawing toilets. I was on my way to becoming a junior designer in the firm of Warren and Wetmore. I still have, and treasure, the first drawing I made in an architect's office. It hangs proudly framed in my son's office today. Incidentally, I was given a ten-dollar raise, to thirty-five dollars a week.

My next assignment was to design ornaments for the New York Central Building. Today it stands as a small monument to classicism backed up against the huge Metropolitan Life Building blocking Park Avenue. Many of the thousands of Renaissance ornaments that adorn that building were my designs.

Not long after my emancipation from toilet design, Mr. Pearce gave me a rather unusual assignment. Mr. and Mrs. Vanderbilt, the same people for whom I had designed the garage ornament, had an apartment on Park Avenue in one of the buildings that had been designed by Warren and Wetmore. They had decided to modernize their apartment, and part of the modernization consisted of building a dressing room and bathroom for Mrs. Vanderbilt. I was given the project of designing the dressing room and bathroom. The only problem was that I had no idea what a dressing room was. I inquired among some of the more experienced designers and was told that wealthy folks did not dress in a bedroom but rather in a dressing room. After a little research, I felt that I was in a position to design a very elegant dressing room for Mrs. Vanderbilt.

The first challenge was the selection of a historic style for the rooms. I reasoned that since William K. Vanderbilt was, in effect, American royalty, I should take my inspiration from royalty in Europe. I decided to carry out the entire project in a Louis XVI style. The dressing room, with its closets and dressing table and armoires, was to be built of Circassian walnut with gold leaf on the delicate carvings. There was to be an intricate cast plaster ceiling, and the floor was to be covered in luxurious carpeting. I designed the bathroom with walls and floors of white Carrara marble with applied gold ormolu. The ceiling was to be tiled in a mosaic Renaissance pattern. The bathtub itself was to be carved from a single block of *verde antico* (green) marble, measuring seven feet long by three feet wide and three feet high. White Carrara steps were to lead up to the bathtub, which was to be partially recessed into the floor. Of course, all the fittings would have to be either solid gold, or if Mr. Vanderbilt complained, gold plated. It is surprising how quickly a ghetto youth can research and find out what the ultimate luxury for a millionaire should be. When the sketches and plans were presented to Mrs. Vanderbilt, she was enthralled. Mr. Vanderbilt ordered the plans to be sent out for bids.

At this time, it became necessary for me to go back to Columbia University to complete my final thesis. I went to see Mr. Holland and asked for a leave of absence. Mr. Pearce urged me to come back after I had graduated and continue as a designer with the firm.

The thesis that architectural students were required to prepare usually called for the design of a large building or group of buildings. The subject for our thesis in 1927 was a design for a Museum of the Peaceful Arts. It was customary at that time, for a senior who was working on his thesis, to select two lower classmen to become his assistants. One of my assistants, a Mr. Ball, was an older man. He had been a pilot and a flying instructor who had decided to become an architect. Our project was due on May 15, and on the last day the entire class worked not only during the day but right through the night, so that the thesis drawings could be presented the following morning. Someone suggested the best way to stay awake was to keep eating ginger. (There were no "stay-awake" drugs at that time.) I ate so much ginger that I still cannot bear the sight of it.

That night Charles Lindbergh flew across the Atlantic. By coincidence, Mr. Ball had taught Charles Lindbergh how to fly, so all through the night the radio blared away, telling us of Lindbergh's flight in the *Spirit of St. Louis*.

I actually never went back to work for Warren and Wetmore, but I did go back to find out how my designs for the Vanderbilt dressing room and bath were faring. Mr. Pearce told me that although the actual designs had been retained, it had been necessary to scale-down the project. Where I had used Circassian walnut, they were now building the dressing room of pine, which was to be painted, where I had called for that *verde antico* marble bathtub, a standard bathtub was being used with a little green marble trim. I was terribly disappointed. After all, wasn't Vanderbilt a millionaire? Why not a solid marble bathtub? As Mr. Pearce described it, when the cost came in Mr. Vanderbilt let out a low whistle and then turned to him and said, "Ronald, you seem to forget that I am a Vanderbilt, not a Rockefeller! Let us simplify the design and build this dressing room and bath at a price that I can afford." Thus my marble bathtub was never built. Papa had been able to fashion a copper tub for a colonel in the czar's army, but Mrs. Vanderbilt's marble bathtub was just not meant to be.

Lapidus's future wife, Beatrice, in riding habit, 1924.

7 First Jobs

During the difficult period with Archie, I met the girl who was to become my wife. One night, at a party, I talked to a pretty raven-haired girl named Beatrice who seemed quite interested in me, in part because, as I later found out, she mistakenly believed I shared her interest in riding.

I called her the following week, and we began to see a great deal of each other. I was more than twenty-one years old, so imagine my shock when I discovered that the bright, charming, and sophisticated Bea was only a little over fifteen.

Bea lived in Bay Ridge, another section of Brooklyn, and I lived in Flatbush, more than an hour away by subway and elevated. One evening I stayed quite late, and I did not get home until after six in the morning. Papa was just getting up to go to work, and he was surprised to see me dressed. I told him that I had to get to school early, and I was on my way out. So out I went. No matter the sleepless night, all I could think of was Bea, whom I loved with all my heart, and loved till the day she died.

By the time I graduated from Columbia, I had been seeing Bea for four years, and I wanted to ask her to marry me. But first I needed a job. How could a scenic designer without any prospects of earning a living ask a girl to marry him? I loved Bea, and love finally won out.

I made the rounds of stage design studios, but in 1927 the Broadway stage was at low ebb. The men I approached for work, some of them famous set designers, urged me to forget about the stage, explaining I would be foolish to try to get into set designing when I could go to work for an architect and, eventually, become one myself.

Regretfully, I gave up all thoughts of the stage, and I soon found a position as a designer and detailer with a firm called Block and Hess. I was asked to develop at large scale the proposed ornaments on a building for an organization known as the United Order of True Sisters that the partners, Block and Hess, had designed. The building had been designed in a late American colonial style and my schooling in classic architecture and ornament served me well.

After this project, I went on to design buildings, but after less than a year, Block and Hess regretfully informed me that although they were very satisfied

Beatrice at camp in the Berkshires, 1923.

with my services, they were no longer needed for the simple reason that there was no more work in the office.

Once again I went job hunting. Jobs were not easy to come by, but I had made up my mind that I would look for a position that would pay a much higher salary than the fifty-five dollars that I had earned at Block and Hess. The sooner I began to earn enough, the sooner I would be able to propose to Bea.

I applied to be chief draftsman in Arthur Weiser's office. When I showed Mr. Weiser some of the drawings I had prepared at Block and Hess, he was impressed with my design ability and my drafting capabilities but wondered whether or not I could take charge of a job with several men under me. I assured him that I could although I had my doubts. He then inquired whether I was familiar with the Building Department in Manhattan and could get plans approved. Again, I assured Mr. Weiser that I was thoroughly familiar with the Building Department and would have no problems in getting the work of the office approved quickly. Mr. Weiser handed me a set of plans together with a sheet of about twenty-odd objections.

"If you can get these plans approved in a hurry, the job is yours," he said. "As soon as these plans are approved, you will be on the payroll for seventy-five dollars a week."

With the plans in hand I went to the nearest telephone booth and called John, a draftsman I knew who studied architecture at night at Columbia.

"John," I asked when he answered, "where is the Building Department?"

I told him that I could land a very good job if I succeeded in getting a set of plans approved by the Building Department. We arranged to meet that evening, and he gave me explicit instructions as to what to do.

The Building Department was on the twentieth floor of the Municipal Building in downtown Manhattan. John told me to go to the plan-desk boy who sat at the entrance and slip him a dollar. The plan-desk boy would then ask the examiner in charge of my particular project to see me. As a rule, an appointment had to be made in advance, but if you took care of the boy sitting at the desk he could persuade the examiner to see a friend of his and help him out. John explained that I would have to present the plans to the examiner and ask him how to overcome the objections, but that I would probably have a very rough time.

Bright and early the next morning, propelled by the thought of seventy-five dollars per week and simultaneously full of apprehension, I went to the twentieth floor of the Municipal Building with a roll of plans under my arm. I managed to slip a dollar bill to the young man sitting at the plan desk, and after a half hour's wait, I was ushered in to see the examiner who had made all the objections. The man with whom I came face to face was of German origin and had only one arm; he had lost the other in the First World War. I informed him that I had come to see him about remedying the objections on the plans from the Weiser office.

"*Ach, himmel*, another one?" he said. "Young man, you are the third one who has come to me trying to get these plans fixed up. They are awful, just awful! You had better find out how to fix them yourself."

Out of desperation I pleaded, pouring out my heart as fast as I could.

"Please, sir, I am engaged to a wonderful girl and I would like to get married, and so would she, but I can't find a job that pays enough salary that would make it possible for us to get married. Mr. Weiser has offered me a job for seventy-five dollars a week if I can get these plans approved. I know that the plans are bad but if I had to correct them on my own I would be working for weeks without a salary before the plans would be acceptable. If you would be kind enough to show me how to overcome the objections, I would be able to get the job, and then you would have the satisfaction of knowing that you had done a wonderful good deed and made two young people very happy."

The German engineer looked at me in disbelief. He scratched his head while staring at me. Finally he said, "*Gott in himmel*, I have heard everything — so many crazy stories — but such a story I have never heard. I am crazy to do this, but I will be a sucker just once. I will show you how to correct these bad plans, although I should not do it."

He gave me a red pencil, sat me down at his desk, pulled out his own set of marked-up plans and started me on the corrections. Patiently and thoroughly, he went through the plans. It took about two hours. He showed me where the exits were wrong, where the steel was underdesigned, where the structure did not conform with the building code, and on and on and on until my set of plans bore exactly the same markings that were on his plans.

"Ya, I think I have been foolish, but I have done it. Now, young man, take those plans back to Weiser's office. Correct the tracings, make the cloth blueprints, and bring them in and I will stamp them approved." He scratched his head and continued, "This never have I done before. I do not know why I have done if for you, but your heartbreaking story, if it is true, is so original that I feel that for once I make an exception."

I rushed back to Mr. Weiser's office and very knowingly said to him, "Mr. Weiser, I think you need me a lot more than you realize. I was up most of the night studying these plans. There are so many mistakes. I tried correcting them all and then went down to the Building Department and found that the examiner agreed with most of my corrections. He helped me to make the remaining corrections, and now we are ready to revise the plans and get the approval." I went to work, corrected the tracings, making all the changes indicated in red on my set of blueprints, and had the necessary prints printed. I dashed back to the Building Department that very same day.

The examiner looked over the plans, checked off all the corrections, and said, "By golly, young man, you have finally finished the plans and I can approve them. Now, don't forget to send me an invitation to your wedding."

NORRIS LAPIDUS DES. 1927

ARTHUR WEISER
ARCHITECT

PRELIMINARY PLANS FOR PROPOSED HOTEL............................ DANBURY . CONNECTICUT...

Rendering of the first hotel Lapidus designed, in Danbury, Connecticut, 1927,
while he was chief draftsman for architect Arthur Weiser in New York.

The next morning I went to work for Arthur Weiser, where I remained for over a year, as the chief draftsman. Most of my work was satisfactory, although I remember one major exception. I was asked to design a hotel in Connecticut, my first opportunity to design a complete building by myself. I worked away at it for days and finally had the preliminary sketches finished. I asked Mr. Weiser to look them over so that I could prepare the final presentation drawings. He sat down at my drawing board and carefully scrutinized what I had done. He complimented me on my design and the plan but told me that I had made one glaring mistake.

"Morris," he said to me, "in modern hotels every guest room has a bathroom. I think that you had better replan the guest-room floors."

I had never stayed at a hotel other than the farmhouse hotels in the Catskill Mountains where I used to go as child with my parents. In those so-called hotels, there was usually a bathroom and toilet at the end of the corridor, and I assumed that was how all hotels were planned. My career thus far seemed to be inexorably involved with toilets, going from the plethora of toilets in the Atlantic City Convention Hall to the *verde antico* marble bathtub for Mrs. Vanderbilt and now to the complete lack of bathrooms in a hotel.

I still had a great deal to learn in my profession, which I became keenly aware of when Weiser was commissioned to plan a twelve-story office building. Work had been scarce, and a young junior draftsman and I made up Weiser's entire staff. As the chief draftsman, really the only draftsman, I had to design and engineer the office building by myself—the steel structure as well as the mechanical systems. At Columbia I had been required to take courses in all of these subjects, but I had paid very little attention. So back I went to my school notebooks—the formulas, the manuals, and whatever source material I could find. Now that I had convinced Weiser that I was a competent draftsman, I hardly dared to go back to him and tell him that this project was too much for me. I spent night after night at home working out formulas and computations so that I would not reveal my ignorance in the office. As I look back to that period, I realize how foolish it was not to make a clean breast of the entire matter. Weiser would have been disappointed, but I doubt I would have lost my job. A consulting engineer could have been retained to complete the engineering of the building.

During this traumatic period, I had my first bout with psychosomatic illness —a problem that would hound me through many years of my life. I developed splitting headaches and intestinal pains. I experienced such enervating fatigue, nausea, and dizziness that it was almost impossible for me to get out of bed in the morning. I remember one morning on my way to the office, thinking how pleasant it would be to lie down on the sidewalk and simply die. The doctor I consulted found me in perfect health. He told me that there was nothing he could do except to prescribe a strong headache remedy and suggest that I try to get more sleep. More sleep! I was up night after night working out those infernal formulas for the strength of the footings, the size of the columns, the beams, and the girders of the office building. I dreamed of water pipes and drain pipes and boilers that could not get up enough heat to keep the building warm.

Somehow I finally got the plans completed. Weiser looked them over and found them quite satisfactory. I was able to get approval from the examiner in the Building Department, and construction was started. The building was close to our office, and I passed by each day to see if the steel frame was still standing. As the concrete floors were poured, I offered up a silent prayer. The building was built and stood there for many years. It was finally torn down to make way for a much larger structure. We now always use consulting engineers for our structural and mechanical engineering, but it gave me a feeling of pride as, years later, I watched the wreckers demolish this small office building that I had engineered and which was so valiantly and strenuously resisting the wreckers' efforts.

One summer day while I was working for Arthur Weiser, I left my office and boarded a Madison Avenue trolley for a job inspection in upper Manhattan. With a roll of blueprints under my arm, dressed in a Palm Beach suit and a panama hat, I was the very model of a successful young architect. With all of the seriousness that only a very young man can achieve, I was reviewing the things that I would say as I carefully inspected the construction job, so that the elderly superintendent would overlook my youth and show proper respect for my superior professional standing. After all, I did have a diploma in architecture.

Having resolved on the proper things to say and do, I sat back and casually observed the few other passengers on the trolley. For a moment I felt that I was back in one of my daydreams. It just could not be. The elderly gray-haired gentleman sitting directly opposite could not possibly be Dr. I. Seth Hirsch — not Professor Hirsch, the head of the Bellevue X-ray department. Perhaps it was just another elderly gentleman who happened to look like him. But I looked again, and it was indeed Dr. Hirsch.

Well, here it was, my dream come true, an almost unbelievable occurrence. No longer would I have to screw up my courage to visit the doctor at the hospital and tell him that his prognostications had been wrong.

Before actually getting up to speak to the doctor, I hesitated. Will he know me? I thought. Will he remember me after ten years?

While I sat there deliberating, the trolley came to a stop. Doctor Hirsch rose from his seat and walked to the rear exit, descended from the trolley and disappeared from my life.

Morris and Beatrice Lapidus on their wedding day, 1929.

8 Marriage

While I was working in the Weiser office, a fraternity brother told me about Evan Frankel. Frankel was a contractor looking for young designers who wanted to make extra money working after regular hours. He needed sketches of storefronts that would induce prospective customers to contract with him for the construction of a store. He already had several young architects he used when necessary, but since he could never be sure of their availability he was constantly looking for new contacts among young draftsmen.

Eventually a meeting was arranged, and I went to the Ross-Frankel office to meet Evan Frankel, who was about a year older than I. He was a handsome young man, six feet tall, with a pleasant face, and he exuded confidence and affluence. He had sharp aquiline features and close-set, piercing eyes that bespoke his keen mind and sharply acquisitive nature. We worked out an hourly agreement for forthcoming work which would be done during free evenings and weekends.

Frankel showed me a set of rough drawings prepared by a well-known architect for the New York florist Wadley and Smythe. The architect had asked several store contractors to submit estimates for this installation. It was the architect's intention to complete the final plans after he had ascertained what the probable cost would be. Frankel asked me to estimate how much time it would take me to complete a set of working plans. I told him about seventy hours at three dollars per hour, or a cost of approximately two hundred dollars. Frankel said that he would take the matter up with his partner, Mr. Ross, and let me know.

Later, I discovered that instead of submitting a budget, Frankel intended to have me draw the plans so that not only could he estimate accurately the cost of building the storefront and the cabinetwork for the interior, but he would also have complete working drawings as an inducement to the architect who would save himself the expense of drawing the plans himself. In short, the architect would be receiving his full fee without going to the cost of preparing final plans. Frankel's partner, Ross, a cabinetmaker who had learned his trade in Russia, agreed with his scheme, and they decided to invest the two hundred dollars as a gamble.

Frankel told me to prepare a complete set of plans within the next ten days. I agreed, but it meant that I would have to work for an average of eight hours a night, after my regular day's work in Weiser's office. I worked each night and two weekends on the project. On a Monday morning I delivered the plans to Frankel. His ingenious idea was successful. The architect, whom I never met, was delighted with this fait accompli, a set of finished drawings and a contract price lower than the other bidders. Ross-Frankel received the contract, and I was asked to continue on the project. Detailing delicate Georgian architraves and columns and pediments with carved pineapple finials was easy for me.

Several subsequent projects from Ross-Frankel kept me quite busy, too busy. Moonlighting after a full day in Weiser's office left me little time to visit with my fiancée. We had agreed that we would not get married until I was earning at least one hundred and fifty dollars a week. I had achieved my goal, but it meant long hours of night work and weekends spent over a drawing board. Both Ross and Frankel liked my work, and more importantly, so did their customers.

Frankel suggested that I come to work for him on a full-time basis, but I told him that I had no desire to leave architecture and go into the store field. I had no desire to be a store designer; to my mind, that was not architecture. At Ross-Frankel, however, I saw the possibility of earning enough to get married, and Bea and I were impatient. So when Evan Frankel finally offered me a job at a sum that was more than my goal — two hundred dollars a week, ten thousand dollars a year — I took it. Furthermore, he practically promised that I would be earning a great deal more within a year or two. At the time the average earnings of a practicing architect, according to government statistics, were seven thousand a year. That was the average, mind you. There were many architects earning five thousand dollars and less per year. As a senior designer, I might be able to earn one hundred and fifty dollars a week in five or ten years. So once again, as I had given up acting and stage design, I gave up my dream of a career and went to work for Ross-Frankel. Evan knew that I was already engaged to Bea and that I was waiting for her to finish her teacher's degree at Hunter College. But Evan had other plans for me. He was a bachelor and had every intention of remaining one for the rest of his life — and as a matter of fact, he never did get married.

Whenever we were together, Evan harped on the subject of the bliss of bachelorhood and the carefree life that it made possible. He drove a sporty red Stutz Bearcat roadster, and in cold weather he wore a raccoon coat. One day he suggested that he and I go out together with two girls to get a taste of what life would be like as a bachelor rather than as a husband tied down by a wife and, eventually, children. He suggested that we meet at his apartment hotel. I arrived early and waited for Evan in the lobby. While I was waiting, two young ladies came through the lobby and went up in the elevator. They were both gorgeous. One, a beautiful platinum blond, was dressed in a black formal riding habit with a black derby perched perkily on the glistening tresses. The other one was in a lovely evening gown. The girl in the evening gown had a milk-white complexion and striking jet black hair and black eyes. Everyone in the lobby followed them with their eyes until they stepped into the elevator. A short time later, Evan drove up in his red roadster and hurried into the lobby.

"Sorry to be late, old man. Let's go right up before the girls get here." So up we went and when we walked into Evan's suite, I was confronted by the two gorgeous damsels. Since I had spent most of my life with family and relatives, I had had very little opportunity to make contacts with such girls as these. I panicked. How in the world could I possibly spend the evening with them? What would I talk about? Evan turned to me and whispered, "Morris, you can take the blond or brunette. Tonight is the opening night of the horse show and I have arranged for four tickets. We'll go to dinner and then on to the horse show — we're going to have a ball!"

This may have seemed like a wonderful prospect to Evan, but for me the prospect of an entire evening with these two girls was sheer madness. I turned to Evan and told him that I was sorry, I was not feeling well, and I had to get home as fast as possible. He thought that I had suddenly gone crazy. Without a further word to Evan or a goodnight to the girls to whom I had not yet been introduced, I bolted for the door. Not only was Evan never able to persuade me that I ought to remain a bachelor, but rather, he convinced me that above all I wanted to marry my sweetheart and settle down. I wanted a family life just as I had always had with my aunts, uncles, and cousins.

My first important project with Ross-Frankel was a large ladies' apparel shop in the recently completed Palmer House Hotel in Chicago. The three-story emporium was to be the largest store in the ladies' ready-to-wear chain known as Mangel's. I developed the entire project in my new office at Ross-Frankel, but as it neared completion, Evan Frankel ask me to go to Chicago to supervise the work. Bea and I were still not married, but the date was set. My trip to Chicago meant a first long separation for us and my first long trip by train. We would not see each other for three months. There were preparations to be made for our wedding, but I would be more than a thousand miles away.

We arranged to meet for lunch the day that I was to leave so that Bea could see me off on the *Twentieth Century Limited*. She intended to cut her afternoon classes at Hunter College and meet me in a restaurant near Grand Central Terminal at one o'clock. That morning I went directly to Grand Central and checked my bag so that I could pick it up after lunch before boarding the train. At half past twelve I left my office and hurried to the restaurant to wait for Bea. At ten minutes to one I was at the entrance anxiously looking over the heads of the hurrying crowds to catch my first glimpse of her. One, one fifteen, one thirty, two o'clock, and still no Bea. I was getting frantic. I stood there tortured and tormented, not knowing what to do. At a quarter to three, I could wait no longer. The train left at 3:01, so I dashed over to the station, signaled to a redcap to pick up my bag, hurried through Gate 27 marked *Twentieth Century Limited*, and ran down the red carpet to the Pullman sleeper whose number was indicated on my ticket. I dropped into my assigned seat, huddled in misery, not knowing what to think. Fury and fear mingled as I tried to imagine what had kept Bea from meeting me. Five minutes remained before the train was to leave.

Suddenly, she came running along the platform peering into window after window looking for me. I dashed breathlessly out onto the platform. We could hardly speak to each other we were so upset. All I heard her say was, "The professor sprung an exam on us and I was unable to leave. I'm sorry, darling, so sorry." She was crying and so was I. We held each other closely. Then came the command, "All aboard, all aboard—Twentieth Century for Chicago leaving—all aboard." We kissed and mumbled promises to write before I jumped onto the platform of the moving car.

Now that I knew all was well with Bea, I relaxed and looked around the Pullman car. The porter had changed into a crisp white jacket. The car was decorated in soft shades of brown, and the upholstery was deliciously soft. The lights were perfect for reading. The carpet was thick and rich. The car smelled of fresh lacquer. When I went back to the dining car as dusk began to fall along the Hudson River, I discovered a new delight. The color scheme was pink, beige, and chocolate brown. The linens were snow white, and the silver and glassware were polished to a shimmering iridescence. The whole car seemed to glow in the late afternoon light.

After a steak dinner, capped off with a succulent, hot apple pie with a large slab of cheddar cheese and coffee, I went back to the observation lounge to read before turning in for my first night's sleep on a train. I watched town after town glide by as the sun set. Each city appeared to be a stage set with lights beaming from the windows of the houses. I read a book and when I felt myself nodding, I knew that it was time for me to go back to my Pullman car and get into my berth. The coverlet was turned down and the reading lamp was lit. After a quick wash in the men's room, I crawled into my berth and fell asleep riding the finest train in the world.

When I arrived in Chicago, I went directly to the glamorous Palmer House. This hotel was to be my home for the next three months while I supervised the final installations in the Mangel store. No expense had been spared in the design and construction of what was then America's most luxurious hotel; it remained number one until the Waldorf Astoria in New York was completed about eight years later. Cast bronze, fine woods, and an abundance of beautiful marbles were used to achieve an elegance in the interiors, hitherto found only in the most luxurious European hostelries. The elegant Empire Room was a breathtaking setting for dining, dancing, and entertainment. The Victorian Room, with its classic columns and glittering crystal chandeliers, was an opulent setting for gourmet dining. The Chicago Room, for men only, with its floor-to-ceiling mural of a three-hundred-sixty-degree panorama of the Windy City, was a daring and successful new concept for quiet, dignified dining. There were other dining rooms, each with its own theme decor where waiters served with impeccable flair and delightfully courteous efficiency.

There was a room in the Palmer House known as the Chinoiserie, which took its name from the beautiful Chinese Chippendale decor. The first time I ate there the waiter handed me a menu that indicated a choice of soups, a choice of four different main courses, as well as a choice of vegetables, and finally desserts. I studied the menu and told the waiter which soup I had selected. After bringing the soup and without any further direction from me, he wheeled in a serving cart on which all four main courses rested in chafing dishes, together with at least four types of vegetables. The waiter noticed that I hesitated in making my choice, and he suggested that I try a little of each. I did just that. While I was sampling each of the different types of food, the waiter wheeled away the serving cart. I looked after it rather wistfully, wishing I had taken a little more. Again the observant waiter noticed my expression and told me that he was simply taking the cart away so that he could keep the food warm and that he would bring it back shortly. This he did, and he urged me to go on with a second helping of all the delicious dishes. With the desserts I was again encouraged to try each of them. The chef seemed to enjoy varying the menu. Each day that I came to the restaurant, I found new and different dishes. The price for this Lucullan feast was exactly one dollar.

Aside from my gustatory pleasures, tasting the magnificence of the Palmer House was my first experience as a guest in a fine hotel. Much of what I used in my designs for hotels years later was inspired by the refinement and luxury that surrounded me during that stay at the Palmer House.

My days were full and exciting. I worked with the engineers and the technical personnel of the hotel as well as with the various contractors and their mechanics in the construction of the new Mangel store. I was in full charge of the project, and it was a heady and exhilarating experience to see my designs come to life as the work progressed. This was what I had dreamed of while I was learning to become an architect. I was living the role of the master builder. Contractors and craftsmen looked to me for advice and approval with a respect that was most flattering for a young man who was only two years out of school. My days were wonderful, but the evenings and the nights were empty and lonely. I made no friends in Chicago during those three months. Away from the job, I was left entirely to myself. After a lonely dinner I might go to a movie or even get to see a burlesque show. There was little or no legitimate theater in Chicago then. Burlesque was in its lusty heyday, and some of the future great comics and film and television actors were the "top bananas" and the straight men in the traveling burlesque companies that came to Chicago. But once back, I found it increasingly difficult to go to sleep. I would read into the small hours of the morning waiting to fall asleep. As soon as I turned out the lights, however, I became wide awake and would start reading again. I tried long walks, hot chocolate before retiring, a warm bath — but all to no avail. One night I found myself pounding the walls with my fists, screaming in desperation and actually trying to tear out my hair. My elegant bedroom in the Palmer House was becoming my prison, my torture chamber. I took to roaming the streets of the Chicago Loop. When the sky started to lighten with the coming dawn, I went back to my room to wait for the new day. Sitting in an armchair, fully clothed, I would finally fall asleep only to awaken an hour later to start a new day on the job.

Desperate and exhausted, I finally went to see the hotel doctor. After examining me and questioning me, he prescribed a sleeping pill that I was to take each night for the ten days left before the project would be completed. His diagnosis was homesickness. The doctor assured me that on the day I boarded the train for my trip home, I would be cured of my insomnia. He was right. The moment I crawled into my lower berth and put my head on the clean, cool, sweet-smelling pillow, I was sound asleep.

When the *Twentieth Century* arrived in New York, I went to the nearest phone to call Bea and took the subway home. I was greeted by my mother and then hurried to Bea's house. There were still small details to be ironed out before our wedding ceremony in the Leveritch Towers, a hotel in Brooklyn. The wedding took place in the afternoon with ten of my friends dressed as groomsmen in cutaways. Ten bridesmaids — all Bea's friends — wore frilly dresses and large hats. The musicians were friends of my younger brother. A fraternity brother, a young rabbi, conducted the marriage services. All went perfectly as Bea had planned it. She had arranged for the musicians to play all the proper music before and during the solemn ceremony, but after the ceremony, the young musicians broke into a popular song, "You're the Top." Our picture appeared in the rotogravure section of the *New York Times* — I in my formal afternoon attire and Bea in her flowing white gown holding a huge bouquet of calla lilies.

After the wedding and an overnight stay at the Leveritch Towers, we left on a cruise, the first of many that we would take over the next sixty years. The first part of our honeymoon was aboard the British *Royal Mail Steam Packet*, and the first port of call was the once beautiful Havana. We visited Morro Castel, the Columbus cathedral, the National Gardens and the racetrack. We dined on the roof garden of the famous National Hotel. From Havana we sailed to Santiago de Cuba, the original home of Bacardi rum. We were offered free drinks and were given six small bottles of rum as a gift.

The next port was Kingston, Jamaica, then still a British colony. We traveled to Old Spanish Town, the oldest city of Jamaica, and visited the famous Castleton Gardens. We were served tea on the lawn of the Myrtle Beach Hotel, with impeccable service by waiters in red-and-white uniforms wearing white gloves. The tea was served from fine English silver in white bone-china cups and saucers, accompanied by thin cucumber and watercress sandwiches, while peacocks strutted among the guests. I did not have even the slightest inkling that years later I would design the finest luxury hotel in Ocho Rios, as well as several others on this beautiful island.

Our trip on the *Araguaya* ended in Nassau, where we stayed at the Fort Montague Hotel. We took a ferry to Paradise Island with its gleaming white beaches. Years later I would help build a bridge from Nassau to Paradise Island, where I designed the Paradise Island Hotel and its large gambling casino. From Nassau we sailed to Haiti, and from that beautiful but poverty-stricken island we finally arrived in Miami. Our stay was at the (now defunct) Wofford Hotel, which was next to the great Roney Plaza Hotel. North of these two hotels stretched the empty island of Miami Beach with its spectacular beaches. This island dredged in from the ocean by Carl Fisher would become my home years later. On those long stretches of beach I would design my still famous Fontainebleau Hotel and the Eden Roc adjoining it. I would also design luxury apartments on Collins Avenue, a large theater, schools, and other structures.

We took a taxi from the port to Miami Beach to the Wofford Hotel. Prohibition was then in effect, but Bea wanted to smuggle in her six bottles of rum. She put the bottles inside her girdle. When the uniformed doorman opened the taxi door and helped Bea out, one of the bottles escaped and plopped to the pavement. The sweet smell of rum filled the warm, balmy air. While I paid the fare, she ran toward the hotel entrance, only to have two more bottles crash to the sidewalk. Surrounded by the heady aroma of rum, we finally reached the security of the hotel lobby. This was our grand entry to Miami Beach.

We spent a pleasant five days exploring the island and acquiring a fine deep tan. At the end of the five days we boarded a ship bound for New York and family. We returned to the Leveritch Towers while we looked for an apartment. We found what we wanted on Albemarle Road in Flatbush in Brooklyn. We furnished it in the Italian-Renaissance style complete with a wrought-iron gate, a bishop's heraldic banner, and reproduction Renaissance furniture, which had been aged by brushing, beating with chains, and even shot with a shotgun to create fake wormholes. The sofa and chairs were upholstered with red damask. Our first piece of art was a cast of a bust of Marietta Strozzi, a daughter of a famous Florentine. Our little apartment reflected the historical style I loved most at that time. Marietta Strozzi still sits on a music cabinet in the living room of my duplex apartment in Miami Beach.

Forsythe shoe store, New York, 1929.

9 New Theories in Store Design

Between 1929 and 1933 I developed new theories about store design. The recently uncovered ruins of Pompeii revealed many types of stores in this ancient city. Through the centuries, stores were either open markets or craftsmen's shops and homes where the merchandise produced within was often displayed in the windows fronting the street. The industrial revolution of the nineteenth century moved the manufacture of merchandise into factories. Shops or stores were built for the sale of various types of merchandise and had storefronts. An object such as a shoe or a hat was hung outside the store and served as a sign.

By the beginning of the twentieth century, stores were becoming more sophisticated. When I entered the field of store design, the newest development was the creation of an arcade giving the merchant more window display areas before the entrance to the store. My designs had to draw customers into the stores. So began my studies, not of design, but of people: how to find design elements that would stop people on the street and entice them into the store.

One early success was the Theresa Pharmacy, built in 1928 in the Ansonia Building. The pharmacist already had a store in Harlem, which was an elegant neighborhood at the turn of the century, but his trade was moving to the Upper West Side along Broadway. He wanted to follow his customers and build a "modern" drugstore. At that time, the word modern had a magic ring. He did not know exactly what a modern drugstore should be like and neither did anyone else. Eventually, he came to Ross-Frankel with his problem. I told Evan Frankel that I knew just what this man should have in his new drugstore. After some convincing of the client by the persuasive Evan Frankel, I finally got the chance to design something other than the pseudoclassic stores that were in vogue.

I decided that since drugs and cosmetics were colorfully packaged, I would use black as the predominant color in the store. The pilasters of the wall cases were designed like attenuated skyscrapers terminating in the wedding-cake silhouettes of the 1920s. The cornice of the cases was embellished with a machine-carved molding imported from Germany. By finishing the skyscraper pilasters and the city silhouette cornice in black ebony highlighted with silver leaf—black and silver motifs were popular then—I achieved a modern look. The ceiling was painted black and was relieved with large, silver-leaf sunbursts fashioned of plaster, from the center of which were suspended light fixtures made of a milky glass held together with lead strips like those used in stained-glass windows. I had designed them in tiers, their appearance again suggesting the skyscraper silhouette. The floor was covered with bright red linoleum. The soda fountain had a fluted silvered front with a black Belgian marble countertop. The show windows were angled in from the two side walls toward a pair of entrance doors. These doors had ebonized wood frames trimmed with silver leaf surrounding plate glass etched with patterns from my designs. In the show windows, instead of the usual ceiling with its silvered glass lighting reflectors, I used frosted glass and placed the reflectors above the glass so that the light source could not be seen. It may have been the first appearance of the ubiquitous luminous ceiling of today. The skyscraper motif, the color scheme of black, silver, and red, the etched glass, the in-sloping windows, and the luminous ceiling were unmistakably *modern*. Since no one had really defined contemporary or modern styling for stores, my version was accepted. Those skyscraper pilasters and lighting fixtures were picked up by other designers and used in stores for the next several years ad nauseam. Happily, the style did not last too long, but the Theresa Pharmacy was something new and opened the doors for newer and better contemporary styling.

For my next few store designs I went totally modern. I was convinced that this was a time when I could say "anything goes." The merchants wanted more show windows, so the store vestibules were made deeper and deeper. The planes of the show windows were arranged in a plan that can be described as zigzag, sawtooth, angled, stepped, or anything else, as long as I was able to give more windows and more space for display. The entrance doors were moved ten feet back from the street, then twenty feet, then thirty feet — there was no limit.

Inside the stores I tried everything. Pilasters were topped by carved female figures or jazzed-up modern whatnots. The cornices were embellished with carved moldings in the latest hopped-up modern. The floor plans for the merchandise cases were tortured and twisted. The merchants were ready for every kooky idea as long as it could be called modern. This was the Jazz Age. John Held, Jr. and the flapper were "in." As long as I jazzed up my designs for the stores, everything was okay.

Three years after I received my degree, I was eligible to apply for a license to practice architecture under my own name. One of the requisites, however, was that the applicant had worked three years for a licensed architect. I wanted to apply, but I had worked for only two years for two architects and one year for Ross-Frankel — which did not count. My problem was to find an architect who was willing to give me a letter saying I had worked for him in a period when I was working for Ross-Frankel.

I finally found an architect whom I persuaded to write this fictitious letter. He was a graduate of Columbia. I had rendered his projects for two years and I was now asking him for a favor that he found difficult to refuse. He was practicing in a suburban city north of New York City. I went to his office to look at his work so that I could answer any question about that missing third year. Thus prepared, I went for my examination — in those days it was oral — with fear and trepidation.

The examination was held in the office of a well-known architect, where five other architects acted as judges. I arrived at the appointed time, but there were two other applicants before me. I had heard stories of the impossible questions that made applicants quake in fear, and justly so because the chance of receiving a license the first time was about one in ten. Most applicants had to take the test at least three times before finally passing. As I sat there waiting, the two applicants came out red-faced and sweating. At last my name was called.

Six interrogators sat in the conference room. I had with me some of the plans that I had drawn while working for Arthur Weiser. One of the sets of plans was the hotel commission in which I had learned that every guest room of a hotel had its own bathroom. I unrolled these hotel plans first. Some of the examining architects were making a decision on the last applicant. I listened to the verdict — not passed. While waiting for the interrogation to begin, one of the examiners was studying my plans of the hotel. He asked me for the name of the client who had not gone ahead with his hotel. When I told him the name he turned to two other architects and told them that he had drawn plans for the same client for the same hotel. He asked me whether we had been paid. When I told him that we had not, he exclaimed to the other architects that the client had never paid him either. A diatribe followed about clients who came to them and never paid their fees.

While this was going on the chief examiner called the meeting to order so that he could read my letters of recommendation from the three architects. When he came to the false letter he paused and asked if I had really worked for this architect. I answered with a quaking heart that I had. I felt that my doom was already decided. Instead, he declared to his colleagues that he knew this architect and that if I had indeed worked for him I had received a thorough training. He asked if any of the examining architects had any questions. As if in a dream, I heard each examiner say that they had no questions for me. The chief examiner thanked me for coming in and informed me that I had passed.

I left the examination in a state of bewilderment and euphoria. I called the architect who had taken a serious risk by falsifying his letter for me. I told him about the chief examiner who thought so highly of him. My colleague told me that he had never heard of this chief examiner, and there was probably another architect with the same name.

The stock market crash of 1929 had meant very little to us at Ross-Frankel, where we continued to do good business. One day we contracted with a new type of client and, for me, a new challenge — a jeweler, with a store on the corner of 125th Street and Broadway. Harlem was still a solid middle-class neighborhood. This jeweler wanted me to design a jewelry store that would establish him as the leading jeweler in Harlem. He wanted me to create for him the most outstanding and modern jewelry store ever attempted.

Our client's store had been well publicized as "Herbert's, the Home of Blue-White Diamonds." He had developed an excellent image through the young communication and entertainment medium — radio. He was one of the first to sponsor a musical program featuring a young Yale graduate by the name of Rudy Vallee. The program was known as Rudy Vallee and his Connecticut Yankees and would catapult the young singer to fame and national recognition.

I began designing a jewelry store that I hoped would be something new, even revolutionary. I wanted an elegant store interior with showcases scaled to the minuscule size of the merchandise on display. The walls I designed were richly paneled with Circassian walnut. A continuous horizontal display area only twelve inches in height and six inches in depth was set at eye level into the flush wood paneling. This brilliantly illuminated band ran around the four walls of the interior, interrupted only by the entrance and an impressive vault door, which I framed with silver-leafed, carved wood ornament. It was the same art deco fruit-and-flower garland carvings that I had used in my previous store designs. The two columns in the store were sheathed with walnut, which was fluted, reminiscent of classical columns, crowned with silvered carvings instead of classical capitals. I designed special lighting fixtures suspended over the sales counter to give brilliance and life to those blue-white diamonds of which Herbert boasted.

I used the same approach in the design of the show windows, scaling them down to the size of the merchandise — watches, rings, brooches, and so on. Until then, it was customary to run show windows from display platform height to ceiling, but I had decided that there was no special reason for doing this and I dropped the height of the show-window glass to just above normal head height so that people could concentrate on the merchandise displayed without being distracted by empty space above. Over the entrance I designed a marquee which, for the first time, used neon tubing as a design element. Neon tubing was a rather new medium used only to illuminate signs. I created a large, faceted diamond with a wrought-iron frame into which prismatic glass was set and illuminated from behind. This, in turn, was surrounded by a blue-and-white sunburst of neon to express the brilliance of the much advertised blue-white diamonds. When finished, Herbert's jewelry store made quite an impact in the jewelry trade.

Herbert arranged for an impressive ceremony that was broadcast on the radio. By then, Rudy Vallee was playing the big time in the new Loew's Paramount Theater on Broadway, where his act consisted of crooning through a megaphone to the ecstatic wailings of his young female admirers. Herbert tried to get Vallee to make an appearance, but despite his debt to Herbert as his first sponsor, he declined. For the first time in my budding career, I was asked to give a one-minute speech on the radio. How sweet it was to have people I knew tell me that they had heard me on their radios! The store was photographed, and illustrated articles appeared in trade journals showing the latest trend in jewelry store design. Ross-Frankel was credited as designer. Aside from my one minute on the radio, my only recognition was a handsome ring that Herbert presented to me. It was inscribed "A token of appreciation to Morris Lapidus, Architect, for designing and building the new home of the blue-white diamonds — 1931."

One day the young lady in our office who was bookkeeper, secretary, and phone operator received a call from a gentleman who wanted to know who had designed a small shoe shop on Fifth Avenue in New York, which our firm had recently completed. She gave him my name. When I called him back, I learned that he was an editor with *Architectural Forum*, the most prestigious architectural magazine at the time. He told me that he admired very much the little shoe shop called The Parisian Bootery and that he was considering publishing it as an example of the contemporary trend in store design. He invited me to visit him the next day and to bring with me photographs of other work that I had designed. The Parisian Bootery, though small, was my first opportunity to embody the simple, clean lines of contemporary architecture scaled to create an elegant modern ladies' shoe salon. The editor was impressed with my work. He promised to consider several of my projects, but he decided to definitely publish one of them. I explained that the credit line would have to read "Designed by Ross-Frankel."

"And who was Ross-Frankel?" he wanted to know.

I explained that I was employed as a designer for this firm and that our agreement was that only the firm was to receive recognition in any work that was published. Although I had a license to practice architecture, I had agreed that I would not use that title and that all designs were to be the property of the firm.

The editor sat me down and lectured me on the ethics of the profession and berated me for having so little self-esteem that I could allow myself and my ability to be used by a firm that had no moral or ethical excuse for taking the credit for my talents. I hungered for the recognition that he was holding out, but I did have an agreement, and the work could not be published with my name, much as I would have liked it to be. The editor, whose name I have forgotten, but whose influence and determination I shall never forget, insisted that either I talk to my employers, or that he would, about proper recognition. In the end it was he who, after a lengthy dispute with Evan Frankel, convinced my employer that they would gain rather than lose by having the credit line read, "Morris Lapidus, Architect for Ross-Frankel." And that is how the first publication of my work came about.

"The Parisian Bootery, though small, was my first opportunity to embody the simple, clean lines of contemporary architecture scaled to create an elegant ladies' shoe salon."

Parisian Bootery, Fifth Avenue, New York, 1928. This was the first store design by Lapidus to be published, in *Architectural Forum*.

Although the rest of the country was hit hard by the Depression, Ross-Frankel continued have work. Most of my colleagues had been unemployed for months and years. Many of them went back to live with their families. Soup kitchens fed men who had once been tycoons. Selling apples on the street corners was an honest way to support a family. "Brother, Can You Spare a Dime?" became a hit song. Bea and I never really felt the Depression, even though my salary had been cut to seventy-five dollars a week. In those days it was unusual to be able to have a nice apartment, a car, and to keep a part-time maid.

Our work was just beginning to slow down in 1932, when Franklin Delano Roosevelt was elected President. Banks closed and we waited. After telling us that we had nothing to fear but fear itself, President Roosevelt set about getting our economy going through a process that has become known as "pump priming." Specifically, it meant the government was pumping money into depressed areas to get the economy, which had practically ground to a halt, going again.

The first pump-priming activity took place in the southeastern part of the United States, and its effects were felt at once by us at Ross-Frankel. We had come through the Depression fairly well, but now with a new affluence developing, we found ourselves busy indeed. Most of our clients were chain-store operators who sold various types of merchandise in stores located around the country. These chain-store operators had suffered along with the rest of the country's economy, but with the injection of money into certain areas, especially in the South, a new prosperity was born. People went to work on government projects and came home with fat salary envelopes. Money was there to be spent, and the chain-store owners wanted to be there to help them spend it. As business increased, the chain-store real estate executives went looking for new locations where money was plentiful.

One of the first areas to feel this new prosperity was Tennessee, where the Tennessee Valley Authority began pouring billions into public works and dams. I soon found myself traveling to cities throughout the South to inspect and measure new locations for which stores were planned. Knoxville was one of the first cities that I visited, but soon I had covered Nashville, Memphis, Chattanooga, and then on to Birmingham, Alabama, as well as smaller towns in that state such as Anniston and Florence, and the capital, Montgomery. The next wave was in Georgia, with Atlanta as the focal point, where we had a number of stores to be designed. Then followed Savannah, Augusta, Waycross, and then into the Carolinas, in cities such as Columbia and High Point. All my travel was by train. I learned a new way of life in these southern towns and a new way of life on the railroads.

My first trip to Knoxville, Tennessee, was in 1934. Main Street had not changed since the Civil War: farmers still brought their produce into town and backed up their horse-drawn wagons under covered sheds where housewives did their daily shopping; the grocery stores still had barrels of flour and rice and even the proverbial cracker barrel; the general stores sold merchandise ranging from lanterns and shovels to ladies' and men's clothing. I came to Knoxville with the real estate executive of the Mangel chain to negotiate a long-term lease for a large store that was then occupied by a family clothing business. The real estate man negotiated a forty-year lease right there on the spot. The merchant was to receive as his rent two thousand dollars a month — an income significantly higher than that he was earning as a storekeeper — and he would be allowed to continue to live in his apartment over the store. The Mangel executive suggested that since the merchant had been selling clothes in Knoxville for so many years and knew the people there, he might like to stay on as a manager of the store at one hundred dollars a week plus a bonus depending on the sales volume. The man was delighted with the proposition, and thus began a new era on Main Street, not only on Main Street, Knoxville, but on Main Streets throughout the United States.

Knoxville in those days was a small town. When I went back to install more stores in that city two years later, it had changed drastically. Gone were the farmers' wagons and the covered sheds. Fine new modern stores lined Main Street. Excellent merchandise was available, and the people had money to spend. Knoxville was only one of the many cities throughout the South that exploded into prosperity in a period of two or three years. As prosperity spread through the country, I was following it, traveling by train to inspect and measure stores and to supervise installations of more chains that sold men's clothing, women's clothing, men's shoes, women's shoes, children's clothing, haberdashery, and every other type of apparel.

Not only was the face of Main Street changing, but the people on it were changing too. Men and women wore the latest fashions. Well-dressed women became a national phenomenon. The wife of a mill worker in Alabama could dress as well and as smartly as the wife of an executive in Chicago or New York. All the theories that I had been developing in stores were no longer only for the large cities. No matter how small the city, I made each store as exciting and architecturally dramatic as the stores on Fifth Avenue or Michigan Boulevard.

In 1934 I had to make a trip to four locations — Chicago, San Francisco, Galveston, and New Orleans — where I would take the necessary measurements to design and build new shops. There was no urgency, and at about this time I was due to take a two-week vacation. Our first son was almost two years old. My wife and I decided to leave our son with his grandmother and two aunts who all lived together, and go to all four store sites, taking our time along the way.

We began our trip by taking the *Twentieth Century Limited* to Chicago. Our next destination was San Francisco, but we took an indirect route by various trains to visit the redwood forests, the Petrified Forest, Yellowstone National Park, Yosemite National Park, and a stop at the Grand Canyon. We stayed at the Yellowstone Hotel, the Old Faithful Hotel, and the Awahnee Hotel in Yosemite.

Our trip through the National Parks in 1934 was an experience that today's vacationers will never know. Few people in those years went to see the wonders of Yellowstone or the Grand Canyon. As we waited for Old Faithful to erupt, there were only a dozen people to witness this natural miracle. In the redwood forest we toured the park on a bus carrying a total of ten people. At the Awahnee we were among about fifteen guests who watched the "Fire Fall." At the Grand Canyon the two of us were alone with two park rangers.

The train travel was a wonderful life. Unfortunately, it took me away from my home too often, too much. It meant long separations from my children and wife. On the occasion of our thirtieth wedding anniversary, Bea arranged for a lovely cake with only fifteen candles. Bea laughed and said to me, "Though we have been married thirty years, I have spent only fifteen of them with you." We all laughed, but I felt a deep pain. It was a poignant reminder of my absence from home for so many long trips. But this was my career, and this was the life I was forced to lead.

Those years of store design and train travel, interesting and financially rewarding as they may have been, were creatively unfulfilling. More and more architects were entering the field of store design. I was no longer one of the select few. What once may have been sensationally new, was now becoming the commonplace and the expected.

There was one brief, exhilarating interlude. Evan Frankel brought a new client to our office. His name was Ben Marden. He proposed to build the most elegant nightclub in the city of New York. Many years before there had been a club in New York called the Palais Royale where Paul Whiteman had been the orchestra leader. The Depression had seen the demise of that elegant night spot. Ben Marden proposed to reopen this club and, once again, make it the chic rendezvous of society.

My enthusiasm for the project and the eloquence with which I described the kind of nightclub I would create if Ross-Frankel were given the commission won Marden over. The staging and the lighting presented a marvelous challenge for me. The Palais Royale would feature not only famous performers but also a bevy of lovely dancers. I was asked to come up with new staging effects: stairways for stars to walk down, platforms for beautiful show girls, unusual locations for dramatic entrances and exits. A huge electrical panel with a formidable bank of switches and dimmers was designed to create a variety of moods and colors. A large ventilation system was installed that blew air at high velocity through a large metal chamber up in the building roof trusses over which dozens of blocks of ice were placed. The air was forced through this chamber under the blocks of melting ice so that it passed through the extreme cold air as if it were blowing through a refrigerator. It was necessary to replenish this ice box with dozens of blocks of ice each day. It was a crude method, but it worked. For the first time that I know of, cooled air was introduced into the interior of a large public room.

An arched, vaulted ceiling was divided with ribs, behind each of which I concealed three rows of lamps, one blue, one red, and another yellow. By manipulating the dimmers, I was able to create almost every color of the rainbow. Newspaper columnists took note of the new type of night club that was being created. For the first time, I saw my name appear in a gossip column. As the project neared completion, Broadway people were allowed in to see the results. Leonitoff, the famous impresario of the great Roxy Theater, where the most resplendent stage spectaculars of the day were produced, complimented me on my artistry and skill. He promised to call me shortly. He told me that he could use a man of my talents as an assistant. The nightclub owners assured me that all their future clubs would be designed only by me.

"Kid, you're gonna be the hottest thing on Broadway when this club opens." I heard this repeated again and again. Finally, the great day came — opening night at the Palais Royale. The most important people in New York attended the gala evening: Fred Keating was master of ceremonies for the star-studded review; the featured stars included a recent import from Paris, Jeanne Obert, The Yacht Club Boys, as popular then as the Beatles were in the sixties, and the Boswell Sisters (Connie was to go on to individual stardom later). The music was by Emil Coleman and his orchestra. The dance routines were created by the great choreographers Doris Humphrey and Charles Weidman. The dancers included Ernestine Hockman and Eleanor King and an unknown male dancer, Jack Cole. The entire evening, including a wonderful program of entertainment and a superb dinner, cost five dollars — a steep price for a country slowly emerging from its most disastrous depression ever. But people came in droves. At the bottom of the printed souvenir program a line in bold type read "Entire decoration conceived and designed by Morris Lapidus."

The post-Depression days were creating an era that wanted more and more stores. I was kept busy, and my staff of draftsmen and designers grew as Ross-Frankel expanded its activities. The publication of my stores in architectural magazines was increasing. Apparently, I was doing something right. My work was not only admired by the critics, but the stores that I designed produced higher sales volume for my clients.

Shortly after I began designing stores, I wandered into a bookstore that sold foreign magazines. I spotted one that gave me my first solid design element. The magazine was published in Germany and was called *Gebrauchsgraphik*. It was a magazine of graphics used for packaging, sign identification, and exhibits. It was like no magazine published in the United States. I immediately paid for a year's subscription and went on to receive this magazine for over ten years. I must admit that Europe was way ahead of us. I used the bold European graphics to create the signs that identified my stores. My first little shoe store on Fifth Avenue used this type of lettering. Element number one in my store design became bold graphics.

The second element in my design came about when the glass industry learned to bend large plates of glass into greater rounds. I used this curved glass at the entrance of store fronts. A pedestrian unconsciously followed the curve and found himself or herself entering the store front vestibule or arcade.

I also began to study human nature. The first book I bought was *The Outline of History* by H.G. Wells, and I started a library of anthropology. In these books I found clues to human behavior. I developed theories based on these studies, one of which I was able to test.

Most store interiors of the early 1930s were monochromatic. They were painted in several shades of beige or gray or, when we wanted to be particularly feminine, in subdued tones of pink. I reasoned that the visual impact of good color had drawing power. Colors could attract or repel. Why not use strong pleasant colors to draw people into stores and make them want to come in and buy? I tried selling this idea to a number of clients, but most of them simply refused to take a chance to find out what would happen. I argued that if colorful posters made people stop and look, why not use the same principle in store interiors? The owner of the Mangel chain stores who had let me have my own way in the Palmer House store listened to my theory that color could attract people. I told him my ideas of using soft blues, warm yellows, and shades of rose. I described using wallpaper with a pattern of large roses on the theory that color would sell more panties and brassieres, more blouses and dresses than in a nice gray store. He was sure that a multicolored store interior would clash with his merchandise, but he was willing to let me try my theory, provided we would not charge him extra for repainting the store in a nice warm gray when the experiment failed.

The first store that was used for this experiment was in Jacksonville, Florida. I was there for several weeks toward the end of the project, personally mixing the paint colors for the painters to be certain that they were all just right. I enjoyed supervising this part of the work, and the painters were amused and pleased to be working with such unusual colors. The night before the grand opening, Mr. Mangel himself came to see the results. He was horrified. If it had not been too late to repaint the entire store before the opening, he would have had the painters replace the colors with his favorite shade of gray. He snorted that the store looked more like a circus than a ladies' ready-to-wear shop.

The next day, Mr. Mangel and I spent time together inside the store and outside on the sidewalk in front of the show windows listening to customer comments. I was vindicated. "Such beautiful colors — such a pleasant store — why hadn't anyone else thought of using such pretty colors?" Other merchants came in to congratulate Mr. Mangel and tell him how clever he had been to realize that color helped sales. They were going to get their stores painted in this modern manner as soon as possible. Mr. Mangel thought that they were all crazy. He still preferred gray.

Through the years I have been chastised by critics for the exuberant use of color in my designs. I decided a long time ago that I wanted to please as many people as possible and if the critics objected, I would have to bear their barbed comments and stick to my own theories of color and adornment for all my work. In my search for emotion in architecture, I went back through human history in my quest for the origin of people's reactions to color and adornment. Throughout the ages, people have loved to use color.

Color enhanced buildings and interiors in many past epochs. For example, although we now see very little color in Gothic churches because time has removed it, brilliant colors were applied to the carved stone and to the carved wood when these churches were built; stained glass flooded their interiors with a rainbow of color. The ancient Greeks and Romans used colors extensively: the rediscovery of the ruins of Pompeii, where volcanic ash preserved the original colors, proved that Roman homes and temples were brightly colored. The beautiful white marble sculptures of the great age of Pericles in Athens were not originally white—everything that was carved was also painted in brilliant hues. Egyptian temples were alive with color, traces of which still can be seen. The Babylonians used brightly glazed brick on their buildings. Persian temples and palaces vibrated with color. But the human love of color perhaps began even much earlier. Primitive men and women used mud to decorate themselves and put on shells and animal teeth for bangles; we are still doing exactly the same thing but in a more sophisticated manner. The cave dwellers satisfied their search for beauty with wall carvings and paintings; we still carry on the same tradition of color and adornment in our homes, our churches, our schools, and in every form of architecture.

Having evolved my theory of color and adornment, I used it in every store that I designed. Once I began studying what made people tick when they went shopping, I began to formulate other principles of design that would help the sales volume of my clients. I studied the effectiveness of the pulling power of storefronts. I concluded immediately that window shopping was one of the foremost pastimes of Mr. and Mrs. America. Main Street USA is, and has always been, the best show in town. Show windows, I reasoned, acted like circus barkers in front of a sideshow tent. They were out there in front of the store twenty-four hours a day with the same type of appeal as the barker's spiel. The trick was to be loud enough, without being offensive, and to show enough to whet the appetite. I warned my clients not to crowd their windows, not to try to show everything. I once drew an illustration for an article that I had written about storefronts, showing a lovely, beckoning young lady with enough draperies to conceal and yet to reveal. The caption read, "You don't have to show everything to get the message across."

This idea was the result of an experience in college on the first day of life-drawing class. When the attractive young female model stepped onto the model's platform and dropped her robe, I went right to work on the paper pinned to my easel. I was there to draw, not to gape. During a fifteen-minute pause from posing, instead of standing there completely nude, she had her robe on and one breast peeping out of the folds. I found myself staring with more than an artist's interest. In short, the message came through—when she showed just a little. Slowly the clients followed my suggestions.

Another conclusion I came to was that people like to meander through a store. The square and rectangular layouts of our buildings and our real estate do not provide sufficient reason for designing stores on a rectilinear grid. I introduced sweeping curved walls into my plans. Curving, undulating paths were created by the placement of showcases and sales tables. The same sweep that appeared in my store work appeared later in many of my apartment houses, as well as in the planning of my best-known hotel, the Fontainebleau, in Miami Beach. I used the same theory when I planned the S-shaped Summit Hotel and the boomerang-shaped Americana Hotel, both in New York.

A catalogue entitled *Forty Years of Art and Architecture*, accompanying the 1967 exhibit of my work in the Lowe Gallery at the University of Miami, was written by Dr. August L. Freundlich, the chairman of the art department and director of the gallery. In it he described me as an "architect by training and a mob psychologist by choice." Dr. Freundlich, better than any of my critics, had summed up, in a few words, what I had tried to do throughout my career.

Besides my theories of color and sweeping curves, I found that I was using three forms as an ornamental expression that seemed to have become a part of my design vernacular. A magazine editor called these rather meaningless forms "woggles." Another pet design element was the use of circular openings in walls and ceilings. Again, one writer called them "cheese holes." Slender poles appeared in my work as design accents, and soon they were christened "bean poles." I went through a design period where my work became identifiable through the ever-present woggles, cheese holes, and bean poles. Even in my latest work, these three forms seem to appear as if of their own volition.

One more theory, or device, found its way into all my work, whether it was the design of a store, or a hotel, or a restaurant, or even a hospital. I called it the "moth complex." We are all familiar with that inexplicable drive in the moth to get as close as it can to a light source. I soon discovered that this same tendency holds true for people. By putting brighter lights in a show window, I could make people stop and look. There might be nothing more exciting in the brightly illuminated window than there is in the poorly lit show window next door, but invariably people react in the same manner even inside the store. I experimented by placing a bright light over one showcase and an ordinary light over another. Twice as many people stopped to examine the merchandise in the brightly lit case as in the poorly lit one.

Faced with an unusual planning problem, I put this theory to use in a ladies's shoe store on busy 34th Street in Manhattan. The store was forty feet wide and two hundred feet deep. I realized that the proportions were all wrong. How could I ever expect a customer to walk two hundred feet, a full city block, to be seated in the rear of the store so that she could try on a pair of shoes. The owner insisted that there be as many fitting chairs for customers as could possibly be installed. Would a woman ever walk to the back of the store? I decided to put my "moth complex" to its severest test. For the rear wall of the store, I designed a large, illuminated wall ornament. The ornament itself had no special significance, nor did it have any display value. When the store opened for business, the store receptionist directed the ladies to the available seats where the salesmen were waiting to help them. It was natural for the receptionist to please the early customers by seating them in the front of the salon so they would not complain about the long walk to the seats in the rear of the store. The ladies were willing, actually demanding, to be seated in the rear. That brilliantly illuminated, meaningless rear wall drew them as light draws a moth. Until the store was torn down many years later, customers still insisted that they wanted to be seated in the rear.

Another innovation of mine and a couple of other store designers was to eliminate the wall that separated the storefront from the interior. Why not open up the front and make the interior of the store a part of a display? Thus the open storefront was born. I devised a special detail that made it possible to insert the glass wall with no moldings to break the surface of the side walls. The sheer glass wall, with no visible methods of support, made the storefront a part of the interior and the interior became a part of the front.

An excellent device for making a small space seem larger was an arrangement of mirrors. I would mirror an entire wall and design whatever was placed against the wall with a half counter or a half ceiling or a half of anything so that when viewed against the mirrored wall, it appeared to double the space.

I was learning many things about merchandising in my career as a store designer. Customers could be made to respond with unconscious reflex actions if the designer understood human nature. Invariably, color and ornament and light acted like magnets and drew people one way or another. Through the years, retail customers may have become more sophisticated, but during my early days in store design I was discovering truisms that I could use again and again in my work to make people like what I had designed for them.

Although I was content to work for Ross-Frankel, Bea never let me forget her belief in my talent and ability. Again and again, she wanted to know when I would finally open my own office. Her faith in my talent was unbounded, but I was still too timid, too introverted. Where was I going to get clients? Would I be able to convince these clients that I should be selected as their architect? I was with a firm that was paying me a very handsome salary. I did not have to worry about bringing in clients or business. I did not have to worry about collecting my fees. My only responsibilities were good designs and finished products. Bea refused to believe that this was how I should spend the rest of my life. She wanted to see me have a career — if at all possible, a brilliant career. Bea was teaching, and she offered to go on teaching indefinitely while I made my early beginnings in the field of architecture. We had saved a little money, and with her earnings I could start a practice and wait for a year or two until it was on its feet as a going financial venture.

During the fifteen years I was with Ross-Frankel, I resigned twice, but each time they persuaded me to stay on. They convinced me that I probably would not make as much money as an independent architect as I was earning as a captive architect. They frightened me with the prospect of hunger and lean years looking for clients, trying to make ends meet, and after I had established myself and had a good practice, I would have all the worries of running my own business. Each time their arguments persuaded me to remain with them. Bea was disappointed but patient.

The popular Steinberg's dairy restaurant on Broadway in New York, 1929.

"*For the first time I used a mirror wall to achieve a dramatic effect in this restaurant. The lighting, which I designed, helped to achieve that modern look I wanted.*"

Swank Showroom, New York, 1929.

Regal Shoes, Fifth Avenue, New York, 1931.

*"I used bronze and curved it to sweep customers into the store.
A pedestrian unconsciously followed the curve and found himself or herself
entering the store front vestibule or arcade."*

Doubleday bookstore, Detroit, 1932.

*"The entire bookstore is a huge graphic design.
Element number one in my store design became bold graphics."*

"Why not open up the front and make the interior of the store a part of a display? Here the entire store forms a single display of cutlery; store and interior are inseparable."

above: Hoffritz for Cutlery store, New York, 1939.
facing page: Mangel's women's clothing store in Jacksonville, Florida, one of several Mangel's that Lapidus designed in the early 1930s.

The Armstrong's showroom, New York, 1933.

"Here I used the 'woggle' shape on the floor, ceiling, and wall. I also used my 'bean pole' to support the table, and two 'cheese holes' on the wall. I went through a design period where my work became identifiable through the ever-present woggles, cheese holes, and bean poles. Even in my latest work, these three forms seem to appear as if of their own volition."

The Ansonia shoe store, 34th Street, New York, 1940.

"This store is a perfect example of my 'moth complex': I used light to draw women back to the rear of the store. The shoe boxes are behind the decorated walls. Note the lavish use of ornament."

Postman's glove and handbag store, New York, 1941.

Bostonian shoe store, Chicago, 1940.

facing page and above: Barton's candy store in Times Square, New York, exterior and interior, 1941.

"My huge sign in neon is in keeping with Times Square — a design that is a graphic display. This narrow store was made to seem larger by my use of mirrors. The doughnut shape, as well as the counter below it, is only a half-round but appears to be a full circle. Numerous 'cheese holes' are used for display."

Lapidus with a model of his design for the Distilled Spirits Institute Building for the New York World's Fair, 1939.

During the 1930s, Ross-Frankel was moving into other types of buildings, and one of their interesting new clients was Seagram, the Canadian whisky firm. When the United States decided that it had had enough of the noble experiment, Prohibition was abolished and Seagram was ready with a large stock of aged Canadian whisky. I designed Seagram's New York offices in the Chrysler Building in a Tudor style, complete with fake fumed-oak fireplaces and pegged linen-fold oak panels.

While working for Seagram, I met the Bronfman brothers, owners of the firm. The head of the firm was Sam Bronfman. Allen Bronfman, the youngest brother and a lawyer by training, was second owner. I eventually met the two oldest brothers, Harry and Dave Bronfman. During the period that I was working on their new offices, I became quite friendly with all four of them.

Their father was a devout Jew who had immigrated to Canada, settling in one of the "dry" provinces. He had a long flowing beard and his trade was mattress making. The oldest son, Dave, got a job as a bellman in a local hotel. In the early years of the century, hotels were used primarily by drummers, or salesmen. In the dry provinces, these drummers usually called a bellman to get them a bottle of whisky. Typically, each bellman knew a local bootlegger. (The term "bootlegging" is derived from an old custom of delivering illicit material by carrying it in tall boots.) Dave did so well with this sideline that when Harry, the next oldest brother, came of age, he too became a hotel bellboy and joined his brother in buying whisky from bootleggers to sell to his hotel clients.

When Sam came of age, he suggested that the three of them buy out the bootlegger and go into business for themselves. They were soon selling illicit whisky throughout the province. When the province repealed its prohibition on liquor sales, they bought a small distillery. Sam was a brilliant businessman, and they became a fairly large distilling company. They moved to Montreal and established that city as their headquarters.

Sometime later they heard that an old line distilling company was for sale. The company was owned by a wealthy family named Seagram, who were more

"The offices were done in an authentic Tudor style.
For Seagram, newly arrived in the Chrysler Building, I wanted
to convey a feeling of age in a most distinguished way.
I designed the sampling room in a modern manner,
with my 'cheese holes,' the undulating wall with a mural,
and a sweeping, curving bar."

New York offices of Seagram, in the Chrysler Building, designed by Lapidus in 1934.
Part of the offices featured pegged linen-fold oak panels (above), while the sampling room
(facing page) was decidedly modern.

interested in breeding and racing horses. Sam bought the Seagram Company, along with its distilleries and main office, which resembled an English castle.

In 1938 the Distilled Spirits Institute decided to exhibit at the New York World's Fair. The four major distillers who were the mainstay of the Institute held a competition to select the design for the Distilled Spirits Institute Building. Seagram asked Ross-Frankel to submit designs. Schenley asked their brilliant young architect, Morris Sanders. National Distillers and Hiram Walker, the other two distilling giants, also selected architects to submit designs for them. National and Hiram Walker agreed that I was to be the designer but Schenley threatened to withdraw their support unless I agreed that the Distilled Spirits Institute Building and its displays were a joint venture with their architect.

I knew Morris Sanders by reputation, an enviable one for a man so young. Although I would have preferred to be the sole designer, I was delighted by the prospect of working with such a talented colleague. Morris Sanders worked and lived in a converted brownstone on East 49th Street. He had created a fine modern building, one of the first of its kind, with large window areas framed with blue-glazed brick.

At first we got along quite well. It was soon apparent to me, however, that my namesake was a stubborn, unyielding man. But I liked his thinking, and I went along with his ideas. We were compatible as long as Morris had his way. Even though my designs had won the competition, I was still too insecure in my convictions to keep Morris from changing my concept to conform with his very strong opinions of contemporary design. He claimed that my designs were too flamboyant, too pandering to the public taste.

"We must educate people, elevate their level of taste, not stoop to their level. I know that your store designs are popular. You give people the kinds of things that they are looking for and understand. You know better. You are a talented and sensitive designer, Morris. Don't be afraid. Be daring, be bold — to hell with popular taste. Let's do something great."

I could not disagree with him, so I went along with the development of his theories of design. But when we were ready to design the interior of the building and the displays, we disagreed vehemently. The Institute wanted to present distilling as a respected industry, almost as old as civilization itself. They wanted to convince visitors to the Fair that the economy was supported by the vast amounts of corn, barley, rye, and other grains that went into distilling and by the dollars spent for bottles and bottling, barrel making, shipping, and advertising. They wanted to demonstrate that a great deal of American history developed because of distilling. The display of the history of distillers was to show that the first grant for a distillery was made by Peter Minuet, the Dutch governor of New Amsterdam. They wanted to demonstrate that the development of the Midwest was due to the distiller's demand for more corn, rye, and barley. The Whisky Rebellion and its importance in formulating tax laws in the Thirteen

Colonies was another historical highlight. This, and more, the Institute wanted to show in dramatic exhibits. Morris demurred. It was all so corny, he claimed. "Why not create nonobjective displays showing the uplifting gaiety and the better living produced by imbibing."

I could not agree with him. This time I was adamant. I would have none of his abstract symbolism, which I did not understand. Certainly Mr. and Mrs. America would never understand it. The distillers were anxious to show the country that drinking whisky was perfectly respectable. It had been sufficiently maligned as a wrecker of homes, a destroyer of men, a demon that had been exorcised as an evil spirit from the body of America. Chastened America was to be made to realize that old John Barleycorn was not a monster after all. That was what my displays and designs were intended to convey, but Morris was against all that.

"Let's show them glory and gaiety. Let's express waving fields of grain and gently swaying corn as an abstract fantasy. Don't be prosaic. Don't be obvious. Let art and the mind be the exciting stimuli," he said.

We were finally forced to bring our widely divergent ideas before the design board of the Distilled Spirits Institute. They listened to both of us, and their decision was unanimous. I was to be the sole designer of the exhibits and the interiors. Sanders was to be paid his full fee, but he was dismissed from the project. I found no joy or solace in the final action. I admired Morris immensely, but his strong, inflexible nature would permit no compromise. We remained good friends in spite of the new arrangement. If the committee wanted trivia, then let me give it to them; he wanted no part of it. I respected him, not only for his talent—and he certainly was an exceptionally talented architect—but also for his convictions of what an architect's duties were to himself and to his clients. Sanders felt that it was wrong for me to stay with Ross-Frankel, to compromise my position as an architect by working for a firm that designed and built stores. At that time, however, I still was not ready to open my own office.

While we were working on the Distilled Spirits Building, Sanders was retained by the Heinz Company to design their building. It was one of the most magnificent buildings that I had seen and would certainly be the most beautiful and exciting building at the World's Fair. Finally, the preliminary plans were ready for presentation to the Heinz Company and, specifically, to H. J. Heinz, Sr., in Pittsburgh. When Sanders returned, he told me that Heinz had made one stipulation. The building was to have a fifty-foot green pickle with the number "57" in neon. There were to be floodlights on the roof of the building to illuminate the pickle at night. I was delighted that the plans had been accepted and said that I was sure that the pickle would in no way hurt the beauty of the building. "That's where you and I differ, Morris," he said. "I will not put a pickle on the top of my building, and Heinz can talk pickle and 57 until he is blue in the face, but there will be no pickle on any building that I have designed."

Distilled Spirits Institute Building, New York World's Fair, 1939.
Completed interior (above), and model of a proposed distillery shown in the exhibit (facing page).

"My design used animation to explain how whiskey is made.
I was the art director who hired the models, designed the scenery,
and worked with the photographer to tell the story of the
history of whiskey in the United States."

For several weeks the argument raged. The ultimatum finally came down to a simple sentence. "No pickle, no building!" I pleaded with Morris to put the pickle up on the roof, but he was adamant, and in the end the building was not built. Heinz took a large space in the Food Building, and the Heinz Building remained a dream on the drawing boards of my uncompromising friend.

During the early 1940s when war became more imminent, there was less and less work in our office. When the war curtailed the use of strategic material, it became virtually impossible for the construction industry to function. Without steel, copper, and other materials, all needed for the war effort, no sizable structure could be built for civilian use. The large labor force that formerly had erected buildings was now employed in shipbuilding and other vital war industries. Stores, however, were built with little or no strategic materials. The War Production Board (WPB) reviewed each proposed project, and if the major materials that were to be used for building were primarily nonstrategic, permission was granted to proceed with construction. The WPB issued documents that allowed contractors to purchase a limited amount of restricted materials. Since wood, glass, plaster, and paint were unrestricted, it was possible to continue to build stores.

At that time, my father and my two brothers were running the family automobile lamp and accessory business. There was a possibility that they might secure a government contract to make a specialized signaling searchlight that would become standard equipment on all landing craft if an invasion of the continents was ever undertaken. When the firm was invited to submit designs and prices, my brothers asked me to help them with the design. They had researched the mechanical aspects, but they needed somebody who could draw and interpret their ideas for fabricating such a signaling device. The prospect of working with my brothers at a handsome fee and the dwindling work in construction, along with Bea's insistence that sooner or later I would have to open my own office, pushed me to the final decision. I resigned from Ross-Frankel and started my own practice.

I signed a contract with my father and brothers to design and assist in the manufacturing of the signaling searchlight. At the same time, I started an architectural practice. I visited an engineer whom I had known through the years and asked if I could share quarters with him. He agreed, and so I had my first little cubbyhole of an independent office at 1841 Broadway near 60th Street in Manhattan.

I had never studied engineering for manufacturing products, so I bought a book showing how to draw nuts, bolts, screws, and so on. I worked with my brothers and father until I was familiar with the signaling searchlight. I made complete drawings and when the searchlight was approved, I developed a manual showing how to assemble it if it should be damaged. I also made an enlarged view showing each separate part of the searchlight and how each part fitted into the whole unit.

While deeply involved with the signal device, I designed my own office in the space I was sharing with the engineer. I wanted everything to be ready, if and when the first client came along. I printed cards and letterheads and mailed a modest announcement stating that I had opened my own offices for the independent practice of architecture. There were no clients on the horizon, but Bea assured me that they would come.

Shortly after I set up my new office, a friend who manufactured chairs, and from whom I had made many purchases in the past, called to tell me that Martin's, a Brooklyn department store, was interviewing architects to carry out some remodeling in their large, six-story establishment on Fulton Street. He had suggested my name to one of the owners, Fred Zeits. I called Zeits and made an appointment.

At last the great moment had arrived. I was going to see my first potential client. I fought off my nervousness and apprehensions. Zeits listened patiently, looking through my portfolio as I described my background and experience. He told me he was considering a change because the architect with whom he had been working for many years had developed too large a practice to continue a personal architect–client relationship. I assured Zeits that I could work closely with him, although I did not tell him he would be my first and only client. He agreed to retain me.

I insisted on an annual contract with a guaranteed sum. We agreed on a minimum fee of thirteen hundred dollars. I was to work at a fee which would equal ten percent of the cost of construction, and my fee would be increased commensurate with the construction costs. We shook hands, and I promised to send a letter of agreement. As I left the store, I hurried to find the first public telephone. I could not wait to give Bea the wonderful news that I had found my first client. My practice had begun.

That first year with Martin's went over the agreed-upon minimum. I collected almost fifteen thousand dollars in fees. My association with Fred Zeits and his brothers lasted for more than twelve years. Martin's grew, and so did my practice. It was with a great deal of regret that I finally had to admit to my first client that, like my predecessor, I too had developed a practice that made it impossible to continue to serve him in the manner that we had agreed upon years before. We remained friends even though we could not continue as architect and client.

I had bought a house in Flatbush, a pleasant residential neighborhood in Brooklyn, and had remodeled it to create a contemporary home for Bea and our two sons. Soon after I started the work for Martin's, a neighbor told me that the Rock-A-Bye children's store a few blocks from our house was going to expand. I went to see the owners with my portfolio. They had heard of me and knew my work, and they were especially pleased to have me design their new and larger establishment because I lived so close by. I prepared a contract that was quickly signed.

Announcement card for Morris Lapidus's first independent practice, located at 1841 Broadway in New York, 1943.
The card shows a montage of his work; clockwise from top left: the Rainbow Shop, Kay Jewelers, reception area in the
offices of Mangel's, dining room in Lapidus's house in Brooklyn.

Lapidus's first office, at 1841 Broadway near 60th Street, New York, 1943.

Martin's department store, Fulton Street, Brooklyn, 1944.

"Here I do away with the storefront. All the merchandise can be seen from the street."

Children's floor, Martin's department store, Brooklyn, 1945.

Bea noticed that I was wearing the same shaggy, brown tweed suit with leather buttons and a belt in the back of the jacket that I had worn when I went to get my first contract signed with Martin's. Tweed suits and bow ties were a manner of dress that I had acquired when I was an aspiring young drama student. The first time, I had not put this suit on intentionally. But when, once again, I went to see a prospective client, I made sure that I wore the same suit. I began to feel that it was a lucky suit. Bea dubbed it the "Signing Suit," and she knew that when I wore it I was about to see a prospective client. For several years, I never went to see a new client without wearing my "Signing Suit." It never failed me. In time it became quite worn and shabby and with a great deal of trepidation, I put it aside and wore a new suit for another client. Despite all my fears, I was awarded the commission without wearing my lucky "Signing Suit."

As my staff grew, I needed to find new quarters. The war had ended, restrictions had been lifted, and there was plenty of work for me. I was crowding the engineer whose offices I shared, but office space was simply unavailable in New York. I went from real estate office to real estate office, but the answer was always the same — there was not a foot of space for rent. When I was out walking, just two blocks from my office I noticed the Empire Hotel. It was in a decent neighborhood, and on an impulse I walked in and asked to see the manager. When I inquired whether he had any space that I could rent, he showed me a modest-sized ballroom and offered to rent it to me by the month or by the year. I rented this ballroom for two years. I installed drafting tables and files and wired the room with lights over each drafting board. I retained my office at 1841 Broadway, but all of my staff moved to the Empire Hotel. (In 1992 my son Alan needed to expand his own office and found, by coincidence, the required space at 1841 Broadway. When I come to New York, I stay in a hotel near his office — the Empire Hotel, now the Radisson Empire.)

A year or so after the office had moved into the Empire Hotel, one of my draftsmen came to me and told me that he could provide a new office for me if I would lend him ten thousand dollars. He told me that he had found a boarding house (a former brownstone) on East 49th Street that he could buy and convert into a small office building. I asked him to show me the building, which happened to be on the same block where Morris Sanders and I had worked on the World's Fair project a few years earlier.

In the end, I bought the brownstone and began the conversion into a modern building, which eventually became my office at 249 East 49th Street. When the building was finished it was published in *Architectural Forum*. I would later have the additional pleasure of seeing that little building featured in the prestigious *Encyclopedia Britannica Yearbook* of 1946 as an example of contemporary architecture.

When the building was completed, I decided to give a party for my friends, colleagues, and a growing list of clients. After all the guests had left, Bea and I, together with an old schoolmate and colleague and his wife, remained to talk about old times and our blossoming careers. The four of us sat in my private office chatting and reminiscing about what had happened to us since we left Columbia. We decided to go out for a late supper. I went down to the drafting room floor (my office was on the second floor) to see that all the lights were out and that everything was secure. Before going upstairs I tried to open the front door only to find it locked. I had designed the door with a T-square pull handle on the outside. I did not want any normal locks, and, therefore, the locking device could only be opened with a key. Too late I remembered that I, the owner of the building, had forgotten to take a key for myself. The awful truth dawned upon me: I had no way of getting out of my own building.

When I had completed the building, I arranged for a caretaker, who had a key to the building. Assuming that everyone had left, he had locked the building for the night. I had no idea where I could reach him by phone, another oversight in the excitement of the opening party. I did not have the nerve to tell Bea and my friends that we were locked in.

I remembered that there was a sidewalk door in the cellar that came up on the pavement on the outside of the building. So down into the cellar I went. I propped a ladder under the door and found that I had installed a chain and lock so that no one could break in. I did not have the key to that lock either.

Then I thought of the stairway that led to the roof. The building code required a roof exit. Surely this door was not locked. Up to the roof I went. I breathed a sigh of relief when the door swung open and I stepped out onto the roof. I walked from roof to roof (fortunately, all the brownstones were built to one height), testing roof stair doors in the other buildings to find one that was open. The first few were locked. Finally, I found one that I could open. I looked down into a lighted room and saw a ladder against the wall. With a sigh of relief, I climbed down the ladder and found myself in a bedroom occupied by a woman who was washing her hair. She stood in the middle of the room petrified, with her mouth agape, looking at the man coming down a ladder into her room. I could not think of anything appropriate to say, so without a word I went to the door leading to the hallway, opened it, and hurried down the stairs to the street. At last I was out.

I knew that my caretaker was the brother of the butler who took care of Katharine Hepburn's house a little way down the street. Surely, he would know where to reach his brother and have him come and let my wife and our friends out of the building. The butler, however, had no idea where his brother had gone. So back I went to the boardinghouse and knocked at the lady's door. Without waiting for an answer, I walked in. Fortunately, she had not thought to lock her door. This time I was more talkative. I said, "Excuse me, ma'am," and climbed the ladder up to the roof. She stood there speechless with a towel in her hands. I crossed the roofs to my building and went back inside. I explained my

Lapidus's house in Flatbush, Brooklyn, 1940.

"I designed and built my home 54 years ago as an interior that would be considered ultramodern today. The linoleum floor was used in Armstrong advertising."

Lapidus's private office in his second architectural office, in a brownstone he redesigned on East 49th Street in New York, 1945.

Lapidus's second office, at 249 East 49th Street, New York, 1945.

predicament and told them that there was nothing to worry about, I had found a way to leave the building. I did not dare tell them exactly how.

They followed me to the roof, whereupon I led them across rooftops. The women were wearing cocktail dresses. I think they were either too shocked or too amused to say anything. Once again I opened the door on the roof of the boardinghouse, told them that they would have to climb down a ladder. By now, the lady had finished drying her hair and was in her nightgown getting ready to go to bed. She must have thought that she was having a nightmare. Now four people were coming down her ladder from the roof, two elegantly gowned ladies and two men. As my guests and Bea trouped through her bedroom and out through the door, I turned and said, "Thank you, ma'am, and good night."

The Sans Souci Hotel in Miami Beach, 1949, was Lapidus's first resort hotel; he was the associate architect.

"When the hotel was opened in 1949, guards were kept at the entrance to make sure that only the guests could get in, and to keep out the hordes of lookers who flocked to the hotel, attracted by the bright colors and light. The Sans Souci became the hotel of Miami Beach."

11

A Protégé, Charlie, and the Sans Souci

Now that I was a practicing architect, I was ready to apply for membership in the New York chapter of the American Institute of Architects. Eventually I received an invitation to meet with the admissions committee. The first question the committee asked was why, after receiving my license as an architect, I waited more than fifteen years before making my application to join the A.I.A. I told them that I never really thought of myself as an architect while I was an employee of a construction firm.

The members of the committee heard me out and told me that they respected my reasons for not applying sooner. They were pleased that I had been honest with them because they had received several letters from members of the A.I.A. advising the committee that my application should be rejected. They told me that one member had threatened to resign if they admitted me. It seemed that some architects refused to admit that store design was architecture. In spite of the letters, I was accepted as a member in good standing of the A.I.A.

At the same time, I became a member of both the Architectural League and the Beaux Arts Institute. All these organizations staged plays to amuse, and even poke fun at, themselves. My long-forgotten thespian ambitions now helped me join in acting parts and eventually writing some of the skits. Within a few years, I became the producer of these playlets.

My practice grew and happily, I prospered. I was still a store designer, but now I could call myself an architect specialist, an expert in retailing. I was frequently called upon to lecture at annual conventions before such associations as the National Retail Drygoods Association. My work was being published in just about every trade journal from *Women's Wear Daily* to *Chain Store Age*, and of course in architectural magazines. I was designing stores as far away as Oregon and Washington state.

During the war years, a ship-fitting company, Aetna Marine, had asked me to design what I thought would be a prototype of the postwar luxury ship, specifically, a cruise ship. Aetna Marine wanted to ensure postwar business through a colorful and exciting sales promotion that could be carried on during the war. One of the officers of the company knew me—from when he was in promotion and sales with a chain store for which I had worked while I was with Ross-Frankel. He felt that my dramatic flair in interior design was what was needed for the future cruise ships. I was given the plans of a Liberty Ship, which Kaiser was building for our country, and told to evolve a conversion from a troop carrier to a luxury cruise liner.

I set to work on what seemed to be a new field for me. I used all my tried and proven theories of exciting forms, unusual lighting, and, of course, lavish color. I decided that just as I had opened up storefronts with wide expanses of glass, I would open up the interior of the public spaces in a ship to a vista of sea and sky. If people were going to take a cruise, they wanted plenty of sea and sky, so why not sell them what they wanted? My old standbys of color, swirling forms, and exciting lighting were included in my designs, even the ubiquitous woggles, cheese holes, and bean poles.

The renderings were finally completed, and I arranged to present them to the board of Aetna Marine. They were enthusiastically received. An itinerary had been worked out for a tour of my work, which was to be shown to ship owners and marine companies throughout the United States. The chairman of the board wanted all of us to go up to lunch in the private dining room at the top of 12 Church Street in downtown Manhattan. The building where Aetna Marine and many of the other shipping companies had offices consisted of two towers connected by several bridges at the upper floors and by a common lobby at street level.

We all went up in the elevator to the club, and our first stop was the bar where the chairman ordered drinks and proposed a toast to me and my exciting version of the postwar luxury ship. Down went one Manhattan cocktail. Someone else proposed a toast to the "Ship of Tomorrow." Another Manhattan. Some other club members joined us and wanted to know what the celebration was all about. The chairman of the board introduced me as the young designer of the postwar ship—another Manhattan cocktail. I looked longingly at the luncheon table that was waiting for us. But the toasts continued and I lost count of the cocktails. I had to go someplace before I fell flat on my face. I made it to the men's room, where I sat down on one of the toilet seats, closed the door of the stall, and fell asleep.

When I awoke a club attendant was tapping on the stall door, calling my name. He offered me a fizzing Alka Seltzer and told me that it was past four o'clock. The party had broken up long ago. I wondered whether I had been missed. I decided to struggle back to the Aetna Marine offices to find out what had happened. In my sodden condition, I started down but found myself in the lobby, so I started up in the elevators to where I thought the Aetna offices were located. But I had picked the wrong tower. Down I went and crossed one of the bridges to the other tower, but I still did not remember where the Aetna offices were. Back down in the lobby, I finally found a kindly elevator operator who took me by the hand, led me into the elevator, stayed with me until I reached the proper floor, and eventually took me to the Aetna offices. It seemed I was not the only dropout. No one had ever really sat down to lunch.

We all finally had one for the road and then I started home. It was an interminable subway ride, although I must have slept through most of it. When I finally got home, reeking like a distillery, Bea wanted to know what had happened. I told her that my ship designs had been launched. She led me to bed, helped me to undress, and before I drifted off to sleep I heard her say, "I'm afraid, my dear, it was you who was launched today."

My designs eventually appeared in all the maritime magazines. They had a great influence on the postwar ships. Many of my designs were copied, but thirty years went by before I was finally commissioned to design ship interiors.

My store work continued to appear frequently in the three important architectural magazines. The two interior magazines, *Interiors* and *Interior Design*, also featured my work often. I was developing new and innovative design concepts. I felt that I achieved the ultimate in my quest for a style that expressed my theories of design in a chain store called The Rainbow Shops. There, I finally designed a store in which all vestiges of rectilinear design disappeared. Everything was curved, including the floating ceiling.

I still hoped that one day I would design buildings that reflected my theories. I also wondered why my store designs, which most architects admired, were never used by architects. Perhaps these free-flowing designs were wonderful for stores but in no way applicable to building design. Buildings, it seemed, had to be boxes no matter if they were art nouveau or art deco or the new International Style.

In 1945 World War II ended and my practice continued to grow. One evening Bea asked me to come with her to her friend Etta Hornstein's apartment. Mrs. Hornstein, a widow, had one son who, since returning from the war, did nothing but sit around the house all day. I met the young man, who appeared listless and depressed. He told me he had been studying aeronautical engineering for two years at college when he was drafted. After the usual army tests, it was decided that he would join the air force as a navigator. After he had completed his training he was sent to England. His missions were over Germany, where he was shot down twice. The first time he managed to escape and return to England. The second time, he was captured and imprisoned by the Germans until the war ended. When he was released he was admitted to a military psychiatric hospital for treatment. He tired of his confinement and sought a discharge from the air force, but the only way he could get out was to sign papers that it was his choice and not that of the air force. He was twenty-four years old.

He was a bright young man, and I offered to employ him. His two-year training in aeronautics had taught him drafting. I told him that he would start as a plan desk man, but that I would personally watch over him and train him as an architectural draftsman. He hesitated at first but finally decided to try to work for me.

Within a year this young man, who had changed his name from Hornstein to Abby Harle, was becoming a qualified architectural draftsman. At that time we were drawing the designs and the working drawings for a large men's and women's clothing store called Bond's. Mr. Rubin, the owner, had become successful by advertising two pairs of pants with each suit.

The store occupied the first three floors of a new office building on Fifth Avenue that was being designed by Skidmore, Owings & Merrill. Abby was assigned to check the firm's drawings. Abby pointed out to me that although everything including structural steel, plumbing, electrical wiring, and air conditioning was clearly drafted, he could not figure out how all this equipment got through the huge girders that carried the upper stories. I traced every conduit, every plumbing pipe, and every air-conditioning duct and found that if they did get through the girders, it was not shown. In the end, the project had to be reengineered and the girders redesigned to allow all of the ducts and plumbing to go through.

Abby became increasingly involved in this large project, and eventually I designated him to supervise the construction. At first he was reluctant because he did not have the experience to act as the architect's supervisor, but I explained that if a question arose all he had to do was call me. When I introduced Abby to Mr. Rubin, he said that Abby was too young for the job. I finally persuaded Mr. Rubin and his staff that I would replace Abby if any errors or improper decisions were made. Abby remained on the job until its completion. At first he called me a number of times each day, but these calls came less and less frequently as he learned and supervised at the same time.

The Bond store gave me an opportunity to experiment with my theories of merchandising. The clothing was on the upper floors; only accessories were sold on the street floor. The huge street floor had many columns which I encased in round faux marbre or scagliola — now almost a lost art — which made them a strong element in my design. These columns achieved a lightness by terminating in large circular lighting areas with concealed down lights.

On the second floor I used free-flowing curved walls and ceilings. On the ladies' clothing floor I used sweeping curves everywhere — walls, ceilings, and merchandise displays. The cabinet cases for all garments for both men and women disappeared owing to the invention of new methods of hanging and lighting men's and women's clothing.

After completing the Fifth Avenue store, we began the plans for a six-story Bond store on State Street in Chicago. The building was designed and planned by a prominent Chicago architect who would incorporate my design for the facade and the interior in his plans. A large stairway extended from the first

Bond clothing store, State Street, Chicago, 1949. Lapidus designed the steel and glass facade and interiors.

floor to the sixth floor. I decided to use a metal and glass facade, the full width and height of the stairway.

The interiors carried my free-flowing designs of the arrangement of merchandise much further than my designs for the Fifth Avenue store. Once again I sent Abby Harle to supervise the work, which went on for more than six months.

In the meantime, Bond's had signed a lease for a large multistoried store in Cincinnati. Although the lease was signed in 1945, the property would not be available to Bond's until 1949. I was given the commission for this store in 1946 although the installation would not begin until 1949. When we signed our contract, I prepared a carefully calculated estimate for building costs of half a million dollars. Our fee was to be ten percent of that amount, or fifty thousand dollars. Over the next three years the cost of construction for all trades rose slowly but continuously. Architectural magazines published monthly indexes of the rising costs for all trades, reflecting the steadily rising costs of construction. We billed Bond's periodically and showed the increasing cost of the project. We always sent copies of these rising cost indexes with each bill. By the time the plans were finished, we indicated on our bills that what had started as a half million dollar budget had risen to one million dollars. Our bills were sent to the vice president of construction and we were paid promptly.

One day I received an urgent call from Bond's summoning me to their executive offices. When I arrived fifteen minutes later, I was ushered into the office of Barney Rubin, the chairman, who was with his vice president of construction and two men from the accounting office. Mr. Rubin, a short man with a polished personality, asked me to be seated. I looked at the silent, frightened faces of the other men in the office. Mr. Rubin showed me my last bill and politely asked me if I had been paid. I nodded in the affirmative. In one instant the polite Mr. Rubin suddenly flew into a terrible rage. He wanted to know why a fee of fifty thousand dollars had suddenly become a fee of one hundred thousand. I tried to explain how the costs of construction had doubled during the postwar period. In a fury he turned to the vice president and asked if he was aware of this. He said that he was. Then Mr. Rubin, now quite beside himself, asked the two accounting people if they were also aware of the increase. They stated that they had carefully researched the prices before paying the additional charges. Mr. Rubin then called for his son-in-law, the president, to come to his office immediately. He arrived and met a tirade of abuse from his father-in-law. Why, he screamed, was he not told of this situation? The president said that since Mr. Rubin was semiretired, he did not think it was necessary to keep his father-in-law informed, since he as the president was in total charge of the vast operation.

By now all of us at the meeting were treated to the unbelievable sight of a wildly raving Mr. Rubin. He slammed his fists against the wood paneling of his office, shouting that he was surrounded by idiots, morons, and incompetents.

"My final solution to store design: no wall cases, no visible lighting of the merchandise, and, most important — a huge sweeping line. This was eventually reflected in most of my future hotel work."

Bond clothing store, Cincinnati, 1949.

He wanted the Cincinnati lease canceled. He instructed his secretary to call and demand that the company attorney be summoned immediately. We all sat there in miserable silence. In a short time the head of a large legal office arrived and was greeted by Mr. Rubin, who demanded that the lease for the Cincinnati store be terminated immediately. The lawyer explained that if Bond's did not go ahead with the construction of the four levels of the store, the company would still be liable for ten year's rent for an empty store. By now Mr. Rubin was calling all of us idiots.

Just then, Mr. Rubin's secretary came in to remind him that on doctor's orders he had to have his lunch and take a nap. He turned to us and told us to stay where we were and wait until he returned. We sat there numbed by his furious tirade, unable to speak. In an hour and a half Mr. Rubin returned and once again vented his fury on all of us. In a sudden change of demeanor, he turned to me and said that I had done my duty by informing his organization of the changing prices and wanted to know why I had not come to him with this information. I stammered that I did not think it appropriate to ignore the people I was working with in his company. In a final burst of anger he told us all to get out of his office. Cowed and hungry, we left. We had sat through five hours of abuse. Eventually work was started on the Cincinnati store and when the project was completed, it turned out to be one of Bond's most lucrative ventures.

When I met Charlie Spector I had no sign, no indication that he would change my life and my career. An architect himself, he was vice president of the A.S. Beck shoe store chain and had designed most of the Beck stores. He selected me to design several large stores for important locations, including one on Fifth Avenue and another in Chicago. He was a warm, outgoing individual about my own age, and we became friends.

One day Charlie called me and asked whether I could arrange to have dinner with him. He wanted me to meet a friend of his from Miami Beach. He felt that a meeting might prove mutually beneficial. Charlie's friend, Ben Novak, had come to him with a set of plans prepared by a Miami Beach architect for a hotel to be called the Sans Souci that Ben intended to build there. He was unhappy with the final result and hoped that Charlie could give him suggestions to improve the plans and the overall design. Charlie suggested that Ben meet me. He told him that he had recently engaged me for special stores because in his opinion, I had a flair for creating exciting and attention-getting structures and interiors.

After dinner, a friend of Novak's took us to his midtown apartment where I saw the plans. The first question Novak put to me was, did I know anything about hotels? I told Ben that I had stayed at plenty, but I had never actually designed a hotel.

I looked over the plans and began to make suggestions. I have always been quite facile with a pencil, and, working on some wrapping paper that happened

A.S. Beck shoe store, Fifth Avenue, New York, 1952.

to be in the apartment, I sketched various parts of the hotel that I thought could be made more interesting. I indicated that the exterior should have an imposing pylon and a circular drive to dramatize the entrance. I suggested that the proposed rectangular, one-level lobby be shaped with various sweeping curves and that the space be broken up by terraces with a number of levels. I felt that a sweeping circular stairway would add to the overall drama. Of course, I was using techniques that I had developed in stores.

All these thoughts I suggested to Novak, sketching as I talked. I reasoned that a hotel was another selling medium. What a resort hotel sold was a feeling of relaxed luxury and a freedom from the everyday humdrum existence that the guests were trying to escape. In short, the merchandise for sale was fun and rest and a good time physically and emotionally. When I was finished, I had quite a number of sketches. Novak was very impressed. He asked me what I would charge to design the interiors of the hotel, and consult with his architect on the design of the entire building. I suggested a fee of eighteen thousand dollars. Even though I knew that the fee was entirely too low, Novak said he was sorry to have taken up my time but that he would be glad to pay me for the sketches I had made. I refused payment and gave the batch of sketches to him with my compliments as a gift and as a favor to my friend Charlie.

Several days later I got a phone call from Novak's partner, Harry Mufson, asking when I could come to Miami Beach. He told me that they had agreed to pay me the fee that I had asked and wanted me to get to Florida as soon as I could. Two days later I was flying down to Miami Beach to begin my first venture in hotel design.

Before long, Charlie's role as a matchmaker was put to a severe test. There were three partners in the project. Besides Ben Novak, there was Harry Mufson, the man who had called, and another Harry, who was a ladies' apparel manufacturer. The second Harry was short; the first Harry was tall. Big Harry had been in the automobile tire business. Only Ben had a hotel background. After I was awarded the contract and was given a copy of the architect's plans, I flew back to New York. When the sketches were completed in my New York office, I went back to Florida to present them to the three partners. They liked everything that I had designed, and they arranged for me to confer with their architect so that his plans could be revised to conform with all my suggestions. After studying my plans, the architect startled us all by saying that everything I had designed was impractical and, in short, could not be built. He insisted that there were to be no changes in the plans.

I was stunned. My new clients were shocked. Had they employed a wild-eyed visionary whose knowledge of construction was so limited that all his recommendations were structurally impossible? We left the office of this gruff, unyielding architect to hold a meeting. The partners asked whether I knew anything about construction. Had I ever built a building? Perhaps I was a great store designer, but if their architect said my ideas were unworkable, then it must be so. He had been the architect for half the hotels on Miami Beach. For a fleeting moment I doubted my own ability. Maybe the architect was right. After all, I really had never designed a hotel or a building. Soon, however, I was furious. I knew as much about construction and architecture as their architect, and I told my clients so. I called their architect a liar and a fraud. How dared he say my designs were impractical? Ben and the two Harrys did not know enough about construction to decide who was right. They liked my ideas, but if the architect said that they could not be built, what were they to do? I thought of Charlie. He had brought me into this situation. Why not get Charlie to come to Florida and act as a judge? My three clients agreed.

The next morning Charlie arrived. I was delighted to see him but nervous and apprehensive as we went to visit the architect. After we got to his office, Charlie listened to me explain what I was trying to accomplish. When I had finished, he turned to the architect and asked him to tell us in detail why these designs could not be incorporated in the plans. The architect spoke at great length about the problems of construction in Miami Beach. The area was man-made. Sand had been dredged from the ocean to cover the mangrove swamps. The land was unstable. All construction was on piles. Circular stairways could not be constructed of concrete. There were strains, stresses, hurricanes—and on and on. I looked at Charlie anxiously. Was I really so lacking in structural knowledge? I was sure that everything that I had suggested could be built, but maybe I was overconfident. Charlie sat there for what seemed an eternity without saying a word. We were all waiting to hear his verdict.

Finally, Charlie spoke. He turned to the architect and inquired whether the architect had a license to practice architecture. Of course, he had been in practice for more than thirty years.

"Then I suggest, sir, that you surrender your license. I have never heard such nonsense before from a man who professes to be a practicing architect."

We left the architect sitting in stunned silence. Out on the pavement my three clients asked whether I could take over the entire project. They wanted to terminate the architect's contract and have me become the sole architect for the entire hotel. I refused. Aside from a question of ethics, I had no desire to hurt another architect, and I was not ready to assume a responsibility which would necessitate opening an office in Miami Beach. We returned to the office of the chastened architect and arranged a guarded truce. We would continue as associate architects, but my designs and my plans would be followed.

In the design for the Sans Souci I once again used my old bag of tricks— sweeping curves, a woggle-shaped carpet, the old cheese holes in the floating ceilings and the curved walls, bean poles hung with cages of live birds. But I also added more. Native coral stone walls splashed with fountains and lush tropical foliage grew in the most unlikely places. A grand circular stairway

Sans Souci Hotel, Miami Beach, 1949. Pool deck and garden (facing page), and lobby (above), with cages of live birds hanging on "bean poles."

wound skyward. Terraces went up and then down for no special reason in an exuberance of motion. Colors adorned the interiors as well as the exterior — bright, vibrant colors that complimented the blue Atlantic, the golden sands, the flaming bougainvillea, the green palms. The gardens and the pool deck were transformed into an exotic fairyland.

At night the illumination I used was handled in accordance with my proven moth theory, and it worked here as it did in my stores. People moved toward light, and light led people to the dining room, the cocktail lounge, and the night-club. The lighting at the entrance made people want to come in and have a look around. In fact, when the hotel was opened in 1949, guards were kept at the entrance to make sure that only the guests could get in, and to keep out the hordes of lookers who flocked to the hotel, attracted by the brilliant colors and light. The hotel was built at a much lower cost than its neighbor, the Saxony, which had opened the year before, and in spite of the lower investment the Sans Souci became *the* hotel of Miami Beach.

I was away on vacation when the Sans Souci had its grand opening. Bea had gone through serious surgery, so we took a South American cruise for rest and recuperation. The four of us — my wife and I, and my brother and his wife — sailed from New York on the *S.S. Brazil*, a ship of the Moore McCormick lines. The itinerary included stops in Trinidad, Santos (Brazil), Montevideo (Uruguay), and finally Buenos Aires. My brother had made the same trip the previous year. He had established a business arrangement with an Argentine cousin who owned a company that imported *Repuestos*, automobile parts manu-factured by my father and two brothers. My father had two sisters who had settled in Argentina with other relatives, so we actually had a large family whom I had never met living in Buenos Aires.

The trip to Buenos Aires took two weeks. During the beautiful ocean voyage, I met some interesting fellow passengers. One day while I was painting a water-color, Commissioner Robert Moses, the man who had built the expressways in New York and Long Island, came over and introduced himself. Of course, I knew him by his reputation. I told him that I was an architect, and we started what became a series of conversations. Mr. Moses and his wife rarely spoke to any of the passengers, always keeping to their suite and eating at their own table. The attention he paid me was an honor.

Another passenger was the newly appointed American ambassador to Argentina and his wife. The ambassador had also booked passage for a well-known teacher of Spanish, a Mrs. Madrigal. The ambassador spoke no Spanish, but Mrs. Madrigal assured him that she could teach him to speak a passable Spanish in two weeks. Their teaching sessions lasted for eight hours each day at sea. We never met the ambassador during our two weeks at sea, but Mrs. Madrigal would come to the dining salon and talk to us about her special tech-nique of teaching.

On October 28 our ship crossed the equator and a special event was held to celebrate the crossing. The passengers who had previously crossed the equator arranged an initiation for the passengers who were making their first crossing. The uninitiated were brought before a court of beautifully gowned passengers who were dressed as a king (played by a woman) and a queen (a man) and the royal court. Since my brother had already been across and was aware that I had been a theatrical makeup man, he arranged for me to make up the royal group. Because of my service to the court, I thought that I would be exempt from the indignities of the initiation. This was not to be, and I went through an initiation that included being doused with the ship's garbage. The initiates, reeking of refuse, were immediately thrown into the swimming pool.

When our ship sailed into the port of Buenos Aires, there was a great crowd of people on the pier waiting to greet the arriving passengers. We noticed a rather large group of people standing to one side. Jokingly we said to each other that there must be a special passenger on the ship. Imagine our surprise when we came through customs that this large group of greeters was our own reception committee. We did not realize how many relatives we had in Buenos Aires. Only the cousin my brother dealt with and some of his brothers spoke English, all the rest spoke only Spanish. Despite the language difference, we were warmly greeted, taken to our hotel, and that evening given a large reception banquet.

After a wonderful week in Argentina, we traveled to Rio de Janeiro where we met more relatives who spoke Portuguese. Some of my second cousins were engineers, and fortunately they spoke English. I wanted to meet Oscar Niemeyer, the Brazilian architect who had become well known in America because of his unusual architecture. One of my relatives, an artist, knew Niemeyer and arranged for me and my wife to visit with him at his home. He spoke fine English and I told him that I admired his work, especially the sketches that I had seen of a series of buildings he was designing for Pampulha, a new provincial suburb. He asked me whether I had a swimming pool. I told him that where I lived in Brooklyn, there was not a lot of space for swimming pools. He had never been to the United States, and from his reading of life in our country, he was convinced that all Americans had swimming pools. Years later, Niemeyer, an avid Communist, was appointed architect of Brasilia, the new capital of Brazil.

A year after the opening of the Sans Souci, I happened to run into Little Harry, the third partner in the triumvirate for whom I had designed the hotel. Little Harry, the dress manufacturer, suggested that I ought to go see the finished hotel and invited me to be his guest. So Bea and I eventually flew down to Miami Beach and stayed at the Sans Souci Hotel.

While I was in Miami Beach enjoying for the first time in my life a vacation in a hotel that I had designed, I received a call from a gentleman who told me that he was building a hotel on the beach and would like to discuss my services. I met him and learned the hotel was actually well underway — the concrete frame was already in place and the roof had already been poured. This gentleman told me that he was quite unhappy with the architect's designs for this hotel and asked whether I would consider becoming the associate architect and interior designer in an arrangement similar to that which I had made with the owners of the Sans Souci. I agreed, and once again I found myself in the throes of designing and doctoring a hotel. This was one of several that followed in succession. There was the Nautilus Hotel, the Delano Hotel, the Biltmore Terrace Hotel (now a Holiday Inn), and the Algiers Hotel. In each of these projects I was the associate architect and the interior designer. I had yet to be commissioned to design a hotel from the very beginning. I was still known as the "hotel doctor."

Biltmore Terrace Hotel, Miami Beach, 1951. Lapidus was associate architect and interior designer.

Previous pages and this page: Algiers Hotel, Miami Beach, 1951.

"What a resort hotel sold was a feeling of relaxed luxury and a freedom from the everyday humdrum existence that the guests were trying to escape. In short, the merchandise for sale was fun and rest and a good time physically and emotionally."

Pool and sweeping, curved line of cabanas, Fontainebleau Hotel, Miami Beach, 1954.

12 The Fontainebleau

Glancing through a New York newspaper, I saw an article announcing that my client Ben Novak was going to build the largest luxury hotel in Miami Beach on what was then the Firestone estate and that his architect was going to be — Morris Lapidus! This was startling news to me. I wasted no time in telephoning Ben to find out what this was all about, and whether, in fact, I was going to be his architect. Ben explained that he simply used the first name that came to his mind when the reporters asked who was going to be his architect. He told me that he would be glad to have me as an associate architect again and as the interior designer, but that he really would be looking for a prominent architect to plan the hotel. Then and there, I made up my mind that if I was going to work with Ben at all, I would not be the interior designer and the associate architect, or the consulting architect, but *the* architect who would design the entire structure.

Ben wanted me for the interiors, but he had no intention of letting me serve as the architect. With plenty of time and patience, I finally convinced Ben that I should become his architect by agreeing to accept a ridiculously low fee. A minimal fee for a hotel such as this would be four percent of its cost. The cost was approximately twelve million dollars, and at 4 percent, the fee should have been four hundred eighty thousand dollars. My fee was eighty thousand dollars. I knew that I could not possibly make any profit. In fact, I was risking bankruptcy, but I had been waiting for this opportunity all my professional life. And so began the saga of the Fontainebleau Hotel.

If ever my dramatic training stood me in good stead, it was during the period in which the Fontainebleau was built. There were times when I felt that I was always on stage. Ben is still convinced that he really designed the Fontainebleau, and I have never tried to disabuse him of that belief. At the very outset, I realized that my client would want to control every feature in the design and the planning of the hotel.

Ben was a hotelier to his very fingertips. He knew hotel operations as few men do. But it went deeper than that. He knew what he liked and, as I was to learn later, what his guests liked. As we jockeyed the design, it was his taste, the taste of his clients, that won out in the end. It was my task to interpret these likes and, at the same time, carry out my own theories of design so that I could create a hotel — interiors and exterior — that revealed my talent and ability, albeit under Ben's direction. I was determined that this new hotel would reflect all the theories that I had evolved during my store-designing days. If I had reached people through their basic emotions and love of color and drama in my stores, I could do the same in my hotel design. I had been successful in my previous work as a consultant, but now I could go much further as the sole architect unhampered by a colleague. My only stumbling block might be my client.

Just as I had broken away from straight lines and rectilinear forms in my stores and early hotel interiors, I resolved that I would start with a building plan that would do exactly the same thing. I prepared twenty-six thumbnail sketches of variously shaped buildings without once using the ubiquitous rectangle. The site was a large piece of oceanfront property with no rectangular street patterns. I had my staff draw curved buildings, round buildings, Y-shaped buildings, snake-shaped buildings, every conceivable shape. The form that appeared most often was the curve. A sweeping curved building was what I wanted and what I hoped I could sell my client.

Ben rejected all the proposed sketches. He was going to dream up his own shape. I waited. One day he called to tell me that he had hit upon a marvelous idea. When we met he told me that the idea had struck him like a bolt out of the blue that very morning while he was sitting on the john. (In subsequent interviews, he became more delicate and told interviewers that it really happened while in his tub having a bath. In any case, he knew what he wanted.)

"Why not have a curved building? No one has ever designed a curved building."

"Why, that's a wonderful idea, Ben," I said with a straight face.

This process was the one I used with Ben throughout the entire planning and design period. I spent hours, day after day, night after night, talking theoretical ideas. Instead of saying, "Let's do it," I simply talked, then let the matter drop. Invariably, at our next meeting, Ben would tell me about his new idea.

The path that I would travel, until the sketches became a reality, was to be long and rocky, beset by one unexpected difficulty after another. There was to be a period of nearly two years — of frustration, helpless despair, insurmountable problems, sleepless nights, and eventually the prospect of financial ruin — from the time when the final scheme was approved until I would finally be told to start drawing the plans.

Ben wanted to build his grand hotel on the lovely Firestone estate. He decided to raise the money to buy the estate from the Firestone interests by leaving the Sans Souci partnership. His partners encouraged him and seemed pleased by his departure. All seemed to be in order, and I became the architect. Ben had negotiated with two wealthy men to become his partners in the new venture: one was the head of one of the nation's large grocery chains and the other was an automobile dealer from Washington.

One of Lapidus's preliminary sketches for the Fontainebleau Hotel, 1952.

The hotel under construction in 1954, with the Firestone mansion in the foreground.

*"My sketch was one of many used to convince my client
to dare to use this unusual form for a hotel.
A sweeping curved building was what I wanted
and what I hoped I could sell my client.
I had my drafting room in the original Firestone mansion;
construction went at a feverish rate."*

Then came the first disaster. The two Harrys, who seemed so content to see their former partner go into a new venture, sued him. The suit claimed that since he had used partnership funds to purchase the Firestone estate, he was bound to take the two Harrys with him as partners in this new venture. Thus began a long series of lawsuits.

I kept working on the preliminary plans. The two new partners wanted no part of a long, involved lawsuit with all the possible legal mudslinging, so they bowed out of the deal. I kept working on my sketches. Ben brought two more partners into the deal, both wealthy, influential men. One had been the builder of the Burma Road during the war, and the other was my former client for whom I had designed the Palais Royale so many years before.

Meanwhile, time was flying and the lawsuits were dragging through the courts. I had already spent over ten thousand dollars of my own money on the designs, but I had not received a penny for my services. I was devoting most of my time to the project, and the rest of my practice was suffering. Since no work on the new hotel could be started until the lawsuits were settled, I found myself with a full set of preliminary plans, an almost insurmountable financial problem, and no indication whether the project would ever be built. More than a year had passed. I needed the money desperately. I pleaded with the partners to at least pay me the ten thousand dollars that represented my out-of-pocket expenses. They said that they would like to accommodate me, but since there was no clarification of the legal situation and no formal partnership, there was a question of who should pay me. I pleaded with Ben, who referred me to his attorney, Henry Williams. He sympathized with me but pointed out that I had been wrong to start the work without a firm commitment or a contract.

Desperately needing the money, I asked Williams to recommend an attorney who would start some sort of proceedings that would lead to the payment of my fee. He said that I did not need an attorney. Although he represented Ben and his partners, he offered to act for me despite the conflict of interest. He told me that he would get the partners to come to his office and let him, their attorney, act as judge and jury. I was to present my case and then the partners would present theirs. He would then decide if I was entitled to any money and, if so, how much. He went further. He assured me that if he found cause for me, he personally, without any remuneration, would see to it that I was paid. It was an incredible suggestion, and I gladly accepted.

In due time we all met. I was my own counsel. I do not know if it was desperation or honesty, or maybe it was that I was once again on stage, playing the part of a great defense attorney. Whichever it was, I won my case. Williams turned to his clients and told them that he was convinced that, legalities aside, they were morally obligated to give me ten thousand dollars to pay for my out-of-pocket costs. If and when the project ever got started again, I would credit the present partners, or any new partners, with the sum I had received against the eventual fee. He turned to me and said, "Morris, I pledge you my word as a lawyer and as a gentleman that I will not rest until I get the money for you." I started to stammer my thanks, but he stopped me, "Don't thank me until you get your money. I promise that you will get it. I like you and your sincerity, although I must admit that you are about the lousiest businessman I have ever met."

I left his office in a daze. My last recollection is the sight of the three partners sitting there staring unbelievingly at their attorney. A month after that strange trial, I received a check for the full amount from the escrow account that Williams held for the hotel.

The lawsuits were finally settled out of court. By this time there was an entire new group of partners, twelve of them, maybe more. I never did get the full count. Ben Novak, my original client, had 25 percent of the project, and Ben Jaffee, from Chicago, also had 25 percent. The rest was divided among the others. My troubles were over, or so I imagined.

On December 17, 1953, Ben Novak called a meeting where I, the general contractor, several subcontractors, and a number of the partners were gathered. We met in the large living room of the Firestone house. Ben told me to start my final plans. He wanted the plans finished immediately so that he could open the Fontainebleau in exactly one year on December 17, 1954. I protested that this was impossible. The general contractor suggested that instead of preparing the plans in my New York office, I set up an office right there in the very room we were meeting in. I was to bring down some of my staff as soon as possible. He said that a blueprint machine would be installed and as I prepared the first plans, prints would be made every day. He was ready to start excavations the next day. I called Abby Harle and asked him to come to Miami Beach, rent an apartment, and act as chief draftsman. The contractor converted the Firestone house into various offices, and I hired a staff of four draftsmen. We were ready to start this impossible task.

When Abby arrived, I went with him to find an apartment. We found a second-floor apartment off Lincoln Road overlooking a pleasant garden with a small fountain. The large living room would double as Abby's own living room and my office whenever I came to the Beach, which was quite often. So I had my impromptu office, my first in Miami Beach. I had the necessary stationery printed and was in business. In a few weeks Abby was in charge of an office that had grown to ten draftsmen.

The new Florida office worked at a furious pace. Prints of partially finished drawings were pulled every day. The very able contractor had started as a graduate architect and had switched to contracting. He was one of the best contractors I have ever worked with, not only on the Fontainebleau but as the contractor on many of my future projects.

Novak insisted that I move to Miami Beach. Of course I refused. We finally came to an agreement. I was to move to the Beach by the middle of the year and

Morris and Beatrice Lapidus in the small Miami Beach apartment they occupied while Lapidus supervised the construction of the Fontainebleau Hotel in 1954.

stay until the Fontainebleau was completed and opened. I discussed this arrangement with Bea and she agreed. We would find a small apartment near the project and make it our home for six months. Of course, we would be able to go to Flatbush for a few weeks whenever we could. That summer our older son, Richard, would graduate from University of Vermont and our younger son, Alan, would be graduating from high school. Bea and I arranged to give them a grand tour of Europe for the entire summer. At the end of the summer when they returned from Europe, Richard would enter Columbia law school and live in the university dorms, and Alan would enter Trinity College.

When the project was about half completed and our sons had left on their trip to Europe, I heard the phone ring in the apartment that I was occupying temporarily in Miami Beach with Bea. I looked at the clock; it was 4:00 a.m. One of our sons might be calling from Europe. Instead, it was the night watchman on the site of the Fontainebleau. A bomb had just exploded on the inside of the hotel. Could I rush right over?

He had already called the contractor and the partners, who told him to call me. I dressed hurriedly, jumped into my car, and sped to the site. The police were everywhere. Searchlights were playing over the naked concrete structure. The smell of dynamite still hung heavy in the hot, humid, predawn air. I told the police that I was the architect, and I was allowed into the vast space that was to be the lobby. Hastily summoned workers were already setting up shoring near a column that had been shattered by the bomb. Soon my engineers were on the site examining the damage. Fortunately, the dynamiters had set their charges against one of the columns that supported a part of a two-story wing. The continuity of the hurricane-proof type of construction kept the wing from collapsing. After a few hours of study, we decided that the damage was not serious and could be remedied in a few days by adding reinforcing rods and pouring additional concrete.

I was curious to know why anyone would attempt to destroy the hotel. Newspaper reporters were soon on the site. Neither the owners nor the contractor knew of any disputes that might have caused someone to blow up the hotel.

Months later, I happened to discuss the mysterious bombing with a man who was in some way connected with labor and gambling. Many of these fringe characters winter in Miami Beach. I was saying to him that it was fortunate that whoever had set the bomb knew so very little about construction.

The man looked at me and smiled. "Mr. Lapidus," he said, "these people know their business. Why should they try to destroy the hotel? They wanted to get a message across — that's all they wanted."

At some earlier time, Ben Novak had made a trip to Europe with his wife and had passed by Fontainebleau, the French royal chateau outside of Paris. Years later, when asked whether he had gone in to see the chateau, he was quoted in an article as saying, "We didn't stop to look at it. I don't go for those foreign chateaux." He liked the name, however, because it sounded "catchy." And so the name of the hotel was born. The fact that the plans for the new hotel were completely contemporary, without the slightest kinship to the great palace of the French kings, appeared to be of no significance. But having embarked on a French kick, my client decided to go further. One day he proudly announced that the interior design of the hotel would be *French Provincial!* French Provincial in a contemporary building? What could I possibly do to overcome this new brainstorm?

I had hoped and prayed for a chance to show the world that I was a talented architect. I had devoted my entire career to modern, twentieth-century architecture. I did not know if I should fight my client and refuse to design in such a style or if I should simply tell him to get another interior designer. I was faced with compromise or conviction. I thought of my old friend Archie, the sculptor, the renegade who had ended up in a mental institution. Archie had refused to compromise, stubborn and unyielding to the very end.

Soon thereafter, I received some devastating news. Morris Sanders, the architect I had worked with on the 1939 World's Fair project, had committed suicide. When I moved into my office on 49th Street, we used to see each other from time to time, and occasionally we would have lunch together. My practice seemed to be growing constantly, but his was dwindling. He often told me that I was a much better architect than my work indicated because I was too ready to compromise with my clients. He also felt that I should not compromise when it came to setting a fee. He would say, "To hell with the bastards. If they don't pay a standard fee, why work for them, and if they won't let you design the kind of building you think they should have, throw them out of your office." I told Morris I was willing to compromise in design and in fees as long as my practice was growing. One day at lunch Morris suggested that we form a partnership. He felt that his unyielding approach to architecture was probably not the best way. He felt that perhaps we could form a good team. He would look after the designs and stay away from the clients, compromising wherever necessary. I knew that this would be impossible. The unbending nature of my good and talented colleague would never work in a practice such as mine. And so we gave up the idea, and Morris laughingly said that, after all, it was only a silly idea and we both ought to forget about it, and we did.

The houseman who took care of my office as well as Morris's came to me with the dreadful news. Morris had sent his family away for the weekend, telling his wife that he had some urgent work to finish. He was dead when the houseman found him Monday morning. All the oven gas jets were still on. The obituary notice in the newspapers said that my friend and colleague had died of a heart attack. I would rather think that he had died of a broken heart. From that day on, there remained no doubt in my mind about compromise.

I collected some illustrations of lovely French Provincial interiors. This handsome style was perfect for small chateaux and country homes but would be utterly ridiculous in a tropical contemporary luxury hotel. I developed a plan to get my client to forget about this inappropriate style, but I need not have bothered. He took one look at the illustrations and wanted to know if I was crazy.

"I wouldn't have these old-fashioned interiors on a bet. I want that modern kind of French Provincial. I want real luxury modern French Provincial."

I did not even blink an eye. All I had to do was try to create interiors that I could convince him were "modern French Provincial." And so began another campaign. I had to give up my original idea of the smart contemporary interiors that I had been developing and try to create interiors that my client would accept. Although I had set up a field office in Miami Beach, most of the actual designing was done in my New York office.

I was living in Flatbush, and every morning I rode to work on the subway. Most of the designs for the Fontainebleau were conceived on those subway rides from Brooklyn to my office in Manhattan. In the play *Three Men on a Horse*, the central character works out the horse-race winners every morning while riding to work on a bus. His phenomenal record of picking winners — on whom he never bets, he just does the handicapping for the fun of it — finally comes to the attention of a group of gamblers. They decide to capitalize on this man's genius for picking winners, and they persuade him to leave his job and make his and their fortunes with his uncanny ability. But for some strange reason, he loses his capacity to pick winners. In desperation, they try everything, until finally it dawns on them that the motion of the bus on his daily morning ride created the proper euphoria for his unusual talent. So it seemed with me. I could do my most inspired designing riding the subway. I might almost claim that the Fontainebleau was designed on the subway and not on a drawing board.

I spent a great deal of time preparing my client to accept my designs for the rather large coffee shop that was to go into the hotel. I encouraged him to talk about what he would like, and then I would sum up for him, so that in the end it would seem as if he was the one who was telling me what to draw. We talked about a Rumpelmayer cafe (I had never seen Rumpelmayer's in Europe and neither had he). We spoke of the elegance of old Vienna at the height of the Strauss waltz era — Dresden figurines, rococo arches, gaslit crystal chandeliers, elegance, Old World luxury.

I prepared my designs and sent them down to Miami with one of my associates. This particular young man was a thorough modernist. He hated the ornamentation that I had imposed on an otherwise simple contemporary interior. When he presented the scheme to our client, he spoke glowingly of the clean contemporary lines and extolled the virtues of the modern planning. Ben called and wanted to know if I had lost my mind. The designs for the coffee shop were emphatically rejected. I apologized to Ben and promised to work out the coffee shop according to the ideas he had given me. The next week I was in Miami Beach presenting the "new designs." They were the identical drawings my young associate had shown Ben the week before. I pointed to the rococo arches, the oversized Dresden figurines, the gay romantic Viennese pavilion over the quick service counter, the pseudo gaslight fixtures dripping with crystals.

"Well, now you've got it. You've got everything just the way I told you. Do me a favor. Don't send me any of your smart kids. You know how to put my ideas on paper. You do it."

While I was creating the style that was neither period nor modern, I still had to arrange all the interiors, especially the huge lobby, to represent a direction. But what was the direction I was seeking? What was the central theme? Whose tastes was I trying to satisfy? Obviously, Ben's as my client, but also that of his clientele, who would be wealthy Americans coming for a winter vacation.

What were the tastes of the vast majority of affluent Americans? What and who were the taste makers of the middle of the twentieth century? Bauhaus and the International School were considered the leaders of design, but were Americans accepting these imported theories of Gropius and Breuer and Mies van der Rohe? The answer was an emphatic "no"! The critics loved it, but the critics were not going to be guests at the Fontainebleau. So where was I to seek that certain style which would satisfy the guests and would represent for them their dream of tropical opulence and glittering luxury? I finally realized that American taste was being influenced by the greatest mass media of entertainment of that time, the movies. So I imagined myself the set designer for a movie producer who wanted to create a hotel that would make a tremendous impression on the viewers. Wasn't that exactly what I had wanted to do when I studied architecture? So I designed a movie set! I never for a moment let my client know what I was doing. For him I was expressing his ideas of what a luxury hotel should be.

Perhaps his ideas and my designs were not really too far apart after all. I must have succeeded on both counts. The guests loved the hotel, and it has been used as a movie background for countless films — from James Bond to Frank Sinatra — and for a number of television shows. A famous director was a guest at the Fontainebleau's opening ceremonies. When I met this gentleman, he told me that someday he would like very much to film a picture at the Fontainebleau because it was a perfect movie set. So at last I had fulfilled my dream of being a set designer, only my sets were not for a play or a stage, they were the interiors of a grand hotel.

One of the many partners of the Fontainebleau Hotel was Jules Gorlitz, a man of exquisite taste. He was extremely fond of antiques, especially antiques of the late eighteenth and nineteenth centuries. He and I persuaded Ben that the hotel, since it was in "modern French Provincial," should have antique adornments. Ben agreed, and we settled on a budget of one hundred thousand dollars to be spent on antique furniture and decorations — lamps, clocks, statues, and so on. Jules and I became the patron saints of Third Avenue, the antique center in

New York. I could hardly walk down that street without having one of the dealers stop me and draw me into the store. At that time the antique market was in the doldrums and business was bad. Dealers offered us beautiful objects at ridiculously low prices. We bought marbles, terracottas, bronze statues, and busts. We acquired elegant lamps, beautiful clocks, a magnificent nineteenth-century piano with marquetry and ormolu work, gilded cherubs, exquisite vases, wall carvings, and a lovely collection of furniture to be refinished and reupholstered. Finally, as the hotel neared completion and the lobby was almost finished, I scheduled the pickup of all the furniture and *objets d'art* by a trucking company.

A large trailer truck was loaded with this cargo and driven to Florida. Several days later Ben called in a raging fury. He told me that there was a truckload of junk outside the hotel and that he would not allow it inside. At first I failed to understand what he was talking about, but then it dawned on me that he was referring to the antiques that I had bought. Both Jules, who was there at the time, and I pleaded with Ben, but our arguments were to no avail.

Late that night I took a plane to Miami Beach. I went over again and again the performance I would have to put on when I got there to try to convince my client that the "junk" was exactly the kind of adornment that he needed for the interiors of the hotel. Ben was waiting for me in the lobby. Much to my amazement, he told me that it had not really been necessary for me to make the trip. He knew just what these antiques were, that most of them were priceless treasures. He told me that he had been upset by so many other things at the time the truck arrived that he really did not take a good look at what was being delivered. He had had many problems—labor situations, work that was not being completed, problems with contractors, and so on—and he had had a splitting headache. When he saw the truck it was only his state of mind that made him say what he did. After all, he told me, he was a connoisseur and did know fine things. He was sorry that he had upset me and regretted that he had put me to the trouble of a needless trip. What, I wondered, had transformed the man who saw only junk one day into the man who glowed with pride at being the owner of such priceless objects?

I learned the story some days later from Jules, who was there throughout the entire event. It seems that after the truckers had unloaded various pieces of furniture, the statuary, the clocks, and the carvings, Ben kept ranting about his idiot architect who spent a fortune buying a truckload of junk. My client was not one for keeping his thoughts to himself. The whole world had to know just what he was thinking, and everyone within earshot of my client knew how he felt.

That evening, Ben was showing some friends around the hotel. The couple had traveled extensively and were people of discerning taste. As they viewed the various pieces of sculpture, the busts, the figurines, the bronzes, the urns, the vases, and all the other beautiful objects, they went into raptures about the assembly of so many lovely things in one place. They were delighted and impressed to learn that such a lovely collection would be integrated in the new hotel. Ben said nothing, but he listened.

Early the next morning when he came to the job he found that the carpenters were using marble busts for sawhorses. Others were standing on the furniture to reach up to their work. He became furious and called for the superintendent. He let him know, in no uncertain terms, that what was happening was an atrocity, that these priceless treasures were being ruined by the stupid workmen. This same superintendent had heard Ben's tirade the day before and could not understand what he was talking about, except that what was "junk" yesterday were priceless treasures today. Ben ordered an enclosure built to protect the antiques and instructed the workmen to stay away from them.

As the project neared completion, I began to realize that accepting my original fee would probably bankrupt me. I was devoting all my time and energies to the completion of the Fontainebleau. I was making no effort to seek new work, and I was losing established clients. The Fontainebleau had become an obsession. As we neared the opening date, I realized that I had poured all my available business capital into the planning of this one project. Fortunately, Bea and I had been able to save some money through the years, our nest egg. I had to start drawing money out of our savings account to remain solvent and to complete my work on the hotel. The project had grown in scope and so had my services. Overseeing and designing all the interiors and arranging for the purchase of all furnishings and decor, as well as paying overtime salaries to my staff, were draining away my life's savings with no hope of making up the loss.

I talked to Ben about this disastrous situation. I insisted that I was entitled to an increase in my basic fee. I reasoned that I should receive an extra fee of eighty thousand dollars, or a total fee of one hundred sixty thousand dollars, a sum representing one percent of a project whose cost had risen to sixteen million dollars. Of course one percent was a mere pittance, but one-half of one percent was absolute madness.

Ben sympathized with me. He was aware that he had demanded the impossible on that December day when he had instructed me to complete the final plans, supervise the construction, and then design and complete the interiors in exactly one year. Ben agreed that I was entitled to an extra fee but said that my request for an additional eighty thousand dollars was preposterous. We haggled, we argued, I pleaded. I was not asking for a profit, I simply wanted to cover my costs. I was satisfied that my profit would not be a monetary one. Ben kept telling me that his hotel would make me famous. Who else would have done what he had done — given an architect who had never designed a total building a commission to design a sixteen-million-dollar hotel that would be the first great hotel to be completed since the Waldorf had opened in 1932? I agreed that the

Fontainebleau might bring me fame and the kind of architectural practice I had been hoping for, but fame would not prevent bankruptcy.

Ben reviewed my costs carefully and showed me that if I were to get an extra forty thousand dollars, or fifty percent over my original fee, I would at least not suffer any financial loss. I accepted. Ben suggested that we wait until just before the opening of the hotel so that he could broach the question of extras to his many partners.

At last the great day was approaching. In a week the hotel would have its well-publicized grand opening. The partners had arrived. Many of them were seeing the completed project for the first time. The partners had a short meeting in Ben's office, and then I was asked to conduct them on a tour of the hotel and the grounds. We walked through the building where workmen were feverishly completing the last minute touches. Drapes were being hung, lamps placed, last pieces of hardware set; painters were touching up damaged spots. Maids were making beds, dusting furniture, and tidying rooms. Porters were wielding brushes and mops and vacuum cleaners. A hotel was being born.

The partners admired the furniture that I had designed, they exclaimed over the grandeur of the glittering lobby with its fine woods, beautiful marble floor and columns, elegant furniture, glowing crystal chandeliers, and the final touch —those lovely antiques, strategically placed to create the ultimate touch of authentic luxury. I then led the group out to the gardens and to the huge pool deck with its large pool and sweeping curved line of cabanas. The partners stood there admiring the bold curving line of the hotel, the fountains and statuary, the pool and deck, all glowing brilliantly in the noonday Florida sun. The palm trees, the sparkling ocean, and the white beaches completed the picture of tropic opulence. The men overwhelmed me with their congratulations.

As we walked along the pool deck, I caught up with Ben and told him that this would be the opportune moment to tell the partners about our agreement and the extra fee we had arranged. He looked at me with a blank stare. He said he had no idea what I was talking about. I protested but he kept saying he did not understand.

The sun was shining brightly, but I began to shake as with a chill. The back of my neck and scalp began to tingle. I actually felt the hair on my head standing up. My palms were sweating and I was freezing again. The sun looked like a black ink spot on a blood red sky. I felt as if I were paralyzed. A sudden fury seized me. A pile of discarded lumber was lying at my feet. I bent down and picked up a length of two-by-eight lumber. There was only one mad thought in my crazed brain—"kill the monster!" I heard myself screaming, "He must die —he must die!" Ben started running, and I followed, wildly swinging the heavy timber. I had no control over myself as I ran screaming and flailing the length of timber. I caught a fleeting glimpse of the startled faces of the assembled partners, then blackness.

The next thing I knew, someone was placing a cold, wet towel on my head. I felt cold water dripping from my soaked hair to my shoulders. I sat there trembling. I heard myself muttering over and over again, "He must die, he must die." Slowly, I realized that I was sitting in one of the hotel offices. The partners were grouped around me looking frightened and solicitous. Jules was standing at my side with his arm around my shoulders.

"Take it easy, Morris. Calm down. We're your friends. Just calm down or you'll have a heart attack. Calm down and tell us what this is all about."

"He promised," I sobbed. "He promised that he would tell you about the extra. He promised and now he says he never said it."

"What extra? Calm down and tell us what extra."

"My extra fee. He promised to get you all to agree to pay me an extra fee of forty thousand dollars. I swear to you he promised."

"So that was what it was all about?" Ben Jaffee said. "Morris, we all agreed a long time ago that you were to have your fee increased. How much do we owe on the original contract?"

"There's a balance of ten thousand due me, Ben."

"So right now we owe you fifty thousand. Is that right, Morris?"

"Right, Ben. If I don't get that money I'm broke — bankrupt. I put all my money into this project."

Ben Jaffee left the room to discuss the matter with Ben Novak. The other partners, seeing that I was regaining my composure, began to tell me what had happened.

"We heard you screaming. It was so sudden, we didn't know what had happened. We thought something had fallen from the roof and hit you. We thought you were hurt."

"Then we saw Ben running as if the Devil was after him. You were chasing him with that timber, screaming."

"Hey, kid, I didn't know you were that strong," said a partner named Herbie. "That timber must weigh fifty pounds."

"Strong?" my friend Jules was saying. "Strong? It took four of us to tackle you and pull you down."

"They must have heard you screaming across the bay in Miami. You sure were wild, Morris."

I sat there listening in dazed silence. Was it possible that all this had happened without my knowing what I was doing? Could this happen to a person, a complete blackout? I could have killed my client with one blow and it would have been murder. I began to tremble again. The second Ben came back into the room and explained that I would get my fifty thousand but that I would have to wait until the hotel had opened and cash started flowing. He would give me fifty thousand in notes for six months. The notes would carry full interest and were negotiable. A lending institution would give me the money immediately.

There was just one hitch — Ben's signature was needed. He was ready to sign the notes, but he would not sign until I apologized.

I refused. He should have been apologizing to me.

Ben Jaffee sat down beside me. He put his arm around me and spoke to me in fatherly tones.

"Listen to me, Morris. I am much older than you. I know how you feel about my partner, but the guy wants an apology. So walk in and say, 'I am sorry,' that's all. Don't let pride stop you. Go get your money. That's what is important. Get that note signed and walk out."

The others urged me to get it over with. I walked into Ben's office. I had no idea what I looked like. My client's normally well-tanned face was a shade of pea green.

"I'm sorry, Ben," I said. "I apologize."

"You should be sorry. Why didn't you talk louder? I never said I wasn't going to pay you. I didn't know what you were screaming about. You were whispering, and you know that I don't hear well." I knew that Ben wore a hearing aid.

"I know that we agreed to an extra forty thousand dollars. But you kept whispering, I didn't understand what you were trying to say to me. I'm your friend. Why should I try to hurt you?"

Perhaps I was hasty, nervous, and apprehensive, worrying about my money. Maybe I had not made my meaning clear. It was possible that, in fact, he had not heard me. I wish I could relive that awful moment and see whether or not I was wrong. He picked up a pen and signed the notes and handed them to me. I walked out of the office.

The last few days before the opening was a frenzy of activity, like opening night at the theater multiplied a hundred times. Every part of the hotel had to be ready to receive guests. The front office, with its receptionists, room clerks, reservation staff, bookkeepers and all their intricate billing machines, was bustling. The sophisticated paraphernalia was being checked with repeated dry runs to make sure everything and everybody would function smoothly when the first guest checked into the hotel. The kitchen worked at top capacity preparing meals to see whether there were any flaws in the equipment. Delicious menus were tried out and the food was offered to the help or discarded. The chef checked and rechecked the huge refrigerator boxes for contents and temperature. Soup kettles and vegetable steamers were tested, the ovens were tried again and again, and an elaborate system was established to ensure a fast flow of food from station to station. The fry chef had to be ready with his potatoes at the same instant that the vegetable chef was ready. The broil chef had to have meats done to the proper degree to comply with the waiters' orders, and the saucier had to bring his sauces to the point of perfection at that moment. The *maître de bouche* and the master chef conferred with the sous-chefs, making last-minute adjustments. In the bake shops the aroma of delicious cakes and breads filled the air. Everything had to be perfect for the Grand Opening Ball.

In another part of the hotel the housekeeper was directing her staff, issuing uniforms that were tried on and adjusted. The housekeeper was getting innumerable telephone reports from each floor requesting additional items — blankets, ashtrays, soap, towels — from the floor managers who were supervising the maids and the porters. Down in the boiler room the chief engineer checked his machinery and his charts to make sure that there was plenty of hot water, that the huge air-conditioning plants and their compressors were performing properly. A breakdown of air conditioning during the opening ceremonies, when the hotel would be filled to capacity with guests and dignitaries, would be an irreparable disaster.

The large laundry was another scene of controlled confusion. New sheets were put through the monstrous washers — no sheet was to be used unless it had been washed at least once. The director of the laundry wanted his washers, tumblers, dryers, drum ironers, and valet equipment in perfect order. All these activities were part of the behind-the-scenes operation, or more properly, the back-of-the-house operation, activities that the guests never see but of which they would become instantly aware if anything went wrong.

The public rooms were scenes of feverish and frenetic activity. Chairs and tables were being set up in the coffee shop, the main dining room, the supper club, the cocktail lounge, and the grand ballroom. In the main lobby and the other public spaces, last minute details were being completed. Through all this tapestry of activity, final threads were being woven by an army of painters, electricians, carpenters, plumbers, drapers, carpet layers, paper hangers, and a host of other tradesmen. The waiters, busboys, and bellmen in bright new uniforms, which I had designed, were everywhere, becoming familiar with the building that would soon cease to be just a building and would be an exciting, new, luxurious tropical resort hotel. I had the heady feeling that generals must experience the night before an important battle.

Opening night with its Grand Ball was almost an anticlimax. Guests arrived in evening attire and I was quickly sought out, congratulated, complimented. For some reason, I wanted to get away from the gaiety, the excitement, the warm feeling of admiration, and be alone. I walked out into the quiet gardens and looked back at the sweeping lines of the building that I had designed. Behind me were the beach and the restless ocean with its waves beating their runic rhythm as a sort of obbligato to music coming from the ballroom. A full Miami moon bathed the hotel and its gardens in soft light with the brilliant lights of the hotel interiors acting as accents to the moonlight. Until this moment, all of this had been mine, all mine. Now I felt like a parent saying his last good-bye to a child he has nurtured to manhood. The Fontainebleau belonged to my clients and the world. My task as the architect and the interior designer was completed.

Grand Ballroom, Fontainebleau Hotel, 1954.

"The guests were waiting for the Grand Opening Ball to begin. It was time for me to go in.
I wiped away a few tears. Why in the world should I be crying at a moment like this?
I had dreamed of an acting career, of making my appearance on stage, entering stage right.
Well, it was time for me to make my entrance, not on a stage as an actor but into a
glamorous luxury hotel as its architect."

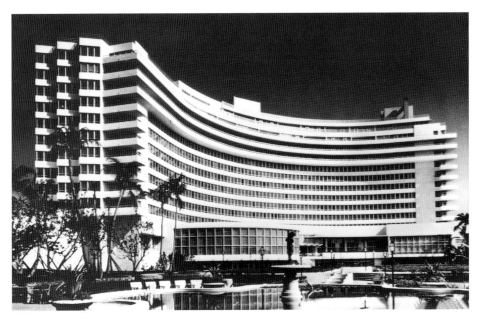

Garden facade, Fontainebleau Hotel, Miami Beach, 1954.

Aerial view of the Fontainebleau Hotel (previous pages), pool and gardens
(above), and rear entrance stairs to the garden (facing page).

Coffee shop in the Fontainebleau Hotel, 1954.

"I spent a great deal of time preparing my client to accept my designs for the rather large coffee shop that was to go into the hotel. We spoke of the elegance of Old Vienna at the height of the Strauss waltz era — Dresden figurines, rococo arches, gaslit crystal chandeliers, elegance, Old World luxury."

Lobby, Fontainebleau Hotel, 1954 (above and overleaf).

*"I finally realized that American taste was being influenced by the greatest
mass media of entertainment of that time, the movies.... So I designed a movie set!"*

*"In the Fontainebleau lobby [overleaf] are the famous 'stairs to nowhere.'
On the back wall is my favorite photomural — this time of a Piranesi etching."*

Front entrance, Eden Roc Hotel, Miami Beach, 1955.

13 The Hotels and the Critics

For the opening ceremonies of the Fontainebleau Hotel, the publicity people decided to invite the mayor of the town of Fontainebleau. He was a very polite, albeit rather bewildered Frenchman who gave me some very original criticism of my work. He spent his time walking around the hotel shaking his head in disbelief at what he saw. He was accustomed to the elegance and the regal splendor of the palaces of the great Louis XIV and Napoleon, but this type of elegance baffled him. In my halting French, I asked him what he thought of the hotel named after his city. *"C'est une bouillabaisse."* I did not know whether this was a compliment or a devastating criticism of the kettle of soup I had cooked up.

"Aimez-vous la bouillabaisse, monsieur?" I wanted to know.

Yes, he liked bouillabaisse, but only once in a while. That wasn't too bad, I thought. After all, the Fontainebleau had been designed for vacationers.

The opening was, of course, well publicized. Travel editors wrote glowing descriptions of this ultra-luxurious hotel. Articles describing the new hotel and mentioning me as the architect appeared in national magazines, including *Life*. Suddenly I was famous. People and old friends that I had not seen in years sought me out to offer their congratulations. One of my earliest store clients whom I ran into at the opening said to me, "You don't have to worry about making it. You've got it made."

But did I really have it made? An old friend and the editor of *Architectural Forum*, who had previously published much of my work, called to tell me that he had been considering publishing the Fontainebleau, but had decided against it. He told me it was too controversial, that it violated all the precepts of building design. Thus I got my first impressions of what the architectural profession thought of my work.

My next call came from the editor of *Progressive Architecture*. This magazine too had published many of my stores. The editor's comments were polite, but he told me that one of their other editors had visited the hotel, and they concluded that they could not possibly publish such a radical piece of work. The final blow came when the editor of *Architectural Record* called to say that he felt he owed me the courtesy of telling me that the Fontainebleau was too far off the mainstream of architecture to warrant publication. I had designed a hotel, my first total building, that the public loved but the architects hated.

With the hotel completed, I was ready to move back to New York. Miami had been an exciting interlude, but there were new stores waiting to be designed. I had no idea when the next hotel commission might come along. As the Fontainebleau settled down to its first weeks of business, I received a call from Harry Mufson, Ben's former partner, and arranged to meet him at the Sans Souci Hotel. He told me that he had just completed negotiations for the land directly to the north of the Fontainebleau and that he was going to build an even more luxurious hotel called the Eden Roc, named after the swimming pool and gardens of the famous Hotel du Cap.

I was eager and ready. I felt that it was proper to tell Ben that I was starting a project for his former partner on the beach front adjacent to the Fontainebleau. Ben was furious. He forbade me to act as Harry's architect. I patiently explained to him that architecture was my profession and my means of earning a livelihood. I was simply showing Ben a courtesy. Ben claimed that I owed it to him to turn down this new commission. Hadn't he been the one who gave me my first opportunity to design a hotel? There would be other hotels, but I was not to design Harry's hotel.

I told Ben a story about an ancient architect: In medieval Europe an architect by the name of Lanfred was the designer of a castle which would be known as Ivry, a vast, strongly fortified tower built by Aubree, wife of Ralph, Count of Baveaux. The good Aubree selected Lanfred as master of works because he was a man whose skill was praised beyond all others of his time in France. When Lanfred had completed the castle with much labor and at great cost, Aubree, fearful that he might build another equal to it elsewhere, had him beheaded.

Then I told Ben about Sennamar, an Arab architect, who built the palace of Kahoovrnack for King Norman Alaouvar, the tenth king of the Arabs. The king was fearful that Sennamar might design a building of equal magnificence for someone and so he dispatched him to Allah with high recommendations.

I reasoned with Ben that I was sure that he was not going to have me beheaded, nor was he going to dispatch me to Allah. In short, I was going to act as Harry's architect. Ben warned me that if I did, he would never speak to me again and that I would be forbidden to enter the Fontainebleau. I left the hotel feeling like Adam being driven out of the Garden of Eden.

Harry had also been banished from the Fontainebleau forever. One day, however, he put on dark glasses and snooped through the hotel. He returned saying he wanted the same atmosphere but "no French stuff."

I tried to convince him to use contemporary, but he did not go for it so I suggested Italian Renaissance. I got some books together and showed Harry the interiors of the Vatican, the Pitti Palace, the Uffizzi, and many others. He liked what he saw but wanted me to leave out "all that heavy ornament."

"As the Fontainebleau settled down to its first weeks of business, I received a call from Harry Mufson. He told me that he had just completed negotiations for the land directly to the north of the Fontainebleau and that he was going to build an even more luxurious hotel called the Eden Roc, named after the swimming pool and gardens of the famous Hotel du Cap."

The Fontainebleau Hotel (1954), and behind it, the Eden Roc (1955) in Miami Beach.

Once again I was caught in the same trap, but by this time I had crystallized my ideas and resolved to refine and polish the approach I had used for the Fontainebleau. I was still designing stage settings, however. People love to feel as if they are on stage when traveling or stopping at an elegant hotel. In most hotels that I designed, I have arranged the levels so that when guests enter the restaurant they find themselves at the top of a short flight of stairs in a position to see and be seen. I invariably place soft pink floodlights in discreet positions so that the guests are actually on stage with a spotlight on them. In the Fontainebleau, guests go up three steps to arrive at the platform, walk out onto the platform, and then go down three steps. I have been waiting through the years for someone to tell me how ridiculous it was for guests to walk up three steps and then down three steps into the dining room when they could have walked directly in, but no one has ever questioned it.

Most of my hotel interiors have grand staircases and most of these stairs go nowhere at all. They might lead to a balcony or a mezzanine, but people love to ascend or descend circular staircases in a grand manner as in the movies of Busby Berkley and the early musicals.

I decided I would not curve the new hotel, the Eden Roc, or use the free forms on the exterior. Perhaps, I thought, the profession and the critics would be kinder if I restrained my desire to use free-flowing forms. Although the front of the building would be slightly curved, the walls were straight. I decided to use a "Y" shape, but my interiors would still be free-flowing curved spaces.

The lobby was a huge circular space with a spiral stairway to nowhere. The main part of the lobby consisted of oval-shaped columns in rosewood with gold stripes separating the convex flutes. There were no capitals or bases. These columns never touched the huge disk-shaped ceiling. The lobby was enclosed by bronze and marble railings interspersed with short, fluted marble columns on which I mounted beautiful bronze figures that I purchased in Milan. Surrounding the railing, I used terrazzo (the entire floor was terrazzo) in a pattern of huge Greek anthemion, which people thought were large palm fronds. A beautiful bronze-and-crystal chandelier hung from the center of the elegant disk-shaped ceiling.

During the year that I was working on the Eden Roc, Bea and I sailed for Europe on the *France*. The Fontainebleau had been open only six months, but it was already famous. I realized the celebrity it brought me when Bea and I received an invitation to attend the captain's farewell dinner. Sitting with the captain was the attorney general of the United States and his wife. His fame rested on the conviction of Alger Hiss as a spy. The other guests were the French minister of culture and his wife, a French cabinet member and his wife, and the wife of the owner of Air France. The conversation was entirely in French. Bea had graduated from Hunter College as a French major, and my French was still good enough to enter into the conversation at the table. Only

Morris Lapidus and the owner of the Hotel du Cap on the grounds of the hotel
in Cap d'Antibes, France, 1955.

Mona Lisa Room at the Eden Roc Hotel, Miami Beach, 1955.

the attorney general spoke no French, and Bea and I spoke to him and his wife from time to time. The dinner was a Lucullan feast, my first taste of fame.

We had a marvelous time in France and Italy. For the first time, I was actually seeing all the famous palaces, chateaux, cathedrals, and lovely cities I had studied in architecture school. We stopped in Milan and Venice to buy bronzes, chandeliers, and glass for the hotel.

While in Paris, we visited the Louvre. There we found a number of artists copying some of the masterpieces. I did not speak to any of the artists, but when I got back to Florida, I met an airline captain to whom I explained my desire to purchase copies being made at the Louvre. He told me that he had become acquainted with some of these copyists on his regular flights to Paris. I asked him if he could get them to make twenty-four copies of great pieces of art all to one size, about twenty-four inches square. I especially wanted a fine copy of the Mona Lisa. He told me that he could do this and bring these copies into the United States because airline captains never had their luggage examined. In the

hotel restaurant called the Mona Lisa Room, I eventually used the twenty-four copies arranged in ornate frames, with the Mona Lisa placed in a prominent position and spotlighted from a concealed powerful spotlight. The entire wall was framed with twisted columns copied from those in St. Peter's in Rome.

About ten years after the Eden Roc was finished an interior designer was engaged to update the room. He decided to use mirrors in each frame and hide my beautiful copies. Only the Mona Lisa was spared.

While in France, Bea and I visited the Hotel du Cap, a very beautiful and expensive hostelry. I met the owner who kindly showed me the entire estate. I remember this visit especially because the owner offered to take us for a cruise around the area. He said that if Mr. Kennedy was not using his yacht we could take the cruise. We went to Joseph Kennedy's cabana, he was glad for the hotelier to use his yacht, and he insisted that we meet his sons, John, Robert, and Edward.

When we stopped in Milan, I met the owner of the company that made the tile for two twelve-foot-wide panels reaching from the ground to the top of the Eden Roc building. We worked out a system to slowly grade the colors of the tile from the darkest green at the bottom to the palest green at the top. The man I bought the tile from was a wealthy and influential Italian. I asked him if he knew Gio Ponti and when he said he did, I asked whether he could arrange for me to meet Ponti, who was then completing the designs for the now famous Pirelli building.

Ponti and I met one morning in his Milan studio. He felt that we in America were designing buildings that had no beginning and no end. His Pirelli building was a tall structure that started in plan with a narrow pointed form at one side, expanded to a full width in the middle and then tapered again at the other side — a form that might be compared to the shape of a Zeppelin. He spoke angrily of the International Style. I told him I too despised it.

While in Italy, Bea and I had hired a driver, Vincenzo, and his car. In Milan I asked to be taken to a fine house that specialized in marble and bronze reproductions. When I made my choice and asked for the prices, I thought they were outrageous. Vincenzo kept telling me that I was getting a good price. The merchant finally beckoned me to come with him into a back room. There he told me that he had to quote high prices because Vincenzo, whom he knew, would come back and get 20 percent of the purchase. We agreed on a fair price and then devised a plan. I would leave his shop and angrily say, in Vincenzo's presence, that the prices were too high. I returned later without Vincenzo's knowledge and made my purchases.

In the meantime, back in Miami, I had converted three stores in an open passageway that led to Abby's apartment into offices for me and my staff of eight draftsmen. It was here that I designed the Eden Roc. At the same time, my New York offices were engaged on twenty-five projects. I had a large office at 256 East 49th Street where all the work was still designed by me. I had a few young designers but I had to direct their energies. Commuting between New York and Florida was a backbreaking job.

I decided that I needed a partner and that my old friend Charlie who had introduced me to Ben Novak would be an ideal partner for a large thriving practice. As vice president in charge of design and construction for a large firm, Charlie was earning twenty-four thousand dollars a year. I met with Charlie and offered him a partnership at no cost to him. I showed him my earnings of over eighty thousand dollars a year and told him that he could count on forty thousand dollars a year and be an architect in the true sense of the word, not an employee. He told me that I was more than generous, but he had to think it over. A week later we met again and he regretfully refused my offer. At A. S. Beck, he explained, he had few responsibilities and a sure income, and he did not want to take the risk.

As the Eden Roc was nearing completion, I received a call from clients — Larry and Bob Tisch and their father Al — for whom I had done some minor

Lapidus with clients and friends on the construction site of the Americana Hotel in Bal Harbour, Florida, 1955.
At left, Lapidus (left) with developer Larry Tisch; at right, Lapidus (left) with Liberace, Al Tisch, and son Bob Tisch.

"Few people realize that not only do many architects not design buildings as they would like to, but that getting the building designed and built to please the client and carrying out the work at a decent fee is a never-ending struggle."

hotel renovations in Lakewood, New Jersey. The three men came to see me in my Miami Beach office. They wanted me to design a hotel for them on an ocean plot in Bal Harbour, a town several miles north of Miami Beach. They wanted a contemporary hotel, exterior as well as interior. At last I could forget about traditional styles. We agreed upon a fee, and I started my New York office working on the preliminary plans.

At that time I was fully occupied with the finishing touches on the Eden Roc so I asked a young associate to prepare preliminary designs. He pulled out all the stops and went hog-wild modern. It was with some trepidation that I took the plans with me to Florida for presentation to my new clients. The father, brothers, and their controller came to my office to review the plans. The reception was rather cool. I felt that something was amiss, but the commission was mine and had already been announced in the local papers. Larry, the older brother, acted as the spokesman. He said he would like to take the plans and study them. They made an appointment to return the next day. The next day at the appointed time the four of them were back in my office.

Larry again was the spokesman.

He told me that they had decided to take the commission away from me and that they wanted to pay me for the work that I had done on these preliminary plans. He told me to name the amount and not to be afraid to make it enough.

I was stunned. This had never happened to me before. I asked what I had done wrong. I told them that if they did not like what we had done for them, we would start again. I again asked what the problem was. I told Larry that such a dismissal would be very damaging to my career in Miami Beach and, in fact, could even end it.

He did not want to argue. He aked me again to name a sum. He said that they had decided to give the commission to another architect.

That night I could not sleep. I tossed and turned, then paced the floor. I asked myself myriad questions: What could have happened? Why are they dismissing me? What have I done that displeased them? Who is the other architect they are going to give the commission to? The next morning when I met them, I still had given no thought to what I wanted for the work that I had done. When the four of them came to my office, there was the same question: What did I want for my preliminary plans?

I told them I only wanted one thing: for them to tell me what I had done wrong.

Finally Larry explained that they liked the Fontainebleau and the Eden Roc. But the sketches that I had presented were obviously not my kind of work. He said they had believed they were hiring me, not my staff.

I breathed a sigh of relief and offered to do a new set of sketches myself.

They left to have a brief conference in private, and I waited. All I wanted was another chance. They came back and made me a proposition: the contract

The Americana Hotel in Bal Harbour, Florida, 1956.

"I had made my decision that I was not going to work in a Miesian International Style. I was not going to be a mannerist, a neo-functionalist, a member of the Romantic school or a designer of wavy roofs or a decorative structuralist."

would be rewritten stating that I would be in complete control of all the designs; I would take no other hotel commissions until their hotel was finished; and I would not take a vacation during the entire time that I was working on their hotel. I asked them to prepare the papers as quickly as possible. When the contract was drawn, I showed it to my attorney. He told me that I would be mad to sign such a contract. My life would not be my own until that hotel was designed and built. I signed the contract.

I have never regretted it—I designed three major hotels in three years. The Americana in Bal Harbour was completed a year after the Eden Roc opened. Larry and Bob remained good clients for years. In many ways this was the peak of my career. I had compromised and compromised. I may not have had the courage of my convictions, but I did design three hotels that have become world famous. People look at a building and think of the architect as a member of a glamorous profession. They think of Ayn Rand's hero, Howard Roark, in *The Fountainhead*—master builder. Few people realize that not only do many architects not design buildings as they would like to, but that getting the building designed and built to please the client and carrying out the work at a decent fee is a never-ending struggle.

During the period when I was feverishly developing the Eden Roc plans and then the Americana plans, I went through a rather trying experience in both my professional and personal lives. The intense amount of work ongoing in my Florida office necessitated my presence there, and at the same time, my presence was needed in the New York office. I found myself commuting weekly between offices. Bea and I finally decided that we were going to leave New York and live in Florida. The choice was obvious because life in Florida is a great deal more pleasant than life in New York.

During the difficult months while the Americana was being completed, the *New York Times Magazine* published an article entitled "Architect Deluxe of Miami Beach," by Gilbert Millstein. I recall flying up to New York that Sunday morning and watching passengers on the flight reading all about me. Reading it, I felt as if I had been through months of psychiatric review, although Millstein had stayed with me only about a week. Within that time he got me to say a good deal more about myself and my work than I ever had before. He recorded his own impressions of me, my hotels, my clients, and Miami Beach itself:

> The hotels of Miami Beach are a branch of show business as profound as, say, a *grande fontaine moderne*, which is a large, cantilevered pastry *d'apres* created by Antoine Carème, chef to Tallyrand, George IV of England, Francis II of Austria, and Alexander I of all the Russias. Not long ago they reached what may very well be their apogee when this season's hotel, the Americana, a fifteen-story structure described by paid partisans as "the brightest jewel in the Tisch family's crown of resort hotels," was dedicated....

Miami Beach was created for the sole purpose of entertaining the well-to-do careworn and it is sedulously devoted to excess. Taken singly, its hotels are, by and large, less examples of architecture than an extension of the carnival midway in concrete, lighted up at night like the entrance to the Tunnel of Love. The total effect is not unengaging, the impression of luxury is not false; the mixing and mingling of motifs is likely to amuse the worldly, enrage the purist and overwhelm the uninitiated; the food is fine, and only the snob could complain. They stretch north from the Roney Plaza, each a little more fantastic than the next, and, like the Americana, they have burst the bounds of Miami Beach and Collins Avenue....

The apocalyptic nature of the occasion was clearly understood by Lapidus. With the addition of the Americana, he now enjoys (with the mildly melancholic reservations imposed by the artist on himself) the distinction of being the architect of what are very likely the three best known and the two most expensive resort hotels in the world. He is the architect and designer also of last year's hotel, the Italianate Eden Roc, and the year before last's, the Frenchified Fontainebleau, but, as he pointed out, it was the first time in his almost thirty years as an architect that anybody had ever asked him to appear, let alone speak, at the dedication of a hotel, his own or anybody else's....

There is more, so much more in the Americana, all of it dreamed and designed, without let, or stay, by Lapidus, not excluding the uniforms of the bellman and bellgirls, which make them look like West Pointers and Pointerettes, in gold-and-black and gold-and-white. In the lobby, for example, which is 160 feet long and 100 feet deep in some places, there stands a terrarium. It is 35 feet in diameter and 40 feet high, glassed in everywhere, except on top, so that the lobby can be rained into without wetting the guests. It contains a concrete mountain 25 feet high and all sorts of tropical flora, including orchids. "I wanted monkeys in there," Lapidus murmured regretfully on the grand tour following the dedication, "but they wouldn't give 'em to me. Afraid they'd get out. They promised me some small alligators." At the foot of the terrarium, three baby alligators could be seen paddling listlessly under the furious lighting....

There is no question that a good deal of Lapidus' work is, as some of his colleagues have said cautiously, flamboyant and theatrical, and there was one brief, ecstatic hour in his life when he achieved, as he puts it, "the heady taste of being the white-haired boy of Broadway." He was called on to design a night club, the old Palais d'Or, an institution largely financed by Arthur (Dutch Schultz) Flegenheimer, a patron of the arts and gangster who was shot down by several of his critics in New Jersey.

Lapidus' critics are of a gentler breed, limiting themselves to oral potshots at his work. "He hasn't compromised; he's capitulated," one of them has said. Others have spoken of his "rank commercialism," his "hearty vulgarity" and his "boarding-house baroque." He is said to have "ridden off wonderfully in all directions" and to belong to "no recognizable school of architecture" while appealing to "a great mass of people who don't know the difference between architecture and Coney Island."

Having said pretty much these things in conversation to a friend of Lapidus, one day, a noted architect, who prides himself on his fairness of mind, appended a troubled reverie on Lapidus: "Whatever you say," he observed, "he's trying to do architecture. . . . but he's not doing just ugly industrial plants. He is apparently so convinced that people want that sort of thing—that rounded, lush form—that he's willing to fight for it, and that's no little achievement. It's all a matter of the judge's qualification to judge. Is the judge without taint? Who can throw the first stone? Ah, the hell, he's a phenomenon. What is he? I think it's worth looking into and finding out.". . . [I later learned that the architect quoted was Philip Johnson. Through the years he was a great admirer of mine.]

"The profession looks at me as a misguided individual fighting windmills," [Lapidus] is apt to say. "It used to hurt me years ago. There is always a conflict going on in me—whether to conform and get accolades from the profession or to say, 'Let me design things people like.' I'm trying to find the answer and I'm just not satisfied with the things that are being done. Either I'm going to forget the rarefied, sensitive tastes of my critics and do what I think is a sort of baroque in good taste, or I'll have to join their ranks, and I'm not ready to join their ranks."

"It's utterly ridiculous" he went on, speaking of the Americana's terrarium, "to have a glass-enclosed hole in the middle of a building, with a silly little mountain sprouting orchids. But it's not done tongue-in-cheek. It's done because people need something to give them a lift. It's the crazy hat for women, the bright tie for men. We've stripped our buildings to the bone and now we say, 'Bravo!' But what is happening is that the man in the street sees only an ugly skeleton.

"Nobody can say that in order to be modern our buildings must be cold, rectangular, barren, simple planes. Nature didn't stop with a skeleton when she made man, nor with muscles and sinews. She gave us skin and pigmented it, and hair and colored that, and we added things of our own and the whole thing ended up as one decorative ensemble. If the modernists stop at the skeletal stage, 99 percent of the human race is going to be unhappy. You can't create a steel-and-glass grid and expect people to be happy in it. Look, for example, at Mies van der Rohe's Lake Shore Drive apartments in Chicago. A lovely laboratory concept. As pure design, it's wonderful, but it leaves people cold.

"What am I selling?" he asked himself rhetorically. "I'm selling a hotel, a luxurious, playful atmosphere. There's nothing else to sell. Let my critics stop and think — what am I trying to do? I am doing just what Louis Sullivan advocated — my forms follow the functions. My hotels are to tickle, to amuse...."

Once a high school debater of considerable powers, Lapidus still displays a tendency to indulge in restless controversy with himself. One such bout recently ran something like this: "Well, where do I go from here? I've designed the Americana. Suppose I don't do anything in the next year or two? What then? What difference does it make? Why don't I just settle down? I can make a lot of money. The work doesn't have to be the best. People will never know the difference. You don't make money belittling your own work. But I'm unhappy when I see just a piece of work. I don't know what the answer is."

I had made my decision that I was not going to work in a Miesian International Style. I was not going to be a mannerist, a neo-functionalist, a member of the Romantic school or a designer of wavy roofs or a decorative structuralist. If my work must have a definition, I would say I would be a neo-plasticist. My buildings would express what was taking place in the interiors, and if the interiors would curve and undulate, my buildings would curve and undulate. After all, people spend most of their time inside a building and the exterior is just an envelope.

In an article published years ago in the *Journal of the American Institute of Architects* entitled "A Quest for Emotion in Architecture," I wrote:

> ... the emotional dimension (of the interiors) — the most difficult to describe and at the same time the most easily recognized. It is a place for looking in, a place for looking out. It is a place for the observer, and a place to be observed. It is a place for being alone, it is a place for crowds. It should be a place for people — in short, it is a living space.

Another unexpected and delightful event that occurred about the same time as the *New York Times Magazine* article came about through a letter I received from Ellery Queen. I knew Ellery Queen was a fine writer of detective stories, and I had read a great many of his stories, but I had no idea who Ellery Queen was. His letter read as follows:

> Dear Lapidus:
> I was going over the current issue of *The Saturday Review* when on page 30 I saw a one-column cut of a man named Morris Lapidus. The face was hauntingly familiar, the name very much so. And when I saw that the accompanying article referred to this Lapidus as an architect — "a fifty-three year old Brooklyn architect" — I said to myself, "It's your Lapidus."

I remember a skinny kid with big dark eyes who went to school with me in Brooklyn. Boys High School? Or was it at Washington Square? No, I think the former. He lived in East New York, not far from a Jewish Temple — I forget its name — where the first jazz band I organized, The Sinbad Syncopators, played its first paid job, a wedding at which I had the naiveté to play "Ave Maria," to the horror of the good rabbi. (He stopped me in the middle of a luscious double-stop). This Lapidus kid and I belonged to more or less the same group. I remember there was a guy with beef and pimples on his face — what the hell was his name? — his brother grew up to be a well-known writer — yes! Josephson. Then there was — no, his name escapes me — he was a radio ham — became a commercial artist — Well, all this is beside the point. The point is, I recall a walk with this Lapidus kid — it must have been back from Boys High — in which he assured me solemnly that he was going to become an actor or an architect. I recall discussing with him the dim prospects of a Jewish boy getting a foothold in a decent architect's office. I recall feeling sorry for a kid who was so determined to joust at windmills. Maybe that was why I felt so simpatico. I had what I thought was a stout lance in my saddlesocket, too — I was going to be the Shakespeare of the twentieth century. Of the two of us — if this *Saturday Review* article is to be believed — yours was the stouter weapon! Do you remember me, Lapidus? My name wasn't Ellery Queen then, God knows. It wasn't even the name that's attached to the end of this letter. It was a name I haven't seen in print now for about thirty years, and here goes. Emanuel Lepofsky, Manny Lepofsky. I lived on New Jersey Avenue, between Atlantic and — Liberty, was it?

Anyway, remember? Or are you another Lapidus entirely?

I immediately wrote a lengthy letter to my long-lost friend. Here was somebody who had been my confidante so many years ago, in an uncertain and troubled period in my life. My letter to him was an outpouring of everything that was in my thoughts during this current period of uncertainty. Years ago it was a troubled youth, now it was the troubled man. I have no copies of my letters to Manny, but I have treasured all his letters to me. Our correspondence lasted for a number of years, until I received a last letter, not from Manny but from his wife, Kaye, telling me of Manny's sudden death from a final heart attack. Our letters were an interchange of our hopes and inspirations, as well as our frustrations and unrealized dreams.

One of my first Caribbean projects was the Arawak Hotel (now the Jamaica Hilton) near Ocho Rios. The clients came to me with plans that had been prepared by a firm of British architects. They were anxious to have me become a consultant or associate architect, since they felt that my knowledge of hotel design and planning would be helpful to the British firm. After reviewing the plans, I realized that the project as planned would be a catastrophe and told my prospective clients that I had no desire to become involved with their project. After a number of conferences, the clients asked whether I would be willing to supplant the British firm and start all over again. I told them that, under the present circumstances, such a move would be most unethical. The clients then suggested that I come to Jamaica and meet the Englishmen to try to work out some method by which they and we could work together to build a good hotel.

When I met the Englishmen I asked whether their firm had designed hotels in the past. Their answer was yes, they had, in India in 1902. I realized they were designing a hotel as it might have been built at the turn of the century, with a staff of hundreds to cater to the *pukkah sahibs*. No modern hotel could operate in that fashion. It was finally agreed that I would design the hotel and prepare all the plans. The British architects would remain as associate architects and supervise construction.

I wanted to create a truly tropical hotel. Jamaica, after all, was not Miami Beach. Here there would be no nonsense about creating "modern French Provincial" or "contemporary Italian Renaissance." I spent months in Jamaica to get the feel of the island, exploring the country to find native crafts I could incorporate in my designs. I found excellent potters and ceramists, as well as expert basket weavers, chair caners, and cabinetmakers. I also found another form of art which I had never really seen before—needlework. The Jamaican women sewed lovely panels, using vividly colored scraps of fabric to depict all sorts of Jamaican scenes. This embroidery was used primarily for pillowcases and small throws, but eventually the women created a very large and very handsome needlework mural from my designs.

Designing a building in Jamaica and supervising its construction were difficult and frustrating. The hotel was built by a British construction firm. Foremen were sent over from England to supervise and direct the native workers. Jamaicans, at that time, were willing to work for English foremen and superintendents, but they simply refused to work under one of their own. One black native was an experienced mechanic. The English superintendent decided that he would make a better foreman than the Englishman on this part of the work, but the laborers simply refused to take orders from him. One day when I was at the job site, this man was killed when a load of concrete block dropped from one of the upper floors.

The Jamaicans had many other quirks, as I discovered. They were deeply superstitious. As a part of the project, I planned a compound for the hotel staff. It was a very pleasant group of buildings with terraces and gardens and an open pavilion for social gatherings. I was mystified when I was told that not one Jamaican would sleep in the bedrooms our clients had provided. They preferred to sleep out in the field near the hotel. We soon found out that Jamaicans have a fear of sleeping on stone. It was only after we laid down wooden floors over the concrete slabs that they all moved in.

One morning we found that a huge boulder weighing over a ton had been dropped into a concrete pit that housed the water-supply gate valve. The valve was smashed, and the water supply had to be cut off. There were no boulders anywhere on the job site. It must have taken more than a dozen men to haul this boulder to the site and then to bring it to the pit and drop it so it would smash the valve. We never found out who had done it or why, but we concluded that one of the foremen had been unduly harsh and this was the workers' way of showing their resentment. Later, after the hotel opened, the water to one of the buildings was mysteriously turned off every night. Each night a maintenance man had to open the valve. Again, someone must have offended one of the hotel employees. It was only after a guard was stationed at the valve that this irritation was finally overcome.

Stealing was another apparently acceptable Jamaican trait, although people resented it if you called it stealing. One had to say that they were *taking* something, which, to the Jamaicans, meant something entirely different. As the building neared completion, it did not matter how many guards were placed on the site. Doorknobs, clothing hooks, hang rods, and shower heads kept disappearing. As the workmen were leaving the job at the end of one particular day, Bea noticed a workman toting a basketful of shower heads on his head. (The Jamaicans have a remarkable ability to carry heavy loads on their heads.) She saw him stoop to pick up some greenery to cover his loot as he continued to leave the site. Bea, who knew how much pilfering was going on, spoke to one of the native policemen dressed smartly in a white pith helmet, a white tunic and black belt, and red trousers. She pointed out the man with the basket on his head and told the policeman that he was stealing hotel property. The policeman saluted smartly and started after the thief. She saw the policeman stop the worker and make him put the basket on the ground. The policeman looked into his basket and then waved the man on. Then he came to report to Bea, "That man was carrying some personal property. He wasn't stealing anything from the hotel." We just had to accept the policeman's word, even though we knew that the worker was stealing. This was Jamaica.

These were only minor irritations compared to the many traumatic events that occurred up until the hotel was complete. One such event was when I hired a car and chauffeur to drive from Ocho Rios to Kingston to meet the landscape architect who was arriving from Miami. We were going to stop at various places along the way, including the famous Castleton Botanical Gardens to study the local horticulture. I especially wanted the landscape architect to see some of the natural beauty of the mountains in Jamaica, which I hoped to recapture on a small scale in the landscaping of the Arawak Hotel. On the way back to the hotel the brakes began to fail. We were driving through the mountains and had between thirty-five and forty miles to go to get back to Ocho Rios. Driving along those curving roads that rose and fell over the hills was a hair-raising experience. Soon, the generator began to fail, and after a while we were driving without lights and without brakes. Why we did not stop and just go to sleep in the car I do not know, except that Bea was waiting for me and there was no way to tell her that we would not be back that evening. We staked our lives on the driver, whose knowledge of the road made our safe return possible, although at times I thought we would go off a cliff or find ourselves in the sea. At last, we reached Tower Isle Hotel and my anxious Bea.

At the grand opening of the hotel, the prime minister of Jamaica was present on the platform, as were all the notables of the islands and the owners of the hotel. A local band, resplendent in royal British costumes, was there to play. There were endless speeches praising everybody. The last speaker was the owner of the hotel who arose to thank the people of Jamaica for the help they had given him. He then went on to thank, not only the government, but also all the tradespeople and the mechanics who had worked on the hotel, even the laborers. Only one person was never mentioned throughout the entire ceremony: the architect.

I was soon working on designs for a hotel to be built on Aruba in the Netherlands West Indies. The Aruba Caribbean was one of the most pleasant commissions I have had. When Bea and I arrived for our first visit to the island we were given Queen Juliana's suite in the only hotel on the island, which had just twelve rooms. What made our suite unusual was that it had a water faucet in the bedroom. It had been installed so that the queen could wash her own hair. There was, however, no basin. The bathroom was in a remote place. There were openings in the walls to allow the *pasada*, the never-ending tropical breezes, to keep the rooms cool, but there were no screens. That first night we were almost devoured by mosquitoes. At first we thought we would move into a guest house, but after looking them over we decided to stay in the hotel, and the government graciously arranged to install screens.

Bea and I spent a great deal of time in Aruba during the design and construction of the hotel, which was located on what I think is one of the finest beaches in the world. The sand is as white and soft as talcum powder, and offshore breezes keep the waters crystal clear. The few trees on the island are called *divi divi*. Because of the continuous *pasada*, their branches grow horizontally, pointing in a northerly windward direction. The island has hundreds of varieties of cactus and the most unusual and largest boulders I had ever seen. I never discovered how these boulders, some of them twenty feet tall, got to this island, and how the fantastic shapes they took were created, whether by the action of the sea or the wind. I used the cacti and boulders to achieve an atmosphere of Aruba around the hotel.

Once again, as in Jamaica, I was able to create a truly tropical hotel. There were no doors or windows in the large reception lobby. The breezes were

Lapidus with First Minister Manley and Minister Days of Jamaica (left to right) at the opening of the Arawak Hotel near Ocho Rios, Jamaica, 1957.

allowed to blow through and were controlled by an ingenious arrangement of screens and baffle walls. I introduced a great deal of color, which reflected the brilliantly colored houses on the island, and I combined this color with all sorts of native coral in weird and fantastic shapes.

Our most difficult problem was to keep out the thousands of wild goats that roamed the island. Barriers were built with tall prickly cactus. The entrance driveway was treated with a contraption known as a deer trap. This device is used in northern climates to keep deer away from certain areas. In spite of all our precautions, the wily goats discovered that by wading into the water along the beaches they could eventually feed on the luscious green foliage that was part of the landscaping that we installed. Finally we had to erect barbed wire on the beach to keep the greedy goats out of the property.

This commission came through the most unusual set of circumstances. I, a Jewish architect, won this commission from the Vatican in Rome! The prime minister of the Netherlands West Indies was a devout Catholic. When he decided that Aruba should have a modern hotel, he contacted the Vatican to find him an architect. The Vatican consulted the most powerful lay leader in the United States, a man named John O'Shay, a prominent attorney, to conduct a search for the best hotel architect. Mr. O'Shay called my New York office asking for an appointment. We eventually met and he told me that after a careful survey he had recommended me to become the architect for what would be known as the Aruba Caribbean Hotel.

The Aruba Hotel was completed in 1956. In 1957 a new type of project came into my Miami Beach office. By this time I had left my small office in the alleyway and moved into an office further west on Lincoln Road. Lincoln Road was the widest street, actually a boulevard, that Carl Fisher had carved out of the newly created city that he had dredged out of the ocean — Miami Beach. Lincoln Road was to be the great shopping thoroughfare of his city still to be built.

Jane Fisher, Fisher's young wife, wrote the story of her husband's greatest work, the creation of a city that connected a group of islands into a continuous sand spit by pumping sand between the islands. Originally, the beach was on a large sand island with bath houses, reached by ferry from Miami, which lay on the mainland on either side of the Miami River. Fisher, a bicycle manufacturer who became an automobile manufacturer, had discovered the dry cell battery that gave the automobile electric head and tail lights. He made an immense fortune and decided to spend part of his wealth to create a new city. A bridge connecting Miami Beach to Miami was built by another northerner, named Collins, who came to the beach to grow avocados.

The city grew and Lincoln Road became the main shopping boulevard. As time went on, the elegant stores began to move out to Bal Harbour, where a new open-air mall was being built. The merchants and the land owners of

"I presented my plans for Lincoln Road to the city at a black tie reception that included 21 information posters and a full model. My motto: 'A car never bought anything.'"

Lapidus presenting his plans for the Lincoln Road open-air mall in Miami Beach, 1959.

Lincoln Road came to me with their problem: how to save Lincoln Road. I suggested an open mall where the center of the street was to be created as a landscaped mall with all traffic removed. I envisioned a parklike mall with pools and fountains and exotic concrete shelters, an open-air-theaterlike structure and beautiful landscaping throughout the eight or nine blocks stretching from the ocean on the east to the bay on the west.

I was given the commission, one of the first open malls in the United States. In the end, only six blocks were closed to traffic. I hired a lighting expert to dramatically light the mall. The mall prospered for many years but as the Bal Harbour mall grew, more shops were left vacant. I am glad to say that after twenty-five years of neglect or abuse, Lincoln Road is being restored. Where I had to work with limited funds, the present architects are respecting my original concept and adding new elements to create a beautiful modern mall. The street is now the home of fine restaurants and elegant boutiques, even before the new work is completed.

The following year I found myself designing more and more apartment houses in both offices. I needed a chief draftsman who had worked in an office that specialized not only in apartment housing, but also in office building. I selected Harold Leibman, who had worked in such an office for some years. He came to work for me and had the same standing in New York as Leo Kornbluth (a persuasive salesman but a lousy designer) in New York and Abby Harle in Miami Beach. I now had three seasoned associates.

One of the largest high-rise residential projects that I designed during this period was Trump Village, on the site of the former Luna Park — that wonderful amusement park in Brooklyn that I first beheld as an immigrant kid, bedazzled by the beauty, the color, the wonder, and the sight of my first electric light. The owner was the same Fred Trump who had come to me years before to design an apartment house lobby. Through the years, I had been his architect on various apartment houses. Now I was the architect for a housing development that would eventually be the residence for thirty-eight hundred families and include a shopping center. Since this large tract of land was not laid out in streets with the usual infrastructures, I had an opportunity to design plazas, parks, and pools. Every time I went to Fred Trump's office I met his young sons who were his "gofers." One of the most eager sons was Donald, who years later became the famous real estate tycoon.

As I look back at my records I find that we were working on so many different projects — laboratories, restaurants, hotels, and, of course, stores. We were also involved in hotel work in the so-called Borsht Belt, a district in the Catskill Mountains that had many Jewish (kosher) hotels. Among them were two famous hotels, Grossinger's and the Concord. In these projects I planned swimming pools, ice-skating rinks, and in the Concord, a night club so huge that it could seat three thousand people at tables.

Eden Roc Hotel, Miami Beach, 1955. Exterior view (previous pages), outdoor restaurant (facing page),
Cafe Pompeii (above), and lobby (overleaf), with another of Lapidus's famous "stairs to nowhere."

*"The Eden Roc was completed one year after the Fontainebleau. The fierce criticism of the sweeping
lines of the Fontainebleau made me decide to use acceptable forms here — to no avail."*

Americana Hotel, Bal Harbour, Florida, 1956. Bar (top), the Medallion Dining Room (bottom), lobby with interior terrarium (facing page and overleaf).

Aruba Caribbean Hotel, Aruba, 1956.

Aruba Caribbean Hotel, Aruba, 1956.

"The Aruba Caribbean Hotel is located on what I think is one of the finest beaches in the world. Here it is framed by the famous divi divi *trees, whose shape is fashioned by the constant prevailing breeze."*

Main lobby, Aruba Caribbean Hotel, Aruba, 1956 (facing page and above).

Crystal House apartment building, Miami Beach, 1962 (facing page and above).

Lincoln Road Mall, Miami Beach, 1960 (bottom), and Lincoln Road before
the mall project, 1959 (top).

Seacoast East apartment building, Miami Beach, 1961.

"The curved shape of the building, one side of which is seen here, has been compared to a four-leaf clover. There are four wings joined at the intersection by the same curve."

The Summit Hotel, Lexington Avenue at 51st Street, New York, 1961.

14 More Commissions and a Book

In 1958 J. Meyer Schine, the owner of the famous Boca Raton Hotel in Miami Beach and of the Ambassador Hotel in Los Angeles, called to set up a meeting with me. My reputation had grown and he wanted to engage me as the architect for the new Ambassador Hotel. The Ambassador was then the leading hotel in Los Angeles. In those days, the hotel was used by the film industry for award ceremonies such as the Oscars and the Golden Globes. This was the largest commission of my career. The meeting took place in Los Angeles with Mr. Schine, his two sons David and Richard, the general manager of all of the Schines' enterprises, and the manager of the Ambassador Hotel. The scope of the project included a thousand-room hotel, two office buildings with a total of a million square feet, a convention center, an opera house, and a merchandise mart. Needless to say, I was overwhelmed by such a tremendous project. It was understood that if this project went ahead, I would join forces with the firm of Daniel, Mann, Johnson and Mendenhall, one of the largest architectural firms in California. The work was to be done both in my Florida office and in Los Angeles.

As the project took shape, we met with the head of the largest real estate firm in Los Angeles; he assured us that most of the one million square feet of office space would be rented long before the building was completed. The convention people told us that Los Angeles desperately needed the huge convention center that we proposed. There was no theater that could be used as an opera house, and a city like Los Angeles considered itself incomplete without one. The famous Ambassador Hotel with its five hundred rooms was now out of date and a thousand-room hotel would be the least we could consider. Even the Los Angeles bus company needed a central transfer center which could be built underground.

After a while I lost count of the number of visits I had to make to Los Angeles. Bea accompanied me on a number of these trips. My younger son Alan was a sergeant in the army, stationed at Camp Roberts at Paso Robles. He arranged for weekend passes to meet us for a family get-together. Meanwhile, the preparation of the preliminary plans was proceeding. I used several

Rendering of the proposed Schine Center, Los Angeles, 1959.

"This Hugh Ferriss rendering shows the proposed development of the 42-acre site, with the original Ambassador Hotel in the upper center."

renderers and model makers but I had always wanted to use the famous Hugh Ferriss to do a rendering for me. As the plans progressed I was able to hire Ferriss, who worked with me on the largest and most impressive rendering of my entire concept. As the project neared completion, we called in Dell Webb, then the largest construction firm in the western United States. I gave them my almost completed preliminaries, and Dell Webb came up with an estimate of the cost of this huge project.

The Prudential Insurance Company had its second largest office just one block away from the Ambassador. The company executives were aware of the proposed project and asked the Schine organization to be allowed to see the final preliminary drawings so they could make a proposal. They said that when we were ready to exhibit the entire project, they would call in their top executives from New York to ascertain the size of the mortgage they could offer.

When we finally met with the Dell Webb executives, Mr. Webb told me and the Schine organization that my preliminary plans were so far advanced that he was ready to sign a contract for the project, no matter what the final plans would show. If this project went ahead its dollar amount—seventy million—would be equal to the entire amount of work my office had done since its inception.

I was told to send all my presentation drawings, renderings, and models to the Ambassador Hotel, where a small ballroom was used to mount an exhibit of my work. We were now ready to tell the Prudential people to assemble their executives so I could make my presentation to them. The Schine executives instructed me to tell the Prudential executives that the cost of the entire project, based on extensive research backed by estimates from contractors, was the sum of eighty million dollars. When the day finally arrived, it took me two hours to give the Prudential people a careful description of the huge project. The Prudential executives were truly impressed and said that they would need two days to give us their answer as to how large a mortgage they were willing to offer.

By this time, Mr. Schine had assembled his entire staff of executives, accountants, lawyers, and his sons. A large luncheon was arranged for the Prudential executives, my future associated architects and, of course, myself. After the meal was over, the head of Prudential announced their decision: the company was ready to issue a seventy million dollar mortgage! I need hardly tell of the state of the Schine executives when they heard that it would be possible to build this huge project without spending a dollar of their own money. Mr. Schine rose to thank the Prudential mortgage company and told them that he and his executives would consider the offer and give Prudential an answer in a few days. Mr. Schine was quite calm. He took the occasion to compliment me on a job well done, then announced that he wanted to take a nap. He said he would join us in two hours. When he left, the entire Schine entourage began to talk of the next steps that would have to be taken. Mr. Mann, my soon-to-be associate architect, talked to me about setting up a joint office.

Finally, Mr. Schine joined us and said that he had an announcement to make. We all waited. "Gentlemen, this is a great day for all of us, but," he paused, "I have decided to drop the entire project." For a moment there was silence, followed by all assembled trying to talk at the same time. Schine's son David, who was as shocked as the rest of us, turned to him and asked, "How can you do this?"

Schine looked around at the stunned faces and explained his worries about interest payments and the possibility of another Depression. It was clear that he had made up his mind although for hours the accountants and executives tried to convince him otherwise. After all the hubbub had subsided, Mr. Schine turned to me again and told me that I had done a tremendous job, but since the project was dropped, we would have to renegotiate my fee. "Of course," he said, "you cannot expect me to pay this large sum."

"Mr. Schine," I said, "I have already been paid in full, so there is nothing to talk about."

It was as if I had pulled a gun and shot him. The next day I left the hotel and all of my presentations behind.

While I was working on the Ambassador, Mr. Schine had awarded me two new projects, a hotel in Messina and a hotel and bowling complex in Chicopee, both in Massachusetts. The work of planning and building went on after the Ambassador project was terminated but my bills were paid at such a slow rate that when I finished Messina and Chicopee, I was owed twenty thousand dollars. I kept billing but there was no payment. I consulted with my attorney, who had to associate with a Massachusetts lawyer. I learned that there was no such thing as lien rights, which I expected to place on the Chicopee hotel, in Massachusetts, but I learned that there was a law called the law of attachment. If a claim was to be filed on the Chicopee Hotel, and papers were produced showing that there was no legal reason for not paying, the state would exercise the law of attachment, which meant that all bank accounts and other holdings of the property in Massachusetts would be attached or owned by the state until the matter was settled in court.

My attorney wanted to know when I wanted to file my claim. The opening of the hotel was to take place the following week, and Mr. Schine had invited me and my wife to be present. He asked me as the architect of the project to be the speaker at the opening. I consented. My wife and I arrived for the afternoon opening affair. After my speech and an answering speech by the mayor of Chicopee, we were all invited to an evening banquet. I had told Mr. Schine that I would have to return to New York as soon as the party was over. Mr. Schine and his sons pleaded with me to stay over that night. I refused their entreaties. I knew that the following morning the state would attach the hotel.

The rest I learned from my attorney. The morning after the opening party, the hotel manager called Mr. Schine in his room and asked him to come down immediately, something was terribly wrong. When he came to the reception desk, he found the state sheriff and his staff in complete control of the hotel. He was told that he no longer was the owner, the hotel had been attached by the state. The next day a senior executive of Schine Enterprises called me and asked for an appointment. He came to my office in New York and told me that Mr. Schine was brokenhearted to think that I had been forced to take such measures because he had constantly refused to pay my bills. This man said that Schine and I could still be good friends if I would come to his office and talk things over. This continued for two weeks as one after another, executives, all of whom I knew, including David Schine, kept coming to see me and making offers of a settlement — a settlement that my legitimate fee would be cut in half. The affair ended when I finally let Mr. Schine cut my fee by five thousand dollars. He paid me and informed me that I would never work for him again.

My first hotel commission in New York, my own hometown, almost proved my undoing. Larry and Bob Tisch had acquired the Loew's chain of movie houses, together with all that company's theaters and real estate properties. The new owners tore down the Loew's Lexington Theater, an old movie house, which occupied the southeast corner of Lexington Avenue at 51st Street. I was commissioned by Larry and Bob to design a hotel on a plot that was half a city block long but only seventy feet wide, a very small area for a hotel. In my first plans I was able to achieve five hundred rooms within the zoning envelope that governed the site. "Not enough," said my clients. The Tisches insisted that, somehow or other, I squeeze eight hundred rooms into this minuscule site. The height of the building was fixed by the width of the street and the depth of the property. There was no possible way to go higher to achieve more guest rooms.

A straight line, I reasoned, is the shortest distance between two points, and it followed that this short line or hall, which was the straight line for the full length of the property, could not take any more rooms. Why not bend the hall, in other words, create a squiggle or an S-shaped building with an S-shaped hall, creating a greater length and, therefore, more rooms per floor. The final building plans achieved the eight hundred rooms.

Within the limited area of the first floor, I was asked to accommodate a reception lobby, a cocktail lounge, a dining room, a coffee shop, a men's wear shop, a women's wear shop, a barbershop, and even some meeting rooms. I finally squeezed in all these spaces, satisfying my clients' requirements, although, in my own mind, I called the lobby a dentist's waiting room because it seemed so small.

During all this time, the avid publicity people at Loew's were ballyhooing this new hotel, claiming it to be the first luxury hotel built in New York since the Waldorf. By no stretch of the imagination could the Summit be classed as a luxury hotel. To conceal the minuscule scale of the lobby, I had used a broad palate of colors, nearly invisible clear plastic chairs, and other tricks, all to no avail. The color was just too much for New Yorkers accustomed to the dirty,

"My first hotel commission in New York, my hometown, almost proved my undoing. The Summit was judged an aesthetic disaster by the critics."

Groundbreaking ceremony for The Summit Hotel, New York, 1959. Left to right: Bob Tisch; CEO of the Loews theater chain; Mayor Robert Wagner; Lapidus; Larry Tisch; and Carl Morse, president of Diesel Construction Company.

grimy grays. The public outcry was so loud and insistent that Larry Tisch finally gave in and asked me to redesign and refurbish the lobby. Reluctantly, I replaced the colorful, free-form designed carpets and the beautiful lucite chairs with a brown carpet and small, brown leather upholstered chairs. The unusual luminous metal ceiling remained, but the lighting above the ceiling was permanently disconnected.

Even though the Summit was the city's first new hotel in thirty years, and even though it added eight hundred rooms to the short supply, the Summit was judged an aesthetic disaster by the critics. "It has a slightly greenish, underwater look about it," sighed Russell Lynes. "Somehow its knees look detached from its thighs; it might be the old Beaux-Arts apartments of the thirties trying to do the twist." A topical review in a New York club called Upstairs at the Downstairs had a clever song that parodied the hotel.

The coup de grace occurred on a one-hour television show moderated by Mike Wallace. His guests included architect Philip Johnson and Peter Blake, an architect and the editor of *Architectural Forum*. Peter Blake summed up my S-shaped Summit Hotel by saying, "Let's not have any more snake dances on Lexington Avenue." Mike Wallace asked the panelists why they so disliked my work. "Why," he said, "must all buildings (in New York) be square boxes and why did they all have to be either red brick or white brick? Why not use curves, why not use color (my Summit Hotel was faced with green and tan terracotta brick), and what was wrong with the exciting colors that were used in the lobby?"

All the panelists said that New York was not Miami Beach, it was just not done and was not acceptable. Philip Johnson finally spoke up: "I have been to the Fontainebleau in Miami Beach and counted twenty-seven colors that Lapidus used in his interiors. I think that any architect who can use so many colors successfully deserves to be studied. I, for one, will pass no judgment, but I will watch his career."

Not long after, I received a very welcome telephone call from Percy Uris of Uris Brothers, one of New York's largest and most illustrious builders. Uris invited me to lunch with his brother, Harold. When we met in their very handsome and luxurious offices in one of their own buildings, I was told that they had acquired a block front on Third Avenue in the 50s where they intended to erect a hotel. They had built many of the elegant hotels in the 1920s and now wanted to go back into the field of hotel construction. They were familiar with my work and asked me to be their architect. I was delighted to get another chance to design a hotel in my hometown. We prepared designs that the Uris brothers liked very much, but in the end they decided it would be safer financially to build an office building. Although they admired the hotel I had designed for them, they had a long-standing arrangement with another architect for their office buildings. Regretfully, I was not going to be involved on the Third Avenue site.

Rendering of the proposed New York Hilton on Sixth Avenue facing Rockefeller Center, which was to be developed by the Uris Brothers in partnership with Laurance Rockefeller and Conrad Hilton, 1960.

Shortly after this disappointment, I again was asked to meet with Percy and Harold Uris. This time they told me that they had acquired a block on Sixth Avenue facing Rockefeller Center between 52nd and 53rd Streets. Again, they wanted to build a hotel. This new hotel would have two thousand rooms, with luxurious lobbies, restaurants, and enormous banquet and convention facilities surpassing everything in New York City. My clients were pleased with my original designs, and an accurate three-dimensional model, complete in every detail, was built. I was authorized to proceed with the final plans and was on my way to designing the largest hotel to be built in New York since the Waldorf Astoria.

While developing the final plans for the Uris brothers, I was again invited to meet with my old clients, the Tisch brothers. They had acquired a large block property on Seventh Avenue between 51st and 52nd Streets. They wanted me to be the architect for *their* two-thousand-room hotel—another mammoth hotel, only one block from the Uris hotel. I accepted the Tisch commission with alacrity but told them that I would have to inform the Uris brothers about this new commission.

I met with Percy and Harold, who naturally were not too happy about the fact that there was going to be another hotel of approximately the same size so close to theirs, but, unlike my former client Ben Novak, they had no objections just as long as I would be sure to use an entirely different architectural approach. I assured them there would be no similarity between the two hotels.

As soon as my preliminary plans for the Tisch hotel, which was going to be called the Americana of New York, were published in the New York press, the Uris brothers again invited me to lunch. They told me that Laurance Rockefeller had asked to become their partner in this new hotel venture, and, reciprocally, he wanted the Uris brothers to be a partner with him on an office building directly across the street from the Uris hotel in the Rockefeller Center Complex. I learned that Laurance Rockefeller was content to have me continue to serve as the architect for the hotel, which was to become the New York Hilton since Conrad Hilton was also to be a partner with the Uris brothers.

Then came the blow. There was one condition that Laurance Rockefeller imposed. I would have to give up the Americana Hotel commission. He simply would not have me serve as the architect for Uris and himself as well as be the architect for the Tisches. I pleaded with Percy and Harold to arrange a meeting with Laurance Rockefeller so that I could convince him that my serving the Tisches would in no way affect my ability to create a superb hotel for the Uris/Rockefeller/Hilton venture. But Laurance Rockefeller would not meet with me unless he was informed that I had given up the design of the Americana Hotel. Percy and Harold told me that I would have to make a choice. Regretfully, I resigned as the architect for the Hilton project. The Uris brothers were most magnanimous and paid me for all my services to date.

In 1960 we began plans for the Americana of New York. To build the fifty-story hotel, the Tisches selected Diesel Construction Company, headed by Carl Morse, which had built the Pan American tower north of Grand Central Terminal on Park Avenue. Carl Morse was to be an important influence in the structural design and the building of this giant hotel. Since New York rarely used concrete in its buildings, Mr. Morse instructed me to design a steel-framed building. All of my construction, however, was of concrete and I had no desire to use steel. A long debate and several clashes followed between Carl Morse and me. I pointed out that with a steel-framed building we would have to assume a space of fifteen inches for each floor slab. With concrete we would achieve a saving of one foot for each floor. With fifty floors for the building I could gain fifty feet in height for more rooms. In a steel building we would have to create girders to go from column to column, then we would need beams to form the framing on which concrete slabs would be poured, requiring fifteen inches at the least.

Morse then argued that wind bracing would cost a fortune in the construction of this tall concrete slab. I used a simple strategy to show how the building could be designed to make wind bracing unnecessary. I took one of my calling cards and tried to stand it upright. Of course it fell over. I then bent my card and the card remained upright. I blew against it, a small version of the great winds that would require the strong wind bracing, but I couldn't blow over the bent card. I had won my first concession. I also argued that a great deal of time could be saved by not using steel. I pointed out that when engineering plans were completed, it would take at least two months to fabricate the steel but with our completed concrete engineering plans finished, work could be started immediately. Round two in my favor. Carl Morse agreed to build the Americana in concrete. When it was completed, it was the tallest concrete building in the world. It was also a most unusual building because it was bent. Lewis Mumford, one of the great critics of architecture, dismissed my building by saying that it looked like an open paperback book.

During the two years that I was designing the Americana and supervising its completion, Bea and I decided to rent a *pied à terre* on 56th Street where I created a beautiful, large patio garden. My office was extremely busy designing religious buildings, laboratories, a number of hotels, and won a competition for converting a decrepit slum into a residential community called Cadman Plaza in Brooklyn. I was also given a new and unusual hotel project — the Sheraton Motor Inn, which was to be built on 42nd Street as it came to an end on the Hudson River water front. In 1961 there were large docking facilities for ocean liners sailing for Europe. Many transatlantic passengers from the eastern part of the United States drove to New York City to spend a week or two in the city before their ship sailed. The hotel was to have a six-story garage to hold the cars until the people came back from Europe. Atop this garage base was an outdoor garden area, the check-in facilities, and a handsome circular restaurant. Floating above the open gardens was a twelve-story hotel. A most unusual feature was a large swimming pool on the roof of the hotel where summer visitors were able to relax with a wonderful view of all of New York City.

The next few years brought so many commissions that there are really too many to mention. The Fontainebleau was the catalyst that brought this great amount of work. The critics still hated my work, whether curved or bent, but clients wanted more and more of the sweeping forms. In 1962 I decided to include the names of my three associates in the name of my firm. My stationery read, "Morris Lapidus, Kornbluth, Harle and Leibman, Architects." The three associates were given 15 percent each of the profits.

Leo Kornbluth was the man that I sent to meet new clients and to supervise the many commissions in the Caribbean. One day he came to me with a new client and a commission to design a hotel directly opposite LaGuardia Airport. The client was a resident of Washington, D.C., where I had become quite busy. A week later a crestfallen Leo came back to my New York office and informed me that the client did not sign the contract and was abandoning the job. Six months later Leo asked for an appointment with me and demanded that he be made full half partner with me or he would resign. I was sorry to lose him, but I would not make him full half partner. He resigned and asked that he be given his 15 percent share of the practice immediately. The sum my accountant arrived at was not satisfactory to him, and he demanded arbitration. After several ugly scenes with flared tempers, a settlement was made, but I was not to see Leo Kornbluth again.

A week after the settlement, I received a call from one of the executives that I had worked with at the Schine organization. He told me they were looking over a set of plans for a LaGuardia Hotel given them by the architect for the project, Leo Kornbluth. It turned out that Kornbluth had been drawing his own plans during the last six months he was in my employ.

A few years later Kornbluth was indicted by the IRS for nonpayment of taxes and for using the well-known madam, Xavier Hollander, author of *The Happy Hooker*. He had been paying her huge fees, claiming that she was his interior decorator. The underlying scheme was that he would employ Xavier to procure hookers for his clients, and she would return the money to him. In due course the IRS investigated her, and under threat of prosecution she told the IRS that the entire affair had been Kornbluth's idea. In another scheme discovered by the IRS, Kornbluth paid engineers much more than their usual fees, and after deducting the taxes that the engineers paid for the exaggerated fees, they returned the money to Kornbluth. The IRS sued Kornbluth and won. He had to pay a huge sum in back taxes and penalties and was sentenced to six months in jail. After his release, I do not know what became of the junior draftsman I had hired straight out of New York University and pushed into a position where I finally made him a partner. I certainly had not been a good judge of character.

In 1963 the American Institute of Architects held its annual convention at the Americana of Bal Harbor. The theme of this convention was "A Quest for

Quality in Architecture." The opening seminar was held in the large ballroom of my hotel. Seated at a long table was the group of architects who were about to conduct the seminar "A Quest for Quality in Architecture."

The distinguished panelists used the Americana Hotel to point out what, in their opinion, was not what they would call "quality" in architecture. Sir Basil Spence, the British architect who reconstructed the world-famous Coventry Cathedral in the 1950s said, "As I approached the hotel, I thought it would bite me." Robert Anschon, a well-known California architect, said, "This hotel is built of thin, cheap, improbable materials. It is incompetent, uncomfortable, and a monument in vulgarity." Another distinguished panelist, Dr. Edward Hall of Washington, an anthropologist, whose convention role was a discussion of man's relation to his environment, commented that a bird's nest was better architecturally than the room he had at the hotel. Another member of the panel, George McCue, the art critic of the St. Louis *Post-Dispatch*, said, "Privacy obviously has not been designed into this hotel. I answered my phone twice when the ringing was in my neighbor's room, and when my neighbor flushes the toilet, I feel that I should run for high ground." By this time, half of the audience was looking at me to see how I was taking the harsh criticism of the hotel that I had designed. At the end of the seminar, there was a question-and-answer period. I sat there trying to make up my mind whether I should speak up or quietly slip out of the convention hall. There was a hush in the audience as I approached the microphone and addressed the panel.

"Gentlemen, my name is Morris Lapidus, and I am the architect who designed this hotel." Some of the panelists looked as if they would like to slip under the table where they were seated.

"I may be stepping into the lion's den, but I should like to pose a question for the eminent members of the panel. This hotel is not, by any stretch of the imagination, an architectural masterpiece, nor was it meant to be one. It was designed for people who want to come here and have fun, a joyous time, and, in speaking to many of the people who have come here, they all have the same remark — 'we love your hotel, we're having a wonderful time.' This structure has been built at a limited cost. That is admitted. But the question I pose is this: Is quality in architecture only that quality which can be seen from the outside, or by the camera's eye, or does quality in architecture also have to presuppose the emotions and feelings of the people who come to this hotel? The two, I am sure, are compatible. People want their architecture to give them pleasure both on the outside of the building and in the interiors. When confronted with a problem where cost and many other factors make it almost impossible to create what the panel seems to think is quality in architecture, isn't it also that sense of quality which reduces itself to human comfort, human emotional satisfaction, and a sense of joy, and isn't that part of quality in architecture also?"

Then came the responses.

Mr. Anschon: "Lack of money is no excuse for lack of sound privacy, but I would say the reason that so many people like your building is that it does have a sense of carnival and fun about it, and this is probably its greatest attribute, and for that quality, I congratulate you, Mr. Lapidus."

Sir Basil Spence: "I presume that a certain amount of vulgarity is necessary to make the average person enjoy himself."

George McCue: "The hotel is perfectly designed to make us feel away from home."

After the convention, I received many letters. One was from the editor of the *Journal of the American Institute of Architects*, who wrote:

> Let me congratulate you on the fine delicacy with which you handled the rather caustic comments on your hotel. It was a neat, kid-glove job, and properly silenced your critics — except that irrepressible Bob Anschon, but even he ended up with a compliment! Personally, I enjoyed your building very much — and I did *not* hear the telephone or the plumbing in the next room.

Another letter was from the president of the American Institute of Architects:

> I want you to know how very glad I am that you rose from the audience and spoke at one of the professional sessions at the Miami Convention. Many of us applauded, not only for your courage, but your excellent good humor. Further, because of your brief speech I believe both the panel and the audience became better informed. My very best wishes to you.... we had an excellent time in your Americana Hotel.

Another letter was from William W. Eshbach, an officer of the American Institute of Architects:

> I am writing this letter as a member of the American Institute of Architects who sat in the audience, an ex-Board member, and as the Chairman of the Seminar Program at the Miami A.I.A. Convention. All three of my hats are off to you for your courage, conviction, diplomacy and gentlemanship (for this occasion this must be a word), all of which were so apparent as you responded to the panel members during the first session of the Convention. The content of your response and the manner of delivery [were] great, and I wish to extend to you my compliments. Beyond this, my wife and I wish to thank you as the Designer of the Hotel, for a very delightful Convention and our enjoyment was in a large measure a consequence of the total environment which you created. The room, the balcony, the cabanas, etc., provided a delightful experience away from home.

Alfred Bendiner, a prominent architect in Philadelphia, whom I had never met, wrote an article for the A.I.A. *Journal* from which the following is excerpted:

I know that I am in the great minority for a Fellow in the American Institute of Architects to be saying such outrageous things and it is liable to get me booted out of the Club and my beard taken away.

From the architectural point of view, we could learn a lot and a lot we have to learn because most of the "low brows" who inhabit these places [referring to Miami Beach Hotels] never heard of Le Corbusier unless it was something which placed in the daily doubles…in reading the clippings in Europe [referring to the architects' convention held at the Americana Hotel] I found that somebody took a pass at the designer of the Host Hotel, a member, named Morris Lapidus. Of course, the newspapers picked that up where they should have been reporting on a "Quest for Quality." I think Mr. Lapidus replied brilliantly indicating as I have, that most old architects are too stuffy to enjoy Miami Beach and shouldn't come in the first place. I envy Mr. Lapidus his architecture because I can't do it, and because he seems to be having all the fun and, what's more, he has a clientele who understands and orders more. He is the Barocco Rococo Architect lost in a world of concrete refined Ictinusis, or is it Ictinusae [Iktinos was the architect of the Parthenon]. He is the hot Mozart School of Design. He knows how to do a pleasure dome that suits the taste of the set which would be bored stiff in the Plaza.… Architects are raised with the snotty idea that we are the kings of the fine art, with creators, sculptors and painters our handmaidens, but if you hang around architects long enough, you must realize many of us are a pretty stuffy front with a lot of sawdust inside and not much understanding of people.

In 1965 I was working on the design of a huge office building in Washington, D.C., commissioned by the Blake Construction Company owned by a father and son team, Jack and Morty Bender. We called the project the "G Street Building," and it was to occupy an entire square block. When I presented my early designs, Morty asked us to start working on drawings. For this job I chose Harold Liebman to act as the chief architect. I used a new system of precast concrete panels, five feet wide by two stories tall. These panels were designed with elastromatic vertical joints so they locked into position, one next to the other, to make a waterproof bond. The same system was used top and bottom to create the twelve stories of vertical panels. (No building could rise higher than twelve stories in Washington.) Each panel was two stories in height with two windows for two floors. The windows were installed in the precast concrete plant. The windows (another first) were set in elastromatic channels cast into the concrete. A special device opened on the side of this channel to allow setting the glass. When the glass is in place the special device closes the channel, sealing the windows. It was an inexpensive way of cladding the exterior of the concrete building and the result was architecturally pleasing.

Once we had worked out all the details, I left the entire job of preparing the final plans to Liebman. When the plans, elevations, and details were completed, Liebman took the plans to our client Morty Bender for his review. A week later, while I was in my Florida office, I received a call from Morty requesting that I come to Washington the following day. When I arrived, Morty asked me to review the plans. Everything seemed in order. Morty pointed to a window and asked me to find the special detail. I hunted through the plans for about ten minutes. The detail was there but not in the proper place on the set of plans. He pointed to another exterior elevation that required special large-scale detailing. Again I had to hunt for another ten minutes to find it. So it went, the plans had no coordination. In my own mind I thought that the arrangement of plans and details were helter skelter; there was not my usual coordination and sequence. The information was there but scattered. I realized that Harold Liebman must have worked in his former office under the supervision of a chief draftsman; left to himself he had produced a confusing puzzle that the builder had to solve to be able to proceed with construction.

I wasted no time telling Morty that I would take the set of plans back to New York and have them drawn in a coordinated manner to make them easy to read. This was the first inkling that Liebman was a long way from being the expert he professed to be. He was not happy, but I showed him my way of doing things and directed him to redraw the plans. Morty Bender was quite satisfied with the revised plans. The building was built and we were given a number of other office buildings to design. But this incident eventually led Liebman and me to a contentious parting of ways.

Not long after, my son Alan, only a few years out of school, took over the operation of my New York office.

Bea, who really handled my finances, had for some time been urging me to write a book on the business side of architecture, a subject grossly overlooked by architecture schools. I had written a manual of operations based on past mistakes which I gave to each new draftsman who came to work for me. I finally came up with a title, *Architecture: A Profession and a Business*, an outline, and my manual and took my book idea to the Reinhold Publishing Company. I asked to see an editor who was familiar with architecture, and to my surprise, I was ushered into the office of just such an editor. He looked over my material and then and there gave me an advance to write the book. *Architecture: A Profession and a Business* was published in 1967 and remained in print for more than twelve years.

After the publication of my book, I was visited by John W. Cook, a student at Yale University, who told me that Vincent Scully, a renowned professor of art history at Yale, had suggested that he devote his thesis to an in-depth study of my work. Professor Scully seemed to be a great admirer of mine, although I had never met him. I was told by students who came to work for me that Scully devoted one lecture a term to my designs. Cook told me that he had already studied much of my work in stores and hotels. He spent a great deal of time in my office photographing my work as depicted in the various photos that hung on my walls, as well as photos that I kept in my albums. Whenever he called me from Yale, I would make time to discuss my theories of design.

He eventually completed his thesis and was awarded his doctorate. When I received a copy of his thesis, I was somewhat shocked by the title, "Morris Lapidus—Architecture As Intentional Nonsense." I discovered in reading his thesis how he came to this peculiar title:

> The Depression in the United States in the early thirties created among other things the window-shopper and the inviting and entertaining shop, and Morris Lapidus was there with an American Main Street architecture. Architecture and architectural historians are getting back to Main Street as the human promenade where priorities redefine themselves. As architecture in 1970 rediscovers the scale of the human enterprise in architecture, the work of Morris Lapidus emerges as a surprising informer to a developing sensitivity and a legacy of complexity and controversy. Lapidus has been ignored or cryptically dismissed by historians, critics and colleagues. Standard works on twentieth-century architecture in the United States ignore him, and critical essays on the prominent architectural form makers of the present do not mention him. However, for forty years he has been constructing in an ambiance of commerce and daily life as an architect who stubbornly remembered a mandate from the populace. While glass and steel shelved us into the mechanical electronic utopia, Lapidus aggressively designed and built intentional nonsense for our response and pleasure.

Some years later Cook, by then a professor of religion and the arts at Yale Divinity School, returned to interview me for *Conversations With Architects*, a book he co-authored with Heinrich Klotz, then professor of the history of art and director of the Marburg Institute in Marburg, Germany.

John Cook and Heinrich Klotz were interviewing eight architects who they thought were the architects whose work had the greatest influence on the direction of twentieth century architecture. They spent a half day questioning me about my theories of design. At the end of the long interview, John Cook quoted a line from the Broadway musical *Mame*. She says in the play, "Life is a banquet and most poor suckers are starving to death." Was this what my work was all about? My answer was that my architecture was a banquet of delight and joy. "If you like ice cream, why stop with one scoop, have three scoops, too much is never enough. Enjoy! Enjoy!"

"The lobby of The Summit Hotel was considered too colorful. Public outcry was so loud and insistent that Larry Tisch finally gave in and asked me to redesign and refurbish the lobby. Reluctantly, I replaced the colorful, free-form designed carpets and the beautiful lucite chairs with a brown carpet and small, brown leather upholstered chairs."

Original interior, The Summit Hotel, Lexington Avenue at 51st Street, New York, 1961.

"The 550-foot-high Americana was the tallest concrete building in the world at that time. Although the building employs no curves, I could not resist introducing a curved structure seemingly separated from the building. Most buildings are seen from street level, and this is what pedestrians see — my signature."

Americana of New York Hotel, Seventh Avenue, New York, 1962 (above and facing page).

Sheraton Motor Inn, 42nd Street at the Hudson River, New York, 1960. View of garage (facing page)
and rooftop swimming pool (above).

Temple Beth El, St. Petersburg, Florida, 1965.

"This project was never built, but I think it was one of the best; it was the ultimate in the use of curves. It was to be a huge merchandise mart, including a hotel, to be part of a permanent World's Fair in Florida on a huge site called INTERAMA.*"*

Rendering of proposed International Trade Center, 1968.

Lapidus (center) explains his scheme for a development on New York's West Side at his one-man exhibit, "Forty Years of Art and Architecture," at the Lowe Gallery, University of Miami, 1967. In the background are concrete tiles Lapidus designed for many of his hotels.

15 Two Exhibits

In 1967 the University of Miami honored me with a one-man exhibit in their Lowe Gallery called "Forty Years of Art and Architecture." The "architecture" needs no explanation, but the "art" does. Throughout my adult life, my chief hobby has been painting. I have worked and continue to work in watercolors, oil, pen and ink, pencil, and many other media. This exhibit gave me my first opportunity to display my artwork together with my architecture.

The director of the gallery was Dr. August L. Freundlich, later the dean of the School of Art at Syracuse University. Dr. Freundlich, in assembling the exhibit and writing the excellent catalogue, researched much of the material that had been published about me and made himself thoroughly familiar with the work itself.

In his clear and concise catalogue, Dr. Freundlich expressed in the simplest terms my drive in the field of architecture. He wrote that I design buildings for profit and in doing so try to give the people who use those buildings what they want. And, as far as I am concerned, what they want, to which I add a sense of joy, is what I have been striving to produce in all my buildings.

It is quite easy to produce this joyous euphoria in a hotel but it is more difficult to achieve the same results in other structures. As the architect for Variety Children's Hospital in Miami, I tried to make the children in the hospital as happy as I could under extremely difficult conditions. It is always traumatic to separate sick children from their parents and put them into a hospital where everything seems alien and hostile. To overcome that fear and apprehension, I created an atmosphere of brightness, of color, of excitement, which pervades every space in the hospital, whether it is the reception lobby, the nurses' stations, the corridors, the hospital rooms themselves, the treatment rooms; all of them are bursting with colorful excitement to make the child feel less isolated, less fearful, and, I hoped, more cheerful than the conditions warranted. In this project, the children were my clients.

Late in 1967 I received another call from Larry Tisch asking if I would fly to Monte Carlo to meet a Señor Sucre, a real estate agent, to look over a site as a possible location for a Loew's Hotel. When I arrived in Nice I was met by Señor Sucre, who drove me to Monte Carlo. Sucre drove an open Porsche roadster as if he were driving the Grand Prix along the upper Corniche. He told me about the unusual site for the proposed hotel. I'm afraid I was more worried about arriving in one piece than listening to his talk. When we arrived, I checked into the Grand Hotel de Paris. After I was settled, Sucre took me down to the harbor where we boarded his palatial yacht and sailed away from the shore so that I could see the site of the hotel that he and his good friend Prince Rainier hoped to build.

From the deck of his yacht he pointed to the steep promontory that dropped from the gardens fronting the Casino to the harbor. This was to be the unlikely site that Prince Rainier had decided would be an ideal location for a dramatic hotel. It would face the Hotel de Paris and be next to the Grand Casino. The problem was how to design a hotel that clung to the precipitous sheer drop from the gardens of the Casino to the waterfront. I was there to solve the problem so that Larry Tisch could build the Loew's Monte Carlo. Sucre also informed me that the roof of this hotel must be on the same level as the gardens. There were to be at least five hundred rooms and several dining rooms, plus a large convention hall that would be located on a small island almost touching the mainland.

I sat on the deck looking at this formidable site wondering how this could be accomplished. After a pleasant lunch on the yacht, we drove to the gardens of the Casino. At first I felt the whole project was a pipe dream. I just could not see how a hotel with more than five hundred rooms could literally be plastered onto this cliff. But Larry was sure that I could solve this problem, and solve it I did. I had brought along some tracing paper and pens and pencils, as well as a small drawing board.

Another problem that this proposed hotel would face was that the lower Corniche ran along the shore line of this property. A more formidable problem was that the main street of the city ran along the upper half of the cliff. This street had to be maintained, running right through the hotel, because it was the street along which the Grand Prix annual races were run.

I spent the next few days visiting the city's engineering department personnel to discuss such mundane problems as water supply and sewage. My mind had already formulated an answer to all the problems. I decided to create three, for want of a better word, "doughnuts," which would be the hotel rooms, around beautifully landscaped gardens. My rooms would not face the sea but face inward to overlook three interior gardens. Only in the third "doughnut" would I be able to design a double-loaded corridor so that there could be rooms on one side facing the interior garden and on the other side facing the sea. As I continued to sketch I eventually decided that the "doughnuts" should be hexagonal, rather than circular.

After five days, Sucre suggested I needed a break. He said that the following day I was to come to his yacht for a sail on the Mediterranean. Although I would have to complete my sketches for presentation to Prince Rainier by the end of the week, the rest would refresh me for the final three days of work.

We had a wonderful day. We sailed out to the deep sea far from sight of any land. Before lunch, Sucre suggested that we go swimming. Two of his sons were along, one about sixteen and the other fourteen. He gave me swimming trunks, and the four of us plunged into the crystal clear waters of the Mediterranean. For me, it was a new and exhilarating experience, swimming in deep waters without any sight of land. After we got back on board sailors helped us shower and don luxurious robes. We had cocktails and a delightful lunch. The staff on his yacht included a French chef.

I worked the rest of the week and finished my plans and sections and a nice perspective of how the hotel would look. I was supposed to dress and go with Señor and Señora Sucre to the royal palace to meet the prince. I had hardly slept for the last two days and told Sucre that I just could not keep my eyes open. I asked him if he, rather than I, could make the presentations. He agreed, so I never met Prince Rainier. The next morning Sucre called to tell me that the prince was most happy and had asked Sucre to convey his congratulations and thanks. I flew home with my bundle of sketches and called Larry Tisch and informed him that I had been given the "go ahead."

After a few days back in New York, Larry and his brother Bob (formerly Preston) agreed on a fee for me to continue to develop my preliminary plans. I instructed a few of my senior draftsmen and designers to work up the plans.

While we were working on the plans Loew's was trying to get a mortgage for the construction of Loew's Monte Carlo. One day Larry asked me to come in to see him in his office. He told me that it was almost impossible to find finances, but he had finally found a German labor union that would make the loan at a satisfactory rate. However, the labor union would make the loan on one condition — there was to be no American architect. Larry had agreed. He offered me a handsome fee for all of my work but my preliminary plans would be turned over to a German architect. I had to accept — there was no use in arguing. I stopped my office on the development of the plans. We were deeply disappointed, but we had to accept the inevitable. The Loew's Monte Carlo was completed and is doing wonderful business. Larry and Bob urged me to come to the new hotel, bring my wife, and stay as long as I wished. I have never seen the hotel.

Among my many projects, I was designing restaurants, and of course, all of my hotels had restaurants. I was invited by the College of Hotel Administration at Cornell University to speak to the students on what features made a successful restaurant. On another occasion a hotel and restaurant kitchen designer asked me to conduct a seminar for foreign restaurant owners who had come to the United States to study the American way of designing modern restaurants. There were restaurant men from Holland, Norway, Denmark, and Sweden, and a gentleman who ran the restaurants of a large English company known as the Lyons group. I later accepted invitations from many of them, traveling to northern Europe on a voyage to the finest dining my wife and I have ever enjoyed. During this long trip I decided to go to Finland to see the architecture of the elder Saarinen. I also wanted to meet one of my idols, Alvar Aalto. I was able to arrange a fifteen-minute appointment which turned into an all morning visit. Aalto's secretary came in again and again to remind the master of previous appointments, but we had such a wonderful time talking, and finishing a bottle of wine, that we spent the entire morning together.

The Englishman, Guy Gluckstein, from the Lyons group told me that his company was embarking on building a chain of the most elegant restaurants in England. The first of this chain was to be called The Diplomat, and I agreed to come to London and become the designer.

The Lyons group was a large conglomerate run by two families, the Gluck-steins and the Palmers. There was a rule initiated by the original owners that only sons could enter their business. No sons-in-law were accepted. My friend Guy told me that when he finished college, he was sent to France for two years to study wines. He was then sent to Switzerland to study with the great Swiss chefs. He was assigned to operate the famous Trocadero, in London's Picadilly Circus.

The Troc, as it was fondly called, was a many-storied catering, banqueting, and restaurant establishment that was used by royalty and noble families to entertain their guests. All the banqueting facilities were Victorian rooms with crystal chandeliers and marble and bronze. Although the Lyons group prospered, the Troc, in a once fashionable neighborhood, was now the only building amidst many cinemas and bargain stores. Only one elegant restaurant was functioning for the now old gentry. It was decided to close the Trocadero and start a chain of fine restaurants in London. Guy, who had run the Troc in its heyday, was to be the head of the first of these fine restaurants, which was to be built on Mount Street, not far from Grosvenor Square. It was an elegant street with fine antique shops and fine restaurants. I was to be the architect.

Guy insisted that Bea and I dine with him and his wife in the most famous and elegant restaurants in London so that I would surpass them in my designs. It was a delightful two weeks and the beginning of two years of visits to London while designing the Diplomat restaurant.

In the design I decided to install an unusual lighting system. The main lighting was concealed in the ceiling over each table. I wanted to light only the table, not the diners. This meant a theatrical lighting source that was not visible. The reflected light from the pink tablecloth would bathe the diners in a flattering light. The other lighting was a well-concealed spotlight that was placed over each gueridon (tables upon which the food that was brought to the diners was placed, under which were serving plates and a gas flame) to add drama to the preparation of each plate by an expert waiter.

I met some English architects to whom I explained my novel lighting system, and they all agreed that it could not be done. I had to use Century Lighting of New York, which specialized in stage lighting, and the Strand Lighting Company in London. They worked out the equipment I wanted and joined forces to form the Century Strand Lighting Company.

In 1970 I received a call from John Margolies asking for an appointment in connection with a proposed exhibit of my work. I met Margolies in my New York office where he told me that the New York Architectural League was proposing an exhibit of my work to be called "An Architecture of Joy."

The young man sitting opposite me was telling me that the Architectural League had voted to present an exhibit of my work as an architect for their first show for the year 1970–71. Naturally, I was startled — startled by the suddenness of this honor and just as startled by the appearance of the earnest young man with whom I was talking. I was not accustomed to seeing long-haired, denim-clad, sandaled and beaded young men in my office. John Margolies was the exhibition coordinator for the Architectural League. For over twenty-five years I had been a member of the League, a staid, prestigious organization whose members included many famous architects, painters, and sculptors. As we talked, he told me that the "Now" generation was trying to breathe new life into the stodgy Architectural League. Their newly elected president was Arthur Rosenblatt, who was the architectural advisor to the director of the Metropolitan Museum of Art in New York, my old client Thomas Hoving, for whom I had designed the Bedford-Stuyvesant Park. Rosenblatt wanted to start his term with an exciting and provocative exhibit of the type of architecture that represented what young people thought was the direction architecture should take.

But why me, I wanted to know. I had been practicing architecture for over forty years. I was practically a senior citizen. Why had the league and its selection committee picked my work when there were so many young architects doing such exciting modern work?

The young man explained that he and his generation identified with my work, that my architecture was the "in" thing as far as they were concerned. He told me the Old Guard at the League had fought against the exhibit right down to the line but in the end had lost.

I hesitated. After all the many years in my profession, should I let myself become identified with these young "radicals," "hippies," "revolutionaries?" I had been labeled a controversial architect for years. The brouhaha started after I designed the Fontainebleau in Miami Beach and it had never let up.

I decided to refuse to allow my work to be exhibited. Why should I get into the middle of this controversy? I was not looking for publicity and I was not interested in this prestige. My architecture was my own, and it represented my thinking regardless of what the rest of the profession thought or felt about it. I was not looking for vindication, nor was I looking for approval by the League or any other members of the profession. My son Alan, who was now my partner, had been sitting in on the conference and finally persuaded me to agree to the exhibit, which he would design.

The planned exhibit engendered more acrimonious debate and an epistolary war. The battle was joined by Sybil Moholy-Nagy, then a professor of architecture at Pratt Institute, with this letter to Arthur Rosenblatt:

> I have been very much upset by the debate on the Lapidus exhibition at yesterday's scholarship committee meeting and have come to the conclusion that I can under no condition participate in such an undertaking and would have to resign from the Executive Committee if it won through. Lapidus is a well-known phenomenon in the profession. After having made his pile and excusing his aberrations with the nauseating clichés of "what the people want" (as if taste pollution did not go the other way from designer to the public), he is now grooming his son to refurbish the image by becoming an "art Architect." And in doing so, he sidles up to these almost unbelievable "young rebels" and agrees to their befuddling interpretation of Las Vegas or Venturiism, Pop camp environment to get himself a show.
>
> Now I am perfectly willing to give the promoters the benefit of doubting their ability to look behind this game; but this is awfully hard to do in the case of Margolies [chairman of the Exhibit Committee] who, whatever he is, is NOT naive. The mere fact that he did a spread on Lapidus for P.A. (a magazine more than ready to promotional clip) already compromises the whole affair. But the most incredible aspect is that the League should cough up money ($7,000 or more) to propagandize Mr. Morris Lapidus. Can you imagine what a boon it is for an architect on the prestige-make and with the type of clientele Lapidus has, when he can point out to every potential hotel and motel client that his work has been artistically pedigreed by the 100-year-old Architectural League in sophisticated, high-taste New York? Come on, this just cannot happen — or if it happens, it will happen without me.

Another letter came from Peter Eisenman, then a member of the League's Board of Directors and director of the Institute for Architecture and Urban Studies. His final paragraphs read:

> To not permit the show seems to give the League an official position vis-à-vis current taste. And while I agree that selection is required by the natural

Lapidus discusses his model for the Bedford-Stuyvesant Park at the "Forty Years of Art and Architecture" exhibit, Lowe Gallery, University of Miami, 1967.

limitations of time, space and energy, it would seem that to accept such a negative position, especially under threat of precipitous action such as resignation, would be to limit debate and to codify taste.

Just recently I applauded both Mrs. Moholy-Nagy and Mr. Franzen [Ulrich Franzen vehemently objected to my show; he is one of our fine young architects] for their letters to P/A on the Venturi article. While I again am in obvious sympathy with their concern and admire their involvement as expressed in the letters that they write, I feel that this show, merely by the debate it has so far caused, will serve to alert a most sensitive area in the architectural community. To force reflection on the question of taste, particularly as it concerns a fundamental problem in the debate between architecture as a populous phenomenon and architecture considered as an elitist fantasy, then the League will have contributed something.

Mr. Lapidus' work seems so consistently "out of focus" and yet so overwhelmingly successful that it provides a good vehicle for such a debate. Far from being the ad hoc populism of Las Vegas, this work is quite deliberately contrived to be in touch with something that advocacy planning has been calling "what the people want." If not a critical issue it certainly seems relevant.

Personally, I think the problem of taste to be more complicated than Margolies' exhibition, but at least it is a beginning.

After reading Eisenman's letter, I began to realize that my work was being used as a focal point, or a point of departure, regarding what is good taste or bad taste and whether architectural design should be "what the people want" or what the architects think they should have. At a lecture I once attended given by Mies van der Rohe, he was asked whether he thought that the public liked his buildings. He responded by saying that it was not a question of whether the public liked his buildings or not. He believed it was the architect's duty to teach the public to like what the architect thought they should have. I have always disagreed with Mies. To me, he represented the Germanic state of mind which dictated to the people what they should like and should not like, the kind of reasoning that gave birth to the Nazi movement in Germany. Mies felt that architects by some divine gift were the only ones who knew what was good for people. If the people did not like his buildings, and many of the people who use and live in van der Rohe structures do not like them, then Mies reasoned that the fault was with the people and not with the architect.

Another interesting letter came from John M. Johansen, a prominent architect and a Fellow of the American Institute of Architects. Johansen created some very unusual buildings that express his own approach to architecture. In his work in schools and theaters, not only is the structure expressed but also pipes and ducts and open steelwork. He treats his work like a stage setting with a lavish use of color, and he achieves dramatic results. He does not design buildings that in any way resemble the type of buildings I do, but I admire his daring and bold approach. His letter follows:

> I write this letter to add my support to the Lapidus exhibit proposed by John Margolies. First, I believe this is a matter which only your Scholarship Committee should deal with. However, it seems that others on our Committee (Sybil Moholy-Nagy) have already voiced their opinion so I may as well register mine.
>
> I take pride in the fact that I "discovered" Morris Lapidus early in 1963 when I spoke to the National Convention held at the hotel he had designed. He is the only man who has directly and perhaps artlessly dealt with popular taste in this country. His work may be considered a new aspect of "formative" art in America that is of native common experience rather than "fine art."
>
> I have described it in lectures as "architectural collage," or as "scenic art," in which interiors and even exteriors are treated as stage scenery to set the moods and experiences as done in the theater. More and more we speak of the division between a natural frame and architectural infill as a new way to conceive the building. Much has been made of amusement park design and how Las Vegas and Disneyland are treated with some seriousness today. Unschooled taste is a valid phenomenon; it could be taken seriously or lightly, but it is nevertheless interesting and must not be ignored. On the other hand, much current work in "good taste," attempts at masterworks and pompous "gifts of form" from the "form givers," are becoming wearisome. Neither form shows a threat to the other serious professional efforts today.
>
> I believe we all agree that breadth of the view is the policy of the Architectural League. And threats of resignation on this issue is hardly mature. With these observations in mind, I urge you to read this letter to your Committee and vote acceptance of the Margolies proposal.

After the opening of the exhibit on October 8, 1970, a series of public seminars were arranged by the League at which my work was critically reviewed by many outstanding architects and art critics. The opening presentation was by Arthur Rosenblatt:

> One of the interesting things that John Johansen, who was my predecessor as the president of the Architectural League, said was that he discovered Morris Lapidus in 1963, when the AIA, the American Institute of Architects, held a convention in Miami Beach, and perhaps John did discover him. In a sense, I have a suspicion that I share some of that discovery with John in that several years ago, when I was with the Parks Department, we were looking around. We had decided that a swimming pool was appropriate for Bedford-Stuyvesant, and we endeavored to raise the money in the Capital budget for

it. We looked around for an architect who would be appropriate to design the most magnificent, the most pleasurable, the most delightful... all the things most municipal pools never have. Most of them look like glorified outhouses, and we wanted something that was so superlative and so fine and by somebody who had done more swimming pools than anybody else had ever done. So we thought we'd get somebody who'd done more and had done better than any of the other people had done, and when we had discussed it with friends and colleagues, they said, "Well, you've got to be out of your mind, and you'll be laughed out of town and it's the most ridiculous and insane thing you've ever thought of." And we went ahead and did it only because these people were wrong so often that there was no reason to believe that they were not again wrong. We met with Morris Lapidus and we decided, I think it was over lunch in the Park, that it was the right and appropriate thing to do.

Needless to say that a book came out later that applauded the action and said it was a brilliant stroke of genius and Ada Louise Huxtable of the *New York Times*, who had looked in some modest measure of disbelief at the thought [of commissioning Morris Lapidus], came around shortly after the project had been published in the *Architectural Record* and said, "My God, you know, this really is a brilliant job and really a superb project."

The second seminar occurred in one of the ballrooms of the Americana Hotel and was attended by an overflow audience of architects, newspaper people, and art critics. There were six speakers, each analyzing, dissecting, and reviewing my work. Charles Moore, the chairman of the School of Architecture at Yale had some nice things to say and some disparaging things, but all in all, I seemed to come off pretty well. Some of the others were more critical. One of the speakers was the editor of *Art in America*, Brian O'Doherty, who spoke briefly about the exhibit and then said he would like to read from an article covering the show which had been written by one of his editors, Mary Josephson, and appeared in the March/April issue of 1971:

Lapidus shares with Warhol the ability to stimulate mountainous issues out of molehills, a kind of creativity by proxy.... The disruption of high art in New York in the early sixties by the Pop artists was mentioned as a precedent for introducing Lapidus into the architectural discourse, but this doesn't really apply. The Pop artist, by finally disposing not of Abstract Expressionism but of its myth, was able to advance new ideas under popular disguise.

As communal fantasy, the appurtenances of Lapidus' hotels become infused with symbolic function. Symbolically, they can be read down to the smallest details as consistent texts that call forth a fantasy, codify it and return it to the users — a Homeric act conducted on the level of banality, but with rare shrewdness.

In his shrewd soundings of this vulnerable organism, Morris Lapidus shows an understanding and respect that have received a lot of lip service and little attention in contemporary architecture, where the symbolic value of the building has been the primary consideration. Here architects can learn from Lapidus. But it will be difficult to rival the way he controls the guest, without a hint of the sinister, but with an immense amiability, a pleasing aesthetic lassitude.... Many of Lapidus' contrasts of soft (furniture, deep rugs, occasional walls) and hard (glistening highlights, mirrors opening up dim voids) seem designed to engage an oral or tactile idealism. The bastardization of styles becomes a medium for visceral and tactile fulfillment, for what might be called a "pornography of comfort."

Another speaker seated at the table was Tom Wolfe, the noted critic and author. Some time after this evening he wrote *From Bauhaus to Our House* (1981) in which he describes what happened at this seminar:

How ... to deal with the barbaric yawps of the major hotel architects, such as Morris Lapidus and John Portman? Probably no architect ever worked harder to capture the spirit of American wealth and glamour after the Second World War than these two men: Lapidus, with his Americana and Eden Roc hotels in Miami Beach; Portman, with his Hyatts all across the country. Their work was so striking and so large in scale it was impossible for their fellow architects to ignore it. So they gave it *that look*. Portman the shrug and that look. Lapidus received that look and a snigger....

In 1970 Lapidus' work was selected as the subject of an Architectural League of New York show and panel discussion entitled "Morris Lapidus: Architecture of Joy." Ordinarily this was an honor. In Lapidus' case it was hard to say what it was. I was asked to be on the panel — probably, as I look back on it, with the hope that I might offer a "pop" perspective. The evening took on an uneasy, rather camp atmosphere — uneasy, because Lapidus himself had turned up in the audience.

Model for the proposed Olympic Tower, a "building in the sky" that was to use air rights above structures along Fifth Avenue between 51st and 52nd streets in New York, 1970.

16   A Most Unusual Building and a Return to the Theater

"The Architecture of Joy" exhibit was the prologue to a fantastic opportunity that came my way in 1970 and seemed to herald a whole new direction for my forty-year career: the chance to design a "building in the sky" *over* the Best & Company site on Fifth Avenue in New York, directly north of St. Patrick's Cathedral.

I had pleaded for this opportunity for two years with Arthur Levien and Arthur Cohen, partners in the Arlen Company, land developers for whom I had been designing housing. They had conceived the idea of erecting an office tower, which would also include residential apartments, in the air space they owned *above the structures* fronting on Fifth Avenue between 51st and 52nd Streets, specifically, above Best & Company on the southeast corner and Cartier's on the northeast. Between these structures, however, stood the Olympic Airlines Building, 37½ feet wide, owned by Aristotle Onassis. The Greek shipping magnate had entered into partnership with Arlen on this project. It was on the Olympic site that the stem of the tower was to be erected, a stem rising two hundred feet into the air, well above Cartier's and Best's, and supporting a block-long building "in the sky."

Admittedly, this was an unusual, daring concept, so unusual and so important that the two Arthurs hesitated to entrust it to me and my firm. So for two years they had employed a succession of architects, six in all, in an attempt to solve the design and engineering problems of this building on a stem. For two years I had seen sketch after sketch, model after model, of the proposed solution for what seemed an unsolvable architectural problem. How does one build a twenty-story building one block wide atop a two-hundred-foot tower only 37½ feet wide?

Alan and I thought we had the answer. Finally, Levien and Cohen decided to let us try where our six predecessors had failed. We were given exactly one week to show what we could do. Fortunately, I had already started work in my Miami office on preliminary designs, and Alan, pushing our New York staff to the utmost, had been developing some of the engineering answers. We combined our efforts toward the end of the week and met the deadline. The solution we proposed was accepted enthusiastically.

Arlen then authorized us to proceed with further studies, detailed renderings, and a comprehensive scale model. Within a matter of months, the entire
presentation was ready for submission, not only to Levien and Cohen, but also
to the two partners who would have the final say: Aristotle Onassis and the
equally fabulous Meshulam Riklas, the Israeli who headed the Glen Alden and
Rapid American conglomerates, owners of Best's.

The meeting was so important to Alan and me that we trusted no one but
ourselves to set up the model and hang the drawings on the walls of the Arlen
executive conference room. I had made hundreds of presentations, but I had
never before experienced such a mixture of apprehensive anticipation and sheer
elation. As we adjusted the floodlights to illuminate the gleaming model, it
looked to us like an aesthetic and engineering triumph. Supported on a slim,
black twenty-story granite shaft was a twenty-story mirrored cube that bloomed
like a lovely flower on its stem. Within this glass cube would be housed not only
the most prestigious office space in New York, but elegant executive apartments
as well; at Riklis's request one entire floor would be given over to an art gallery.
At the base of the cube, on the twentieth floor of the stem, serviced by high
speed nonstop elevators from the street level, would be a huge sky plaza, an
unrivaled display area for sculpture (Riklis was an avid collector), a spacious
reception area for visitors, and a congenial lunch-hour meeting place for people
employed in the building.

Our concept also included a high-vaulted shopping arcade, running from
51st to 52nd Street behind the shaft, and also behind Best's and Cartier's. It
would be a pedestrian mall, which, like the cube-flower on its stem, would also
be one of the first of its kind in the city.

As we adjusted the last of the lights, Arthur Levien and Arthur Cohen came
in. Soon after, Aristotle Onassis arrived with several other shipowners, followed
a few minutes later by Meshulam Riklis and his architectural advisor. As the
creative spokesman, I explained the concept of our version of Olympic Tower to
Riklis and Onassis while Cohen and Levien, our sponsors, listened intently.
After I finished, there was complete silence. I quaked. Onassis finally spoke. He
was enthusiastic about the concept and its proposed implementation. Riklis
conferred with his advisor before he, too, gave his unqualified approval. Alan
and I looked at each other with unabashed joy. At last I, an architect who had
been practicing for more than forty years, was going to be permitted to create a
building that might make architectural history, and my son, only thirty-five, was
to be an integral part of the project.

Onassis further declared that he was so pleased he wanted us to design the
new Olympic Airways Fifth Avenue offices, and he asked if we would also be
available to design Olympic offices in other parts of the world. Immediately
after this historic meeting, Alan and I started work on the final plans for
Olympic Tower.

An architect gets few one-man shows in his lifetime. So it was with happy anticipation that I picked up the *New York Times* on the morning of October 15, to read the review of my show's opening by Ada Louise Huxtable:

> I had a much better time at the Morris Lapidus show that has just opened at the Architectural League than I've ever had at a Lapidus Hotel. "The Architecture of Joy," a tribute of sorts to the High Priest of High Kitsch who virtually invented the Florida hotel (somebody had to), is an absolutely dandy little exhibition … conceived and coordinated with a straight face by John S. Margolies.… It is accompanied by the strains of Muzak and the outraged cries of those League members who feel that the show is an unpardonable breach of standards.
>
> The show is being presented as an exercise in mid-American, mid-20th-century popular taste and art and what 90 per cent of the American public really likes and wants. (If three people say you're drunk, lie down, says Mr. Lapidus; if 90 percent of the American people like these buildings they're right, says Mr. Margolies. Will the real American architecture please stand up?)… However, one man's joy is another man's hell. I have never felt more joyless than in Miami in the midst of all that joy. I was depressed in direct ratio of esthetic illiteracy and hokey pretensions to the shoddiness of the execution. I got a terrible case of the Fontaineblues.
>
> Undeniably, Mr. Lapidus has elevated a kind of taste to a kind of art, even if it is made of plastic, mirrors and spit. He is something of a genius, and how he does it fascinates. It also instructs.
>
> His work is often wonderfully pratfall funny — these are the best esthetic sight gags in the world — and its intimate revelations of the pop mentality are mind-blowingly fine. He can teach taste-straightjacketed architects a lot about human needs and responses to environment and design for public pleasures.
>
> To those who have always loved what he does, it is superglamour. To the young and older professionals who have recently come to love it, it is super-camp. They savor every nuance of legitimate psychology and outrageous parody and translate it into homilies about the pop scene that are sincere but not without the scent of patronage.
>
> The current vogue is for turning an appreciation of the lessons of Lapidus-land into a canonization of the results, elevating them to some kind of esthetic pantheon. That is intellectual baloney. It is still uninspired superschlock.

Superschlock! I was just putting down the paper when the phone rang. It was Alan calling from New York. He was somewhat upset, with what I considered commendable filial loyalty.

"Have you read it yet?"

"Yes," I said, "it's not very flattering."

"Flattering? It's the worst thing anybody ever said about you. What are we going to do, Dad?"

"Nothing. She's entitled to her opinion."

"Huh? What are you talking about?"

"The Huxtable review, of course."

"Dad, I'm talking about the editorial. The lead editorial. Read it and call me back!"

Wondering how a lead editorial in the *New York Times* could possibly concern me, I picked up the paper again. Captioned "Good-bye to Fifth Avenue?" the editorial read in part:

> Now speculation threatens the end of Fifth Avenue. By definition, Fifth Avenue is that elegant, glittering, sophisticated artery that is the retail heart and shopping showcase of New York. News of the sale of the Best & Co.'s building to developers for the construction of a new office tower opens the prospect for similar deals along the street. Like the other avenues, Fifth Avenue is to be turned into bland blocks of banks sleekly embalmed in corporate pall. . . .
>
> Even negotiation may not save Fifth Avenue's polished image. The Olympic Tower planned for the Best & Co. site by Aristotle Onassis and Arthur Cohen will be a product of the Miami Beach hotel architect, Morris Lapidus, known more for tinsel than for polish. As they said when the Summit opened in New York, Fifth Avenue is awfully far from the ocean.

What upset me was not the old Summit joke, but the editor's dismissing the tower as "a product" of a "Miami Beach architect" without, to my knowledge, ever having seen a sketch of my design.

On a dull autumn day I received a call from my Arlen clients asking me to come to their offices for a meeting. Their offices on the fifty-fourth floor of their building on West 57th Street overlook the Hudson River and New Jersey in the west and from the windows facing north one could view Central Park all the way to the northern boundary at 110th Street. The park was completely denuded of its green summer mantle. The meeting was attuned to the dying day as my clients formally informed me that I was being dismissed as the architect for the Olympic Tower project. It was with a heavy, anguished heart that I learned that the attacks by the *New York Times* had convinced Onassis, who was supersensitive to adverse publicity, to find another architect for his tower. He made it plain that under no circumstances would he allow the building to be erected if I remained on the project. My clients told me that the concept of the building in the sky had been abandoned. Best & Company was to be demolished, and a conventional building would be built on the site. A new architect had already been commissioned. I thanked my clients for their efforts on my behalf and sadly left the office. When I came down to the street, I felt that I wanted solitude and decided to walk to my east side office by crossing Central Park.

A much more pleasant meeting awaited me with the committee from the Bedford-Stuyvesant neighborhood. They had just learned that their park, which Alan and I had designed, had been nominated for the Bard Award, which The City Club of New York awards in alternate years for urban improvement.

I had spent a great deal of time in New York. Now that the Olympic Tower was finished for us, I returned to my Florida office which was doing well under the guidance of Abby Harle, or so I thought. There were a number of projects — apartment houses, hotels, schools and hospitals. When my secretary found me alone in my office, she told me that she had been inundated by calls from various stores that were claiming that they were holding large unpaid bills that Abby's new wife was incurring.

I called in Abby to discuss his wife's debts. He broke down and told me that he had a bad marriage and wanted a divorce. He asked whether he could transfer his activities to my New York office. I told him that my son, Alan, was in complete charge of New York and did not want Abby working under him.

At about this time we were heavily involved with a number of projects in Washington, D.C. My young client Morton Bender was constantly urging me to open an office there. He told me again and again that he knew a number of builders whom he could recommend to us if we were to open an office. I suggested to Abby that if he wanted to get away from Miami Beach I would open an office in Washington where he would be in full charge. Abby was overjoyed.

I went to Washington and found space in a small office building that would be a fine office with a moderate-sized drafting room, an office for Abby, a conference room and a reception room. Abby was enthusiastic and spent time in Washington outfitting a complete office. He returned to Miami Beach to straighten out his affairs but he was supposed to be in Washington the following Monday.

That Monday when I arrived at my office in Miami Beach, Abby was still there. He explained to me that when the time came for him to leave, his wife admitted that she had been completely wrong and said that she would change her extravagant ways if they could make a new start together in Miami Beach. Abby told me that he had decided to stay in the Florida office. I reminded him that I had fully equipped an office for him in Washington with a year's lease. The end result of a long conversation led nowhere. He was remaining in Miami Beach. Not knowing what to do, I called my attorney, who insisted that I take the first plane to New York.

When I arrived in my New York office, I found my attorney and my accountant waiting for me. They heard me out and their advice was to fire Abby Harle immediately. So ended an association that had lasted more than sixteen years, the last of the three young men whom I had nurtured to become my partners was gone.

I now had one partner, my son Alan.

The New York office was doing well under his direction and I asked him if he would like to change the name of the firm to Morris and Alan Lapidus. He thought that the original name, Morris Lapidus Associates, should be maintained.

A year before all of this happened, I had been contacted by the International Executive Service Corps, an offshoot of a government-sponsored corps of retired highly trained personnel who travel to developing countries in need of their expertise. Among the group were former bankers, oil engineers, executives of commercial enterprises, safety engineers, and government specialists. These retired experts received no salary but all their traveling expenses were paid, and they were given a generous daily stipend. I was invited to the I.E.S.C. head-quarters in New York where they explained that they were supported by arrangement with the U.S. government, which paid a sum equal to half of their costs, and the other half was paid by our country's major corporations. I was asked to join the corps as an expert in hotel design. My first assignment would be a six-month stay in Singapore, where I would help develop plans for luxury hotels.

I told the I.E.S.C. gentlemen that I was far from retired and could not stay away from my practice for such a long time. They were most anxious to have me and I agreed to stay for one month. I was given the manual of operation and all the requirements, including clothing. I was given airline tickets with which I could make whatever stops I wanted on my way there and back.

My work in Singapore turned out to be both exciting and stimulating. I was put in touch with the cabinet ministers, who entertained my wife and me lavishly. They were gracious hosts and most appreciative of the information I gave them. When I left I was presented with a tea service of Salanga pewter made in Singapore. We returned by way of India, spending two weeks seeing many interesting cities and of course the Taj Mahal, the burning gats on the Ganges river, and countless elaborate palaces. When I returned I received a beautiful silver platter inscribed "For service to Country."

During the following years, I spent most of my time in my Florida office while Alan conducted our practice in New York. We had numerous projects including, in 1973, a rather unusual hotel in Jamaica in an area that gave this hotel its name, Trelawny. Once again I tried an unusual approach to the design of a hotel and its planning. It earned the name "A Butterfly," because that is what it looked like from the air.

A project that originated in Miami Beach, where I did the preliminary planning, but was completely executed in my New York office, was the creation of the Theater of Performing Arts. Years before I arrived in Miami Beach, boxing

Trelawny Hotel, Trelawny, Jamaica, 1973.

"Once again I tried an unusual approach to the design of a hotel and its planning. It earned the name "A Butterfly," because that is what it looked like from the air."

had been a popular sport, and the city built a large boxing arena which could seat three thousand people. As an afterthought the city decided to add a large theater stage. It was a complete stage with a proscenium that was forty feet wide and thirty feet high. The stage was fully equipped with a fly gallery with twenty lines (pipes) that were hung in the fly gallery and from which scenery could be suspended. These lines were lowered by means of ropes and pulleys in true theater tradition. The arena was surrounded on three sides with balconies, while the fourth side was the stage. As the enthusiasm for boxing waned, the arena was used for theatrical presentations, and when I arrived it was used by a new and growing opera company.

The arena was a terrible place for shows and even worse for operas. The City of Miami Beach gave me the commission to transform the arena into a theater. Our budget was six million dollars for the renovation. We associated with a theater consultant from New York. The first thing we did was to remove the three balconies that were made for looking at a boxing ring and build a true balcony at the rear of the audience space. The flat floor was torn up and a sloped floor installed to achieve good sight lines. The quarters for the boxers were removed and the walls that had formed the arena were moved in to give the audience room for assembly between acts.

The city selected the acoustical engineers, whom I hired to assist me with the acoustics. They asked me to remove the ceiling, exposing the large steel trusses that spanned the former arena. Even with the ceiling removed, which allowed the height to go to the roof, the acousticians told me that there was still not enough volume for acceptable acoustics. In order to solve the problem, the trusses and the roof would have to be raised about ten feet. Our engineers determined that the cost for this extra work would be a million dollars. I went before our city council and explained the problem and asked for an additional million dollars. After due consideration I was told to do the best I could, but there was no money to raise the roof.

Our office in Florida was quite busy and I decided to give my New York office the task of producing all the working drawings and detailing, the hundreds of details to convert a boxing arena into a true opera house and a Broadway type of theater. The finished project was named TOPA (Theater of Performing Arts). The theater opened and seemed to be a success. The opera company loved its new quarters.

Then the trouble began. People complained about the acoustics (we had warned them) and also about the sight lines which made it difficult to see the stage. Once started, the complaints continued to increase, and after a year, I, the architect, was sued for a million dollars.

According to our contract the suit was to be settled by arbitration. The arbitration took more than two weeks. The city claimed that I had not created good seating and sight lines and that the acoustics were simply awful. My insurance company employed competent lawyers to represent me and the city engaged a prestigious firm of attorneys to represent them. My son Richard, an attorney, represented me in my claim for extras that the city refused to pay.

After visiting the theater and checking the acoustics, the sight lines, and several other complaints, the arbitrators found in my favor. Not only was the city to get no money from me, but they ruled that because of this frivolous and unfounded suit, the city was obliged to pay for all of my legal costs. The arbitrators also ruled that the city was to pay all of my claims for extras.

To complete this sad tale, the lady impresario who was successfully booking concert after concert persuaded the city to redo the theater and to raise the roof. The city floated a twenty-million-dollar bond issue and retained James Stewart Polshek, the architect who had just redone the venerable Carnegie Hall in New York, to redo my TOPA. When plans were completed, the costs were estimated at twenty-five million dollars, twenty percent over the amount the city had committed through a bond issue. There were lawsuits against the architect and the contractor who was to monitor costs. Polshek was discharged and another architect called in. He introduced escalators to replace the original ramps and for the rest he did a confectionery job on TOPA, now called the Jackie Gleason Theater. He did not raise the roof!

My work in the Theater of Performing Arts led to another theater commission. A wealthy citizen of Miami decided that he would buy a building known as the Olympia Building, which contained the largest movie house in Miami, and give it to the city as his gift. It was his wish to convert the huge Olympia Theater, which had been closed for some years, into a fine concert hall. I do not know what he paid for the building and the theater, but my work entailed a cost of six million dollars for the conversion, all at no cost to the city. It was a wonderful experience for me, especially since I had never lost my love of the theater. The Gusman Center for the Performing Arts is now used extensively not only for concerts but also for ballets and most often as a large modern theater.

A year or so later, my wealthy client decided to build another large concert hall as a gift, this one to the University of Miami. Here I was designing not only a most unusual concert hall but also the music school of the university, which is housed within the total structure. I employed one of the finest acousticians (who taught at Columbia University) with the result that the Gusman Concert Hall is considered one of the finest concert halls in any college. In this building I was able to use my theory that the exterior must be an envelope to enclose the unusual spaces that form a concert hall. For me, the exterior appearance must express what is happening in the interior.

Earlier in my story I spoke about the ship design that I prepared during World War II. Sometime in the early 1970s, I had occasion to show my designs for a postwar ocean liner to an acquaintance who had started the first Caribbean cruise business with a shipowner who had a fleet of ships that sailed from

Gusman Concert Hall, University of Miami, 1974.

"In this building I was able to use my theory that the exterior must be an envelope to enclose the unusual spaces that form a concert hall. For me, the exterior appearance must express what is happening in the interior."

Norway to Liverpool, England, carrying Englishmen and Norwegians to the coast of Spain. These Norwegian ships sailed only during the summer season, then were dry-docked for the winter. My friend wanted the ships for those winter months when Caribbean cruises were most popular. An arrangement was made by my friend in Miami and the shipowner in Norway. After the Norwegian ship arrived in Miami, my friend (who was originally an Israeli and whose family had been in cargo sailing ships for two generations) signed a contract with the Norwegian, and hence the first Norwegian Caribbean Line was born. I sailed on the first trip, and this one-week cruise was such a success that another Norwegian ship arrived in Miami. What made these weekly Caribbean cruises so popular was that gambling on the high seas was allowed.

After three years of this successful venture the two partners had a falling out; and the Norwegian shipowner kept his ships and my Israeli friend found himself once again without a ship.

A few days after this event occurred my Israeli friend called me from London and asked if I could leave for London that night. He and his associates were about to purchase two Cunard ships that had been docked in Southampton. He remembered my ship designs and wanted me to be in London the next morning and proceed to Southampton to ascertain if the two Cunards could be converted to cruise ships.

The next morning, I arrived in London and took a train to Southampton to examine the ships. After a day spent in going over the ships, I told my friend and his associates that these former luxury liners were too old for conversion to cruise ships. They told me that they were also looking at another ship that was docked in Italy, the *Empress of Canada*. I went to see the ship and told my Israeli friend that it could be converted. They asked me how long the work would take. I knew that the *Empress* would have to be refitted in the Italian shipyard and then sailed to Miami. This would take about a month, giving me that time to design the interior. I could have the necessary furnishings and all of the decorative material waiting at the dock when the ship, which was renamed the *Mardi Gras*, arrived. I told them that it would take two weeks for me and my staff to ready the ship for sailing.

And so the sales staff went to work selling the cruise and setting the date for the sailing of the *Mardi Gras*, which was now owned by a company called the Carnival Cruise Line. Now, twenty years later, the Carnival Cruise Line is the largest fleet of ships sailing to Mexico and the Caribbean islands.

During this time another commission came to me for a large hotel located on a mountainside in Puerto Rico. I first went there alone to see how we could design a hotel on this dramatic and unusual site. The site was on the eastern tip of Puerto Rico and was surrounded on three sides by the Caribbean Sea. I decided to build the hotel on three levels, starting at the entrance road and descending in three tiers, each one a part of the hotel complex and finally

El Conquistador Hotel, Fajardo, Puerto Rico, 1965.
The hotel is built on three levels, with a funicular (top) running from
the top of the site to sea level, where a reef-enclosed swimming area
(bottom left) is a protection against sharks.

finishing at the beach. These waters are shark infested and we had to build a reef enclosing a large swimming area.

I decided to plan a straight line of rooms and a sweeping curved structure that would contain a large dining room and a large gambling casino at the top. At the middle level I proposed an oval pool surrounded with guest rooms and cabanas and a third level at the beach.

I prepared the preliminary plans and took Alan with me when I presented them. The plans were accepted, and I told my client that the plans and the supervision of the construction would be under Alan's care. New York needed the work. Alan did a great job of completing the project, which had a funicular traveling from the top to the sea level of the hotel complex. I realized that I was getting too old to do mountain climbing.

I kept sending work to New York because that city was undergoing a severe recession. By 1975, however, there was not enough work for two offices. I finally decided to close my once prosperous office in New York. I asked Alan to join me in my Florida office. He gave this some thought, but his final decision was that he preferred to start a small practice (although there was no work on the horizon) and try to get along alone until things turned around in New York. So sadly, I had to say good-bye to my last partner. I was now alone in my Florida practice.

Alan went through three awful years. It was only when Atlantic City voted to allow gambling that his practice began to grow. He eventually became the architect for Donald Trump's Trump Plaza, and his office began to grow into a good-sized practice.

International Inn on Thomas Circle, Washington, D.C., 1975.

"The open and shut dome was admired and even elicited a number of letters
inquiring if this device could be used in some odd places....
The most unusual request came from the White House. Lyndon Johnson's engineers
wanted to know if such a dome could be built at his home in Texas."

17

Africa, Another Exhibit, and a Last Hotel

In 1975 I found myself in my Miami Beach office, practicing architecture without any partners. My office was doing well, but I was seventy-three years old, and I had to make up my mind if I would continue alone or call it quits and retire. What was I going to do with myself if I retired? I liked painting and golf, and Bea and I liked to travel. But I could do all that while I practiced so why retire? The possibility of new projects to design is the lure constantly on the horizon for an architect, so I went on with my practice without any partners. We were kept busy designing more and more apartment houses, but soon came a new challenge in the form of a group of hotels in a place I hardly knew — Nigeria.

Before I embarked on this unusual venture, I was working on the design of an interesting hotel in Washington. My now favorite client, Morty Bender, had decided to build a hotel on Thomas Circle. Once again I used my preferred form, a sweeping curved building. I had decided to place a large swimming pool in front of the hotel, and the building curved around it. I had designed a very large metal and glass dome that covered the pool and included a curved roofed glass passage from the hotel to the pool. I provided heat for the winter and spring and fall seasons. But I wanted an open pool during the summer. I designed the large glass dome over the pool so that it could be opened in the summer and closed in cool and cold weather. The dome was built in ten sections. Two of the sections were stationary and each section, one on one side of the dome and the other on the opposite side, created a thirty-foot-high arch over the pool and the pool deck. The rest of the dome had eight moveable sections, four on one side and four on the other side. These parts of the dome were like curved slices of an orange. Two sections moved to meet the other two sections to form half of the dome, one section sliding over the other. On the opposite side the four sections moved to close the dome. Moving these huge slices of dome and making them watertight was a problem that I solved by using small electric motor-driven trolleys that moved each section into place. A steel channel track in the form of a true circle was laid around the pool, and the trolleys pulled the huge sections easily.

The open and shut dome was admired and even elicited a number of letters inquiring if this device could be used in some odd places. A shipyard wrote to inquire if such a dome could be placed on the top deck of an ocean liner that was being built. The most unusual request came from the White House. Lyndon Johnson's engineers wanted to know if such a dome could be built at his home in Texas. Nothing came of all this, and after ten years the dome and the swimming pool were gone. Maintaining this unusual domed pool was just too costly to keep operating.

The Nigeria project began with a man who had made inquiries about me through a number of acquaintances. He called me from London to tell me that he would like to come to see me and wondered if I would be willing to design some hotels for him in Nigeria. This is the kind of thing that makes an architect's life interesting.

Leon Taman, a typical Englishman, arrived at my office where we talked about his plans to build several hotels in Nigeria. My first question was, why Nigeria? He told me that he was doing business in that country. What kind of business? I wanted to know. He told me that he manufactured pharmaceuticals in England and had become the largest seller of pharmaceuticals in Africa. For several hours he explained how oil had been discovered in Nigeria and described the tremendous boom that was taking place in this once underdeveloped country. His own business was also booming, and he knew that American, German, and other countries' scientists and oil experts were arriving in droves and there were hardly enough hotels to accommodate this great horde of people.

We spent several days discussing ways and means to build hotels in a country that had never produced building materials. Shiploads of material were arriving in Lagos, the capital of Nigeria, but there were no docking facilities to unload the cargo. The result was a state of chaos and a harbor full of ships waiting, in some cases for months, to unload.

During our long discussions, I finally asked Mr. Taman how he, apparently an Englishman, had become involved with this African country. Gradually, I learned the fascinating story of this man's life. His grandfather had traced his ancestry back to the expulsion of the Jews from Spain in 1492. Leon's forebears left Spain, as did thousands of Jews, and spread throughout the world. These Spanish Jews are still called Sephardim, or the dispersed. Many of them, centuries later, still speak a fifteenth-century Spanish called Ladino. Some have forgotten their Spanish background and, though still observing Judaism, have learned to speak the language of their new countries. Leon Taman's ancestors had settled in Italy. In the nineteenth century Taman's grandfather became a provisioner for ships that sailed from an Italian port. To this port came Lord Kitchener, the English general who commanded an expeditionary force to reconquer the Sudan. Kitchener needed a provisioner to accompany his army to the Sudan, and that is how Leon Taman's grandfather finally resettled his family in Khartoum, the capital of the colonized Sudan where Leon Taman was born. As a young lad he spoke Italian, English, and six different Arabic dialects.

It was a boy's pastime to capture and skin all sorts of snakes. Leon discovered that the snakeskins that he and his Sudanese friends skinned could be taken to Italy where snakeskins were in great demand by Italian shoemakers. At that time the best shoes in the world were Italian. Traveling with his Italian passport, which the family never gave up, Leon arrived in Italy with a large stock of valuable snakeskins. He sold his merchandise at a very good price and was asked to come again and again with stocks of snakeskins. He paid his Sudanese friends handsomely and urged them to bring more and more snakeskins to him for export to Italy. By the time that Leon was sixteen years old he was on his way to making his first million.

Later on, he found that most of the essences made from African flowers were used to make perfumes and lotions, so he decided to go into the perfume business. He moved his young family to the city of Brighton in Sussex, England, where he built a factory with all of the equipment for the manufacture of perfume and lotions. When the first factory was completed he learned that the perfume business was a securely closed industry which, try as he might, he could not enter. After a little research, Leon found that he could use the retorts and the batching tanks to manufacture pharmaceuticals instead of perfumes. He employed a retired English Army Surgeon General to head his new venture called International Generics. What better place to sell his product than Africa, where he spoke many of the Arabic dialects. Eventually, he owned several plants that produced different types of generic pharmaceuticals that were sold throughout Africa.

Leon needed a system of construction that could be employed in Nigeria where building materials were in very short supply. The only product of which there was an unending supply was concrete. A few years earlier, I had met a chemist who came to me with a chemical which, if added to the batching of concrete, would produce a lightweight concrete with unusual strength. He had been experimenting with batching and blowing this mixture over a frame built of metal (aluminum) struts and expanded aluminum perforated metal lath. The use of large blowers for the cement resulted in enclosed spaces that needed no structural reinforcing or structural steel support. I first used this method to create reasonably large rooms for adjuncts to my apartment houses. These enclosures or large rooms were used for meetings and entertainment, and they stood by themselves, complete with walls and a roof. The form of these spaces was designed in a continuous manner with the walls curving up to form the roof. I later used this new method of construction in a Puerto Rican hotel to create a large freestanding dining room, with the walls curving up in a graceful form to become the roof. I showed Taman pictures of this form of construction that needed no structural supports. Actually, I was creating a concrete shell with nothing but metal lath forming my structures and using strong power blowers to apply the lightweight concrete to form my enclosed spaces. Leon was enthusiastic about this unusual method of construction. He asked me if I could design a one-story hotel with all of its rooms and amenities to give him a modern hotel. I was quite sure that using this dome shape I could design an interesting and unusual one-story hotel. By designing a central building as the core, I could spread a large number of wings which contained the hotel rooms.

So once again I was off to London to meet Taman. I checked into the Dorchester Hotel where my client had an elaborate suite. A message instructed me to take the Brighton express from Waterloo Station the following morning. It was a pleasant one-hour ride to Brighton where I was met by Taman's chauffeur. I was driven to International Generic's offices where Taman was waiting for me. I met some of the officers of the firm and was made especially welcome by the chief executive officer, the former surgeon general of the British army, a jolly gray-haired Scot. I also met Leon's executive secretary, a beautiful English woman who was really an executive running a large part of the company. We spent time talking about the Nigerian hotel project and then adjourned for a lunch in a delightful English pub. We spent the rest of the day planning for my trip to Nigeria.

The next day I once again took the train to Brighton for more discussions of the scope of the project. I learned that Leon and I would fly to Lagos where we would be met by International Generic's Nigerian manager. I also learned that while staying a few days at a hotel in the outskirts of Lagos, we would drive to Lagos where we would be able to meet with some Nigerian government ministers and then board a plane for a three-day trip around the country to look at possible sites in other cities for a chain of hotels. In short, I was to spend a week in Nigeria seeing most of the important cities, while Leon would carry on negotiations for the proposed hotels.

I spent another pleasant day in Brighton and had time to visit the Royal Pavilion, designed by John Nash in 1815 for the Prince Regent. It looked like an Arabian potentate's palace, with Moorish domes and fantastic details. Then once again it was back to the Waterloo train and my final night in London. The next night I met Leon at Heathrow Airport and we departed for Nigeria.

When we arrived the next morning Leon, a perfect English gentleman, was instantly transformed into an Arab. We were met by two Nigerian diplomats. They greeted Leon like a long lost brother. They spoke Arabic and embraced. Leon held out his hands to our greeters and I could not help seeing the quick, subtle way in which a fistful of English pounds disappeared into the hands of the Nigerians. (Such bribery is standard throughout Nigeria, and in many other developing countries as well.) This legerdemain accomplished, the dignitaries escorted us to waiting cars and a ride to a government building in Lagos. I did not understand the greeting and the language. I was eventually introduced as the great American architect who was to be the designer of Leon's chain of hotels. There were more dignitaries, all in flowing jalabias and Arab headdress. The discussions lasted for hours, all of it unintelligible to me. We were finally driven to our hotel. There Leon introduced me to his Nigerian manager, an Irishman who had worked a number of years for International Generics.

That evening Leon explained how his company operated. I.G. had a fleet of vans with the interiors fitted out like the interior of a drug store. These vans traveled their allotted routes, stopping at local drugstores. The local pharmacist would pick out the pharmaceuticals he needed from the van. The drivers of the vans were pharmacists who spoke the different dialects of each country in Africa.

We stayed in Lagos for several days while negotiations continued. Since I had no part in these meetings, I was driven around the city and its environs. Lagos was choked with people, not only Nigerians, but hundreds of nationals from the four corners of the world working and establishing business contacts. It was a city of dirt, poverty, wealth, and mobs of people. The car in which I rode moved more slowly than the pedestrians who overflowed the streets.

Finally Leon, the Irish manager, his wife, and I boarded a large plane with a comfortable lounge and a nice dining room. Each night we stayed at a local hotel. The manager's wife shopped early and cooked our meals for the next day's flight. We never ate in the hotels we stayed in.

We visited six of the largest cities in Nigeria and we were taken by the local ministers or mayors to examine possible sites for the new hotels. When we made our selections, the officials gave us city plans which gave me the information that I would need to draw preliminary plans when I got back to my office in Florida. I always asked to see historical buildings to gain some knowledge of material that I could use in my designs. But Nigeria, it appeared, had never produced any important architectural style other than primitive places of worship.

We returned to our hotel in the Lagos area and after the customary Arab farewells, we flew to England and I continued on home. This project meant many visits to London and Brighton and one more trip to Nigeria to take care of some formalities. The first of four Nigerian hotels was built in the city of Abeacuta and was called the Ogun State Hotel.

For a few years, I was the architect for the Mount Sinai Hospital in Miami Beach. Designing specialized hospital buildings meant studying various phases of surgery and medicine. These studies required that I don green surgical clothes in order to observe actual operating and surgical procedures — another architectural project that took me far away from architecture.

In 1978 I received an invitation from Linz, Austria, to participate in an exhibit under the auspices of the dean of Linz University (Hochschule für künstlerische und Industrielle Gestaltung in Linz), Dr. Rudolph Kirschschlager, and the

Lapidus on the floating steel stairway he designed for the "Forum Design" exhibit, Linz, Austria, 1980.

"Since Linz was known for its skill in fabricating the most unusual structures of steel, I designed as my central feature a curving stairway built of steel, which had no visible means of support. It was my legendary stairway to nowhere!"

assistant dean of the school of steel fabrication, Helmuth Gesallpointiner. Linz was the chief steel-making city in Austria. The exhibit was to be called "Forum Design" and was to open in the spring of 1980. I was told that it would be an exhibit of all phases of design, including clothing, automobiles, and manufacturing. I received a brochure showing a huge temporary exhibit hall and two wings which would be built of a steel skeleton, over which a special nylon would be stretched. The design of this large exhibit complex would be the work of Haus Rucker Co., a prominent and daring architectural firm in Austria.

In the main hall there was to be an exhibit of the most important young American architects organized by Robert A. M. Stern. In addition to Stern himself were Michael Graves, Allan Greenberg, Charles Moore, Stanley Tigerman, and Robert Venturi. In the wings of the exhibit hall there were to be individual exhibits of the most famous designers in the world, and I had been selected as the only American architect.

I was overwhelmed by this invitation, but I did not feel that I could represent American architecture. I responded with a polite letter expressing my appreciation the honor but added that in my opinion there were other, more deserving architects. Although I was asked to reconsider, I just could not accept this honor. Philip Johnson was selected to take my place.

A month later I received a letter saying that Philip Johnson had decided to withdraw and was asked again to reconsider designing an exhibit that would symbolize American architecture. This time I accepted. Since Linz was known for its skill in fabricating the most unusual structures of steel, I designed as my central feature a curving stairway built of steel, which had no visible means of support. The stairway curved up to a large multicolored wall, where the stairway entered a door-sized opening. There was no way of seeing where the stairway went after it entered the opening. The stairway actually led to another curved stairway, floating down to the floor level where the first stairway began. A visitor descending the stairway had to walk through a gallery where my work was on display. It was my legendary stairway to nowhere!

There were nine exhibit spaces in the wing where my exhibit was placed. The first exhibit was by the venerable Raymond Loewy, the fourth space was mine. The other spaces were exhibits of European architects and two American designers, Sol Lewitt and Rebecca Horn, both artists, not architects.

The opening of the exhibit was an exciting affair attended by thousands including Bea and me. We had arrived in Linz two weeks early so that I could check the final details of my exhibit. We then visited Salzburg, went on to the Schloss Fuchel outside of Salzburg, and took a ship on the Rhine to Schluss Durnstein, arriving in Linz in time for the opening.

The next day I had lunch with Alessandro Mendini, the managing editor of *Domus*, the prestigious Italian architectural magazine. He was a most pleasant individual who spoke perfect English. Several months later I received a copy of

Domus (October 1980) and to my complete surprise and delight, the full-color cover of this very large magazine showed a picture of me! On the editorial page Mendini wrote:

Dear Morris Lapidus:

...At Linz I saw you moving about in the space allocated to you, as you came down the mock theatrical flight of steps as if you were the star of a musical, forty years leading designer of American luxury hotels. The flight of steps started from nowhere and led to nowhere, a self-critical path of coloured chalks closed in itself. Sweating in their Austrian boxes, other designers visualized their dreams of post-modern designs, just as architects sweating in their Venetian boxes, raised the facades of the Via Novissima, a place where true architecture corresponds to its own chrysalis and to its own appearance. [He was referring to the 1976 Venice Biennale.]

　...Why is it that right now your hypersensitive and much debated personality as a "rational fantasist," interior designer and post-modern architect before his time, has swung back into the limelight? In your recent autobiographical book, *An Architecture of Joy*, you say: "Design must express the most elementary human emotion: the desire for, love of and need for ornament." Perhaps in these words lies the whole of your vocation for designing "Hotels." Whilst the house is where the "forever" and the real reside, the hotel is on the contrary where one lives for a few days in "an ornamental state." The hotel is an island of artificial joy, an illusive mechanism, a stage for the conscious comedy of ourselves as mass, charter-flying men and women. Escapism, exoticism, eroticism, and "retro"-futurism, a captivating medley of styles, uses, customs and cuisines, an acrobatic virtuosity of swimming pools covered, open, openable, nocturnal, hanging, waterfall-like. Halls and triumphal stairways for acting out our own parts in Florida, Jamaica, the Bahamas, Puerto Rico, Georgia. Maybe you represent our own possible sin. I too, with friends, arranged at Linz and in Venice, under the general programmes two small "limit-exhibitions" of the "banal object, environment and architecture"; the kind of design that is acquiescent instead of repressive towards the masses. But we were afraid. In fact, rather than optimistic design hypothesis we showed test-tube situations because we believe the method of which you are a precursor is as necessary as it is dangerous.

Soon after the Linz "Forum Design," Leon Taman came back to me and asked if I would be interested in going with him to Hollywood. He told me that he had acquired ownership of the Jerusalem Broadcasting Station. He explained how the station in Jerusalem operated. Television broadcasts from Lebanon giving day-by-day descriptions of the never-ending war, could not be sent to America directly. Instead the broadcasts were received in Jerusalem, where they were edited and sent via satellite to America. The Jerusalem studios were used by all American and English broadcasting companies to transfer the on-site reports. But Leon Taman wanted one not for the news but for the movies.

Broadcasting was closely associated with the motion picture industry. Taman intended to build a broadcasting complex and, at the same time, create an Israeli motion picture industry. The Israeli government was amenable to the project. They offered Leon a plan to subsidize the proposed complex by paying half of the cost. The other half would be financed by Taman. He thought that I would be the ideal architect to design the project. I knew nothing about broadcasting studios and sound stages; therefore a stint in Hollywood to study movie making and broadcasting was in order.

I had acquired a knowledge of merchandising, the hotel industry, distilling, surgery, and ship design, so why not learn about the making of movies? I jumped at the opportunity and in a few days we flew to Los Angeles. Leon envisioned a movie complex with sound stages, broadcasting studios, and a large hotel for actors working in Israel as well as for the legion of broadcasting officials. The producer he engaged became my teacher, and after Leon left, I stayed on for ten days. We visited the various studios, and I became familiar with the construction of sound stages, the older and the newest techniques of lighting and acoustics, the studios where the "soaps" were produced, the huge costume warehouses, and the back lots the size of small cities.

I flew back to my Florida office for a short stay, then left for Israel, where I went to see the large hillside location for the complex on the outskirts of Jerusalem. Most of the complex would be built on a site that had a commanding view of a valley and a river below. I took photographs and surveys of the site, and once back in my office we began to plan one of the most interesting projects that I had ever worked on. The site was so large that we had to build a large model showing the entire hillside and the valley below. We made site plans and also preliminary plans of the sound stages, the broadcasting tower, the hotel, and buildings where film could be developed and edited. Finally the entire project was created and air-shipped to Jerusalem.

I arrived in Jerusalem and set up a really large presentation for my client and officials of the Israeli government. The chief architect of Jerusalem was there, and he finally gave his blessings for the entire project. The engineers, the construction company officials, and the quantity surveyors went about pricing the project. When the final estimates were presented to the government of Israel, they gave their verdict — how often I had heard the same thing in my career — "drop the project." Israel could not come up with their half of the total cost. Leon Taman, wealthy as he was, could not undertake the sole financing of the project. So another great project remained a concept on paper and a beautiful model.

But the dropping of the motion picture project was not the end of my association with Leon Taman. Some years earlier, Leon had bought a partially finished hotel structure in Herzlea, a suburb of Tel Aviv. This partial concrete frame was started about ten years before, then left unfinished and abandoned. Finally, years later, but before I met Leon, he had completed the hotel. When Bea and I came to Israel we stayed at this hotel. It was noted for the constant breakdown of its two miserable Italian elevators. We always stayed on the lowest floor.

It was Leon's idea to one day build a new hotel at the opposite end of the property. The old hotel and the new hotel he envisioned were on a high bluff overlooking a wide and beautiful beach on the shore of the Mediterranean Sea. With the movie studio project abandoned, Leon decided to build a new hotel with a swimming pool and then rebuild the old hotel tower. The new hotel was to be called Daniel Tower and I was to be the architect. It was going to be an elaborate hotel with large meeting rooms and a good-sized cinema which would have its own entrance, and be accessible from one of the largest lobbies I had ever designed. There were to be four specialty restaurants, a large formal dining room, and a convention hall. The rebuilt hotel and the new tower were to have two hundred hotel rooms and rising above them, ten more floors of large apartments which would be sold.

Another feature of the hotel was the requirement that the entire population of the hotel be able to descend to basement or cellar spaces if the hotel were to be bombed in an enemy attack. These spaces could be put to any use that would not interfere with the required spaces for hotel occupants during an attack. What we did was to create one of the most elaborate health spas we could think of. For example, a very large pool (which could be emptied during an attack) had machinery to create huge waves for the swimmers. There were to be therapy facilities and a great number of individual massage rooms. When the hotel was completed, Japanese masseurs would be brought in to cater to the guests.

At every phase of the design Leon asked me if more elaborate and costly elements could be incorporated into my plans. Throughout my career as a hotel architect I had never had a client who continually asked me to spend more money in designing a hotel and its interiors.

For example, the floor of the huge lobby had a fine white Carrara marble. Was there a more expensive material? I was asked. Polished black granite was much more expensive, I replied. The entire floor was made of black granite. Was there anything more expensive than my fine fruitwood paneling in the lobby? Yes, we could use bronze — so we used bronze. The large curving exterior of the cinema was to have a hundred-foot mural designed by one of Israel's top artists. Wasn't there a more expensive way of decorating this large wall? Yes, you could use a sculptured wall all in an aluminum cast, but the costs would be prohibitive. Let's do the sculpture in cast aluminum. I could go on and on.

In the dining rooms I designed a fantasy of a Hawaiian night club with a stage and a waterfall and native Hawaiians to entertain. Another restaurant and a bar was designed as a true Arabian interior, with expensive rugs, hundreds of specially woven cushions, and elaborately carved low tables with brass and ivory inlays. I designed a spiral stairway, one of the most elaborate I have ever attempted, that went through three levels, with glass balustrades and a rich and elegant lighting fixture. This would be the last hotel that I would design and the most expensive.

The hotel was completed after I retired, but I came to the formal opening. "Do you like it?" my client asked. Of course I said that I did. I complimented Leon on his achievement. I had not supervised the final phase of the hotel. By this time Leon had built a large staff of designers and construction supervisors. I visited this project twice in its final stages and all I could do was wonder what my hotel career would have been like if all my clients had spent money as if it had no meaning.

By 1982 my office consisted of just three men. Another recession was again occurring throughout the United States. In my mind I felt that it was time to retire. I was now eighty years old. Why try to stay in practice? In this troubled time a new project came to my office. Through contacts I had made a few years earlier, a large construction firm in Germany sent one of their executives to see if I was interested in joining them in a large project in China. They knew of my work in hospitals and, of course, my work in hotels — two elements necessary for the project. I had to decide whether to retire and end fifty-four years of practice or once again start on a project which would undoubtedly be one of my largest.

The German firm had been contacted by a high-ranking Chinese official who explained what they had in mind. They knew that there were thousands and thousands of Chinese who had left China. These emigrants had a distrust of medicine other than the ancient Chinese medicine they had always known. China wanted a large modern hospital that practiced traditional medicine available to Chinese expatriates, making it possible for a return to their homeland to seek traditional medical care. They also wanted a large hotel in which these visitors could stay while being treated by Chinese doctors until they were cured and could return to their adopted countries.

They also wanted a modern hospital with all the vast new equipment, such as CAT scans, MRIs, X-rays, and the latest in all aspects of surgery. In these proposed facilities, traditional medicine and modern medicine would be available, not for the Chinese in China, but for the hundreds of thousands of Chinese who had left their native land. The German firm that had been selected to build this project had spent weeks conferring with the doctors, both the traditional practitioners and the modern doctors. The Germans had learned that there were two groups of universities — those that graduated traditional doctors who practiced traditional medicine, and those that graduated modern doctors who practiced modern medicine. My German visitor showed me two brochures in which the two schools had listed in explicit detail all the facilities and equipment that would be required. I was astounded by the volume of material.

My German visitor informed me that one of Germany's hospital manufacturers, in fact the largest such institution, would work with me to help draw the preliminary plans. My trip to Germany and my stay there would be paid for. The fee for my preliminary plans was not what I wanted, but retire? Of course not. So began a good-sized project for me and my small staff. I made at least six trips to Germany for long, drawn-out conferences. All contact with China was the work of one of Germany's largest construction companies, which was already engaged in large construction projects in China as well as in other parts of the world. These preliminary plans took up nearly two years of work for me and my staff.

At last the preliminary part of the project was completed. The two German companies began the long process of costing out the entire project, the two-phased hospital and the large hotel and all of the other amenities that would be required. The final sum was staggering. All this material was taken to China. A few weeks of nail-biting waiting ensued. I finally heard from Germany — the project was dropped. The Chinese government could not possibly raise such a huge amount of money.

The same day in 1984 that I heard from Germany, I made my final decision to close my office. I was now eighty-two years old. When Philip Johnson heard of my decision he wrote to me that "an architect should stay in practice until he [is] carried out in a brown box."

Closing an architect's office is not an easy task. In the first place, there are usually unfinished projects. I had two. The first was a conversion of a small movie theater — the Colony Theater on my Lincoln Road project — into a theater for the performing arts that I was doing for the city of Miami. The rebuilt theater was to be used for dance and concerts. The second commission was for an apartment house in an apartment-house complex.

I decided to ask the city if it objected to my assigning the movie theater to my senior draftsman who was in charge of the project. They approved the change, providing I would keep my Errors and Omissions policy. I told them that I would, so this project went to my draftsman, a licensed architect who would start his own office. I told him to take whatever furnishing and equipment he needed as a gift.

The apartment house I gave to another architect in my employ who was in complete charge. I also told him to take what he needed to furnish his own new office. Other professionals when they retire just leave their office to their partners. I had no partners and had a rather large office or really a suite of offices, consisting of what had been a twenty-man drafting room, a large secretarial office, several small offices, as well as my own handsomely furnished office. I also had a large conference room with a specially built table that I had designed with twelve fine chairs. I had a large complex "plan desk" fully equipped with supplies and equipment for shipping large and small objects, and a fireproof filing vault with my latest projects. I also had a large storeroom where I kept the tracings of all my work for the last forty-one years of my practice, as well as renderings and models.

My secretary began to go through my extensive files to take out the correspondences of my last few years, my tax returns for the last ten years, and other material that she thought should be kept. She packaged and wrapped this material and placed it in two files, which I had to keep. I told her to take as much of my secretarial equipment for herself as she wanted. I notified a number of young architects that I knew and asked them to come to my office and help themselves to everything else that my two senior draftsmen had not already ticketed. Some of my special chairs and my office set of sofas I had delivered to my home where, with the help of Bea, I created a work room in the lower level of our duplex apartment. It is here that I wrote my memoirs.

I had two more things to dispose of. The first was a large collection of enlarged photos of my best recent work that I had displayed in my conference room and other spaces. My son Alan came in to help choose the best of them. The curator of Miami Beach Bass Art Museum took the rest for their archives. Another most valuable record of my years of work dating from my beginnings at Ross-Frankel to my latest projects were photos collected in thirty-two white leather albums. Alan had these shipped to his large office in New York.

Last of all, I engaged a trucking company to come and take the thousands of sheets of my life's work to the city incinerators. It took two large trucks to consign all the material to the flames.

I saved some of my awards and licenses to keep in my new workspace at home, where they still hang.

Morris and Beatrice Lapidus at the Great Wall of China, 1970.

18 Life After Architecture

Now that I was finally retired, Bea decided that her long years of managing my finances and handling our investments were over. She gave me the materials and put them in my charge. I really never managed our family financial resources, but I was glad to relieve her of this burden. After reviewing all our holdings I discovered that we held a portfolio well in excess of two million dollars. During my long years of work in my profession and endless periods of traveling to carry on my far-flung practice, spending so much time away from home, Bea had created a social life for herself and of course me. We could now share everything, wealth and a full social life together. All of this I truly owed to her.

Although I was retired I still had an unfinished commitment to complete the Daniel Tower Hotel in Herzlea in Israel. The plans and interior decor were completed and the project was well along in its final construction phase, but I would still have to go to Israel to supervise the final completion until the hotel was ready to open.

While I was setting dates for my future trips I got a call from one of the ship lines for whom I had served as an "enrichment lecturer" in the past. They asked me if I would be available to board a ship which sailed from Pireus, the seaport of Athens, with stops in Cyprus and Haifa, a port city in Israel. The layover in Haifa would make it possible for me to travel to Herzlea and spend a day checking progress on the Daniel Tower Hotel. This invitation to go on a two-week cruise was most opportune and of course I agreed to be in Athens in two weeks when the ship sailed. I called the supervising engineer in Israel and gave him the date of my arrival in Haifa and asked that a car be waiting at the port of Haifa for the short ride to Herzlea. All was satisfactorily arranged. Before setting out for our trip (Bea always accompanied me on my lecture tours — all of our expenses paid), the executive of the ship line called and asked if I would accept an offer to repeat the same cruise for another two weeks. Of course, I accepted this assignment immediately. I was now able to arrange for a second inspection of the Herzlea hotel two weeks later. We left for Greece for a pleasant cruise that would last a month.

Throughout my career, I was a student of human nature. During my store days, I had developed theories to guide my designs by trying to understand how

"Once again, architecture was the medium that enabled me to meet so many historic figures. During the evening I spent a great deal of time talking to the ex-prime minister, Harold Wilson, who had lost his election recently."

Lapidus, former prime minister of Britain, Harold Wilson, and developer Leon Taman (left to right), at a banquet at Lapidus's Daniel Tower Hotel in Herzlea, Israel, to celebrate the anniversary of Israel's founding, 1986.

to please men and women with my architecture. In my retirement, I wanted to write a book which would overcome the criticism of my architecture by the architectural press and the critics who never accepted my theories of what architecture should be. I had assembled a collection of works of science, history, and many related subjects that would be my source material and my references. I had already decided on a title — *Man's Three Million Year Odyssey.* My book would be the story of the forming of our planet (geology), the rise of the human species (anthropology), a study of man's religion (mythology), the origins of art and music over the millennia (history). All of this would be my daily occupation but would not interfere in my life with Bea — our social life, opera, theater, concerts, and our love of travel.

During one of my last trips to supervise the Daniel Tower Hotel I was present when Israel celebrated an anniversary of the founding of that young country. The almost completed hotel was the site of the banquet of that celebration. Leon Taman who hosted the affair invited me to be there as his guest. Seated at a long dais were the most important notables of the government of Israel. At the center was the aged former prime minister of Israel, Golda Meir. Next to her was the former prime minister of Britain, Harold Wilson. The other Israeli notables were Shimon Peres, Yitzhak Rabin, and Abba Eban.

After the dinner and the many speakers, the notables on the dais were invited for an after-dinner reception in Leon Taman's luxurious apartment at the top of the hotel, an apartment I had designed and furnished. I was introduced to each of the guests as the architect for the new Daniel Tower Hotel. Once again, architecture was the medium that enabled me to meet so many historic figures. During the evening I spent a great deal of time talking to Harold Wilson, who had lost his election recently.

In 1988 we felt the wanderlust of traveling and booked for a three-and-a-half-month round-the-world cruise on the *Sajafjord,* now being operated by the Cunard Lines. In the intervening years between the completion of the Daniel Tower and our departure for our round-the-world trip, we had made a number of crossings on the Queen Elizabeth II for which I was engaged as a lecturer.

But I was not through with architecture. In 1989 I received a call from Berlin The caller was Martina Düttmann, who told me that she was the architectural editor for a publishing firm in Basel, Switzerland, called Birkhäuser Verlag. She informed me that this publishing house had received so many calls from European architects asking if they had published any books about my work. Ignored by the American press and American critics, the European architects were anxious to find material about my work. Indeed there was such an interest in Europe that Birkhäuser had decided to publish a monograph of my work.

Ms. Düttmann asked if she could see any of my plans. I told her that I had destroyed all my plans and sketches when I retired in 1984. She was devastated and wanted to know if there was any material left. I told her that the only records of my career were in the thirty-two albums that my son Alan had retained in his architectural office in New York, and that since 1966 Syracuse University's George Arents Research Library had kept an archive section of some of my plans and articles.

Ms. Düttmann asked for my son's office address in New York and the address of the archive library at Syracuse. She wrote for appointments and without delay flew to New York and Syracuse to gather all the material she could find, bringing her daughter Friederike Schneider with her. She spent several days in Alan's office making her selection of photos and then flew to Syracuse. I did not meet Martina Düttmann until after the book was published because she returned directly to Berlin to await the arrival of the large shipment of material. When it arrived she called me to tell me that this record of my work had so impressed her that she had decided to write the book herself rather than give it to an architectural writer. She also informed me that the book would be published in two languages, English and German, and that her daughter would be the graphic designer.

We finally met in 1991 in Rotterdam, where the Netherlands Architectural Society had mounted an impressive exhibit of my work, using the photographs borrowed by Martina Düttmann. When she arrived on the opening day of the exhibit, she presented me with the first copy of the large monograph of my work.

I was totally unprepared and speechless when she withdrew the book from its envelope. It was beautiful. It was a large book measuring (as I later learned) nine and a half by twelve inches. The cover was a handsome montage of two of my finished works in black, white, and pale blue. The biggest surprise came when I read the title— *Morris Lapidus: Architect of the American Dream*. The title stunned me. Why had Martina used such an unusual title? Was I really the Architect of the American Dream? After the few moments it took me to recover, I thanked her profusely for the handsome book.

The next day we were tourists. I stayed close to Martina until the afternoon when she left to catch a plane to Berlin. This woman who knew so much of my life and architecture had in two days become like a close and loved friend. When we parted I kissed her on both cheeks in the European fashion. I have spoken to her by telephone, but we never met again. Our phone conversations were about the book that I had written in 1967 called *Architecture: A Business and a Profession*, now out of print. Martina asked if she could have permission to translate this book into German. I was glad to say yes, but the last chapter, which referred to the coming age of computers, needed updating. Alan agreed to write two new chapters on this newest development in the practice of architecture.

When I finally had the time to look at and read my monograph, I found a beautiful tribute to me, my life, and my work in the introduction written by Martina. Also included is a long interview that Hans Ibeling, director of the Netherlands Society of Architects, had conducted with me the year before when he visited me in Miami. The rest of the book presents hundreds of photographs of my work, some of them showing my early work which even I had forgotten. The graphics and the manner of presentation are stunning.

During this otherwise happy period, I realized that Bea was weakening. She had had a few health problems, but none were life-threatening. We had had such a full and wonderful life together. How could I help her? She slowly sank into a depression and all she now talked about was her desire to die. No matter what I said to her and what the doctors told her, she felt that rather than live a life such as she now lived, she would be happy to just die. Over a period of a few months she rapidly declined and showed no interest in her life. One evening after being assisted to bed by our wonderful housekeeper of many years, she sat up and stared off into space. I asked if I could do anything for her. She did not answer but slowly lowered her head to her pillow and closed her eyes. My beloved wife of sixty-three years had died as she wanted.

Morris Lapidus and his son and partner, Alan, in their studio, 1965.

"My work never tried to follow the changing trends; it was always a sort of plastic form that was molded by the most important feature of my buildings, the interiors, for which all buildings are designed."

Epilogue

The publication of my monograph seemed to open a floodgate of recognition throughout Europe. The European architectural magazines, one after another, published my work together with articles about my theories of modern architecture, an architecture that pleased people. Most of the illustrations were of my work during the fifties and sixties.

A short time after I returned from Europe I received a letter from Sidney Le Blanc requesting a photograph of the Fontainebleau Hotel for a book she was writing on twentieth-century architecture entitled *The Whitney Guide to 20th Century American Architecture*. I sent her an aerial view of the Fontainebleau. She sent me a letter of thanks, adding, "I would also like to take this opportunity to convey my respect for your work and the clarity of your comments. When I came upon your chapter in *Conversations With Architects*, by John Cook and Heinrich Klotz, I felt that you were practically the only breath of fresh air in the entire 20th century of architecture — it was a bright spot in my two years of research on this project — and I wish you luck with *Architect of the American Dream*. I look forward to seeing it."

In 1993 Wallach Gallery at Columbia University in New York City mounted an impressive exhibit of my work entitled "Morris Lapidus — Mid Century Architect." This exhibit lasted six weeks and at the opening I had a pleasant surprise when I ran into Philip Johnson. The last time we had met was thirty years before on the Mike Wallace television show. We took to each other like old friends. After the opening the dean of the Columbia School of Architecture, Bernard Tschumi, invited Alan and me along with some of the faculty and Angela Giral, the head librarian of the Avery Library, to a quiet and pleasant dinner party. It was seventy years since I had entered Avery Hall to begin my study of architecture.

During the last few years Ms. Giral had written and called me a number of times asking for photographs of my work for the library's archives. She told me that it was a distinct loss not to have the work of one of Columbia's most prominent architects represented at Avery Library, one of the country's best architectural libraries. I decided that I would collect all of the photographs of my best work and mount them together with a short story giving the date and pertinent history of the commissions. It took more than six months to collect nearly two hundred photographs and specially mount them before I could send them to Avery Library. I went to Columbia with Alan where Angela Giral showed us how the collection would be housed.

In 1994 I received a letter from the National Park Service. H. Ward Jandl, deputy chief of the Preservation Assistance Division, inviting me to an international conference entitled "Preserving the Recent Past." This event, at which he expected over eight hundred participants, including architects, landscape architects, engineers, preservation authorities, and historians, would take place from March 30 to April 1, 1995. The purpose of the letter was to ask me to be one of two keynote speakers at the opening of this important conference, the first such conference in the United States. The conference would be held at the Palmer House Hotel in Chicago. Of course, I accepted his invitation because it was a great honor to open the conference, but also because I would be returning to the Palmer House where I first arrived sixty-seven years before to supervise the construction of one of my first large stores.

At last I was being recognized by our government (and by the architectural profession) as an outstanding architect. I had pioneered a new architecture, which was hated by the profession and the American critics. I had defied the "International School"; I had defied the "Art Deco School"; I had ignored most modernists. In fact, I held fast to my principle that an expression of my interiors dictates the design of my exteriors. My work never tried to follow the changing trends; it was always a sort of plastic form that was molded by the most important feature of my buildings, the interiors, for which all buildings are designed. I believe that will be the model for twenty-first-century architecture. I have seen this trend in Europe and especially in the work of the Italian architect Renzo Piano, who has designed buildings using the plastic properties of a lightweight ferro-concrete to design new and innovative buildings. He has carried forward what I started with my design of the Fontainebleau.

When I arrived at Palmer House I called Bertram Goldberg, whom I had met years ago and who was to be the second and last keynote speaker. He invited me to his home that evening for a pleasant reunion and an excellent dinner with his wife and two sons.

The next morning, the opening day of the conference, I went to the grand ballroom of the hotel where I was escorted to the dais facing a sea of assembled guests. I was supposed to address this large convocation for thirty minutes. I never use notes in my lectures or speeches. I spoke of my long career, recounting my early days in store design, during which I formulated my theories of design. I described how I finally became a true architect designing hotels, apartment houses, hospitals, theaters, and houses of worship. I told of my difficulties with acrimonious critics and even the architectural press and of my determination to follow a path in architecture which I firmly believed was the architecture of the twentieth century. I painted a picture of what I believed would be the course of architecture in the twenty-first century.

At the end of my thirty-minute talk I flashed a rapid sequence of slides of my work covering the last fifty-five years. I finished my talk with a plea to preserve what was some of the finest work in Chicago and the rest of our country, be it bus stops or great office buildings or state capitols. Much to my amazement, the large audience stood to give me a long ovation. It was a great event in my long life and my life in the field of my beloved profession.

Another unusual event took place six weeks after I returned from Chicago. New York University, which I attended in 1921 to begin my study of drama, invited me to an alumnus banquet in New York to receive a lifetime achievement award. I was officially a member of the class of 1925, and so seventy-five years later, I was presented with a beautifully engraved silver bowl.

As I look back at my more than ninety years of life, I become more and more convinced that Martina Duttmann's perception of my career led her to call me "Architect of the American Dream." My story began as an immigrant infant brought to America's hospitable shores in 1903. I learned the language, rose from poverty through our educational system, struggled for recognition in my profession, sought a modicum of wealth, and most important, found acclaim for my work. That was and is and will always be "The American Dream," and I have lived that life.

Bibliography

Publications by Morris Lapidus

Books

Architecture: A Profession and a Business (New York: Van Nostrand Reinhold, 1967).

An Architecture of Joy (New York: E. A. Seeman, 1977).

Man's Three Million Year Odyssey (New York: Vantage Press, 1989).

A Pyramid in Brooklyn (New York: Vantage Press, 1989).

Reviews

Architectural Record 168 (August 1980): 65–66.

Booklist 74 (October 1, 1977): 259.

Articles

"Lobby Demarcation," *Interiors* 103 (April 1944): 40–41.

"One of the Functions of the Functional Store Is to Attract," *Interiors* 106 (June 1947): 98–99.

"Public Rooms for Tomorrow's Ships," *Interiors* 105 (December 1945): 60–65.

"Quest for Emotion in Architecture," *AIA Journal* 36 (November 1961): 55–58.

"Quest for Living Space In Architecture," *AIA Journal* 41 (February 1964): 37–38.

"The Retail Store and Its Design Problems," *Architectural Record* 97 (February 1945): 96–102.

"Store Design, a Merchandising Problem…." *Architectural Record* 89 (February 1941): 113–36.

"Store Modernizing Without Metals: With Timesaver Standards," *Architectural Record* 92 (October 1942): 71–78.

"With a Tight Hold on the Purse," *Interiors* 105 (November 1945): 84–89.

"Forum Design: Preview of Exhibition with Linz, Austria with Commentaries…." *Architectural Design* 50:3/4 (1980): 42–66.

Secondary Sources

Books

Armbruster, Ann. *The Life and Times of Miami Beach* (New York: Knopf, 1995).

Cook, John Wesley. *Conversations with Architects* (New York: Praeger, 1973).

Davern, Jeanne M., ed. *Architecture 1970–1980: A Decade of Change* (New York: Architectural Record Books, 1980).

Design for Modern Merchandising: Stores, Shopping Centers, Showrooms (New York: F. W. Dodge Corp., 1954).

Düttmann, Martina, and Friederike Schneider, eds. *Morris Lapidus: Architect of the American Dream* (Basel: Birkhäuser Verlag, 1992).

Emanuel, Muriel, ed. *Contemporary Architects* (New York: St. Martin's Press, 1980).

End, Henry. *Interiors Book of Hotels and Motor Hotels* (New York: Whitney Library of Design, 1963).

Fernandez, Jose. *Specialty Shop: A Guide* (New York: Architectural Book Publishing Co., 1950).

Freundlich, August L. *Forty Years of Art and Architecture*. Exhibition catalog (Coral Gables, Fla.: University of Miami, 1967).

Huxtable, Ada Louise. *Kicked a Building Lately?* (New York: Quadrangle, 1976).

Lundberg, Donald. *Hotel Restaurant and Business* (Chicago: Institutions Magazine, 1970).

Placzek, Adolf, ed. *Macmillan Encyclopedia of Architects* (New York: Macmillan Publishers, 1982).

Sky, Alison, and Michelle Stone. *Unbuilt America* (New York: McGraw-Hill, 1976).

Stern, Robert A.M. *Pride of Place* (Boston: Houghton Mifflin Co., 1986).

Articles

"Americana of New York," *Interior Design* 34 (January 1963): 78–85.

"Ansonia Shoes in a Florida Setting," *Architectural Record* 101 (May 1947): 108–09.

"Arcade Store Front," *Architectural Forum* 81 (October 1944): 99.

"Architect and Color Photography," *Progressive Architecture* 34 (June 1953): 117.

"Architectural Offices," *Architectural Forum* 86 (May 1947): 90–91.

"Armstrong's New Showroom," *Interiors* 110 (June 1951): 100–03.

"The Art of Display," *Interiors* 105 (April 1946): 89–113, 142, 144, 146.

"Aruba Caribbean," *Interiors* 119 (November 1959): 90–97.

"Baroques for Shoe Selling: Ansonia Store, New York," *Architectural Record* 100 (August 1946): 89–91.

"Bedford Stuyvesant Community Pool," *Architectural Record* 155 (June 1974): 98–99.

Booth, William. "For Architect Morris Lapidus, A Kitschy, Kitschy Coup," *The Washington Post*, July 2, 1995, pp. G1, G6.

"Brick, Stone and Wood for Automobile Showroom," *Interiors* 106 (January 1947): 107.

"Buildings for Recreation," *Architectural Record* 155 (June 1974): 96–104.

"Bulova Watch Co., Rockefeller Center, M. Lapidus, Architect," *Architectural Forum* 72 (February 1940): 86–88.

"Chicago: Bostonian Shoe Store," *Architectural Record* 103 (April 1948): 135.

"Children's Shoe Sales Unit," *Pencil Points* 27 (March 1946): 85–86.

Cohen, Scott. "Morris Lapidus, Miami Beach Architecture," *Interview* 16 (September 1986): 148–50.

"Commemorative Water Display: Report of the Jury," *Beaux Arts Institute of Design Bulletin* 25 (January 1949): 10–12.

"Commercial Buildings: Architectural Record's Building Type Study No. 198," *Architectural Record* 113 (May 1953): 162–86.

"Continental, Paramus, New Jersey," *Interiors* 118 (February 1959): 72–75.

"Corporate Executive Offices, New York City," *Pencil Points* 27 (July 1946): 46–47.

"Crazy Hat, Bright Tie," *Time*, May 9, 1960, p. 76.

Cuff, Daniel P. "Morris Lapidus: Taking Miami Beach to Israel," *The New York Times*, July 5, 1981, p. 7.

"Department Store," *Architectural Forum* 81 (October 1944): 92–93.

"Design for Retailing," *Illumination* 7 (1948): 16–21.

"Display and Sales Building, New York," *Progressive Architecture* 30 (September 1949): 64–66, 97.

"Doubleday Doran Book Shop, Chicago; M. Lapidus, Architect," *Architectural Record* 79 (March 1936): 211–13.

"Elmer and Amend, New York," *Architectural Forum* 81 (October 1944): 98.

"Executive Offices with Problem Windows, Holly Stores, Inc., New York," *Architectural Record* 111 (June 1952): 144–45.

"Executives' Bar, Seagram Distillers Corporation, Chrysler Building, New York, M. Lapidus, Architect," *Architectural Record* 87 (January 1940): 90–91.

"Exhibit of Building Materials," *Beaux Arts Institute of Design Bulletin* 24 (September 1948): 34.

Farkas, G. "Debate on the Fontainebleau," *Interiors* 115 (September 1955): 8.

"Forty Stores," *Architectural Forum* 88 (May 1948): 93–144.

"Forty Years of Lapidus at Miami University," *Interiors* 126 (November 1966): 12.

"Forum Design — A Performance," *AD* 80:3/4 (1980): 50–51.

"Fontainebleau Hotel, Miami, Florida," *Interiors* 114 (May 1955): 88–95.

"Free-flow Plan in Tight Areas," *Architectural Record* 99 (February 1946): 100–06.

Freundlich, A. L., "Plaudits for Mr. Lapidus," *Architectural and Engineering News* 9 (May 1967): 116.

"Garden City Branch for Martin's," *Architectural Record* 113 (May 1953): 166–67.

"Glass-walled Apartments Convert Old Brownstone to a Modern Money-maker in New York City," *Architectural Forum* 93 (October 1950): 159.

Gueft, O. "Americana Hotel, Miami Beach," *Interiors* 116 (April 1957): 102–13.

"Hotel Arawak," *Interiors* 118 (May 1959): 92–99.

"Hotel Fontainebleau, Miami, Florida," *l'Architecture d'Aujourd'hui* 26 (September 1955): 46–48.

"House Remodeling," *Architectural Record* 91 (February 1942): 38–39.

Huxtable, Ada Louise. "How a Pool Grew in Brooklyn," *The New York Times*, August 13, 1972, p. 18.

"Interior Location Sets Special Problem," *Architectural Record* 100 (September 1948): 111.

"Jewish Communal Center, East Rockaway, New York," *Progressive Architecture* 33 (January 1952): 99.

Josephson, M. "Architecture: Lapidus' Pornography of Comfort," *Art in America* 59 (March 1971): 108–09.

Ketchum, Morris, Jr. "Current Trends in Store Design," *Architectural Record* 103 (April 1948): 109–44.

Lapidus, Alan, et al. "Florida — Had Enough?" *Design and Environment* 4 (Spring 1973): entire issue.

"Lapidus to Design Onassis Building," *Progressive Architecture* 51 (December 1970): 22.

"Lapidus to Design Two New York Hotels," *Interiors* 120 (September 1960): 22.

"Lapidus' Latest," *Architectural Forum* 117 (October 1962): 13+.

Lynes, Russell. "Design: New York Hotels," *Art in America* 51 (April 1963): 58–61.

"Mangel's Montgomery, Alabama," *Architectural Forum* 81 (October 1944): 92–93.

Margolies, J. "Now, Once and for All, Know Why I Did It — Morris Lapidus: The Give'Em What They Want School of Architecture," *Progressive Architecture* 51 (September 1970): 118–23.

Mendini, A. "Dear Morris Lapidus," *Domus* 610 (October 1980): 1.

"Men's Apparel Shop," *Pencil Points* 25 (August 1944): 59.

"Men's Clothing Store, Rego Park, Long Island," *Pencil Points* 25 (August 1944): 70–71.

Millstein, G. "Architect de luxe of Miami Beach," *The New York Times Magazine*, January 6, 1957, pp. 26–27+.

"Morris Lapidus," *Current Biography* 27 (April 1966): 26–28.

"Morris Lapidus," *Current Biography Yearbook* (1966): 233–35.

"Motor Hotels: Building Types Study No. 264," *Architectural Record* 128 (July 1960): 145–58.

"Municipal Swimming Pool, Bathhouse Recreation Complex, Bedford Stuyvesant, Brooklyn," *Architectural Record* 142 (August 1967): 112–13.

"My Way … Il ritratto di Lapidus," *Domus* 615 (March 1981): 8.

"New Kind of Pied-a-terre: Chicago's Forty Stories of Apartment Hotel," *Interiors* 118 (November 1958): 118–19.

"A New Star by Morris Lapidus: Citizens Federal Savings and Loan Bank," *Architecture* 57 (January 1976): 33.

"New York Architectural Offices in a Remodeled Brownstone," *Architectural Forum* 86 (May 1947): 89–91.

"New York Store for London Character Shoes," *Architectural Record* 100 (August 1948): 92–94.

"New York: Corporation Executive's Office," *Pencil Points* 27 (July 1946): 46–47.

O'Brien, Ellen. "An Architect, at 92, Finally Has Gotten Satisfaction," *Philadelphia Inquirer Magazine*, November 3, 1995, pp. 1, 10, 11.

"Office Buildings: Architectural Record's Building Study No. 187," *Architectural Record* 111 (June 1952): 121–51.

"Open Display Behind an Open Front: Men's Clothing Department of a Store in Brooklyn," *Architectural Record* 96 (November 1944): 100–01.

"Paterson, New Jersey Clothing Store," *Architectural Forum* 88 (May 1948): 121.

Pawley, M. "The Emperor Did Have Clothes After All," *AD* 41 (February 1971): 72.

"Personalities," *Progressive Architecture* 42 (January 1961): 53.

"Portrait," *Architectural Forum* 86 (May 1947): 52; 88 (May 1948): 56; 93 (July 1950): 62.

"Portrait," *Architectural Record* 101 (February 1947): 193.

"Portrait," *Interiors* 112 (August 1952): 8.

"Portrait," *Pencil Points* 27 (July 1946): 14.

"Portrait," *Progressive Architecture* 29 (October 1948): 135; 30 (September 1949): 65.

"Postman's New York Makes the Most of a Narrow Frontage, M. Lapidus, Architect," *Architectural Record* 87 (March 1940): 57–59.

"Recreation: A Change for Innovative Urban Design, Building Types Study No. 374," *Architectural Record* 142 (August 1967): 109–24.

"Remodeling Under Difficulties: A Shoe Salon," *Interiors* 103 (February 1944): 32–33.

"Resort Hotel, Architectural Record Prize," *National Institute for Architectural Education Bulletin* 34 (June 1958): 28–31.

"Resort Motor Hotel in Jamaica: Colonial Plaza Motel, Orlando, Florida," *Architectural Record* 128 (July 1960): 160–61.

"Retail Store and Its Design Problems," *Architectural Record* 97 (February 1945): 96–102, 107+.

"Rock-a-Bye Children's Clothing and Furniture Store, Brooklyn," *Architectural Record* 99 (February 1946): 100–07.

"A Room That Was Too Successful," *Interiors* 105 (May 1946): 70–71.

"Rooms of Tomorrow, 1966," *Interiors* 125 (October 1965): 132–37.

Sanders, Joel. "Kontaminierd Moderne," *Stadt Bauwelt* (March 1995): 600.

"Scaling the Heights: Housing Projects for Brooklyn Heights," *Progressive Architecture* 46 (November 1965): 54.

Schweisheimer, W. "Luxus-hotelbauten in Miami," *Bau & Werk* 13:9 (1960): 520.

"Selected Details: Door Frame for Martin's Store, Brooklyn," *Progressive Architecture* 30 (March 1949): 91.

"Shoe Store, Washington, D.C.," *Progressive Architecture* 31 (March 1950): 63–66.

"Showrooms for Pearls Need No Adornment," *Interiors* 105 (January 1946): 90–91.

Silverstone, M. "Fontainebleau, Miami's Hotel of the Year," *Interiors* 114 (May 1955): 88–95.

"Small Store for Large Displays," *Architectural Record* 99 (February 1946): 106–07.

"Store Design: Architectural Record's Building Types Study No. 188," *Architectural Record* 111 (July 1952): 149–78.

"Store Design: George & Lester's, Racine, Wisconsin," *Architectural Record* 112 (July 1952): 164–65.

"Store Design: Reference Studies on Design and Planning with Time-saver Standards," *Architectural Record* 89 (February 1941): 113–36.

"Study Gives Thirty-three Rules for Pediatric Design," *Modern Hospital* 106 (March 1966): 78–79.

"Success Story with Illustrative Notes," *Interiors* 106 (October 1945): 54–61.

"Summit, New York, New York," *Interior Design* 32 (October 1961): 142–63.

"Symphonized Children's Store for Martin's Brooklyn," *Architectural Record* 100 (August 1946): 81–88.

Tretiack, Phillippe. "Lapidus in Florida," *Architecture Interieure Crée* 202 (October– November 1984): 64–67.

"Troop Transports for Peacetime Travel," *Interiors* 103 (January 1944): 54.

"Twenty-five Million Dollar Tingle: Summit Hotel," *Architectural Forum* 115 (September 1961): 7.

"Warehouse for Building Products: U.S. Plywood Corporation Prize, Report of the Jury," *Beaux Arts Institute of Design Bulletin* 29 (February 1953): 11–13.

"Washington, D.C.: Latest Schulte Plan for Corner Location of Luncheonette: Interior Luncheonette at Nams, Brooklyn," *Architectural Record* 100 (September 1946): 110, 138.

"What Do You Think of the Summit?" *Interiors* 121 (October 1961): 132–39.

"Wholesale Showrooms," *Architectural Forum* 81 (October 1944): 98.

Whoriskey, Peter. "8 Over Eighty," *Progressive Architecture* (July 1995): 79.

Wolfe, Kevin. "Morris Lapidus," *Metropolis*, December 1995, pp. 25–29.

"Women's Apparel Shop," *Architectural Forum* 83 (December 1945): 82–83.

"The Year's Work: Morris Lapidus," *Interiors* 101 (August 1941): 29, 39.

"The Year's Work," *Interiors* 102 (August 1942): 29–54.

"The Year's Work," *Interiors* 106 (August 1946): 75–100.

"The Year's Work," *Interiors* 107 (August 1947): 89.

"Yesterday, Today and Tomorrow: Rooms by H. End and M. Lapidus," *Interior Design* 36 (October 1965): 192–97.

Articles on Exhibitions

"From Architects Comes Art," *Progressive Architecture* 48 (April 1967): 64.

Huxtable, Ada Louise. "Show Offers Joy of Hotel Architecture," *The New York Times*, October 15, 1970, p. 60.

"Johnson, Roche, Rudolph and Lapidus: Subjects of Two Exhibitions," *Architectural Record* 148 (November 1970): 37.

"Joy Boy: The Architecture of Joy, Morris Lapidus, Architectural League of New York Exhibition," *Architectural Forum* 133 (October 1970): 67.

"Lapidus Phenomenon at the Architectural League," *Interiors* 130 (November 1970): 22.

"Monuments to Showmanship: Morris Lapidus at the Architectural League, New York," *Interior Design* 41 (November 1970): 72.

"Show a Success, But the Backers Walked Out," *Progressive Architecture* 51 (October 1970): 28.

Works

1944

Martin's Department Store, Brooklyn, New York

1945

Namm's Department Store, Brooklyn, New York
Crawford Clothes Shops, various U.S. cities
Bond's Clothing Stores, various U.S. cities

1946

Ludwig Baumann Furniture Store, Jamaica,
New York, and various U.S. cities

1948

Columbia Mills Showroom, Syracuse, New York

1949

Sans Souci Hotel, Miami Beach

1950

Fresh Meadow Country Club, Long Island,
New York

1951

Jewish Center, Long Island, New York
Ainsley Building, Miami
Biltmore Terrace Hotel, Miami Beach
Algiers Hotel, Miami Beach

1952

Laurel in the Pines Hotel, Monticello, New York
Flagler Hotel, Miami Beach
Hicksville Shopping Center, Long Island,
New York
Trump Village Housing, Brooklyn, New York
A. S. Beck Shoe Corporation, New York

1953

Ocean Haven Shopping Center, Brooklyn, New
York
Shopping center, Jackson Heights, New York
Harrison Country Club, Harrison, New York
Sand and Surf Hotel, West End, New Jersey
DiLido Hotel, Miami Beach
Shopping center, Pritchard, Alabama
Shopping center, Clearwater, Florida
Shopping center, Bradenton, Florida
Airport hotel, New York
Tamarack Lodge, Greenfield Park, New York

1954

Rainbow-Whitestone Beechurst Shopping Center,
Whitestone, New York
Westchester Highway Hotel, Westchester,
New York
St. Augustine Store Center, Florida
Nautilus Hotel, Atlantic Beach, New Jersey
Surf Club Hotel, Atlantic Beach, New Jersey
Broadway Maintenance Office Building,
Long Island City, New York
Fontainebleau Hotel, Miami Beach

1955

Bee Hive Department Store, Patchogue, New York
New Rochelle Country Club, New York
Kutsher's Country Club, Monticello, New York
Eden Roc Hotel, Miami Beach

1956

American Fore Office, Brooklyn, New York
Charlotte Harbor, Punta Gorda, Florida
Federation of State, County, and Municipal
Employees Building, New York
Aruba Caribbean Hotel, Netherlands Antilles
Americana Hotel, Bal Harbour, Miami Beach

1957

The Saxony (apartments), Jamaica, New York
The Highlander (apartments), Jamaica, New York
Shelbourne Hotel, Miami Beach
Voyager Motel, Miami Beach
North Plaza Shopping Center, St. Petersburg,
Florida
Biscayne Terrace Hotel, Miami
Mayfair Apartments alterations, Akron, Ohio
Fort Lauderdale Hotel, Broward, Florida
Sea Isle Hotel, Miami Beach
Executive House (apartment hotel), Chicago
Blauvelt Country Club, Nyack, New York
Continental Restaurant, Monmouth, New Jersey
Bay Harbor Isle Apartment Building, Bay Harbor
Isle, Florida
Deauville Hotel, Miami Beach
Sunny Isles Shopping Center, Sunny Isles, Florida
Arawak Hotel, Jamaica

1958

Daytona Beach Hotel, Florida
Mayfair Hotel, Palm Beach, Florida
Concord Hotel, Kiamesha Lake, New York
Lucerne Hotel, Miami Beach
Leisure Lake Hotel, Leisure Lake, Florida
Colonial Plaza Hotel, Orlando, Florida
Massena Hotel, Massena, New York
Chicopee Hotel, Chicopee, Massachusetts
Brookhaven Laboratory, Long Island, New York
State Office Building, Fall River, Massachusetts
Harrison Hot Springs Hotel, Vancouver

1959

Lobby of the Blair Towers, Washington, D.C.
Lido Beach Hotel, Lido Beach, New York
Golden Triangle Hotel, Norfolk, Virginia
Clason Houses, New York
New Madison Avenue Office Building,
New York
Three Chopt Apartments, Norfolk, Virginia
Syracuse Motel, Syracuse, New York
Stadium Lanes Bowling, New York
The Narrows Shore Road Apartments,
Brooklyn, New York
Bank of Miami Beach
Condado West Hotel, San Juan, Puerto Rico
Shaare Zion Temple interiors, Brooklyn,
New York
Kansas City Motel, Missouri
Ambassador Hotel, Los Angeles (project)
Newark Motel, New Jersey
Motel/Boatel, New Port Richey, Florida
Shelburne Apartment Hotel, Hartford, Connecticut
International Inn, Tampa, Florida
Fresh Meadows Country Club, Lake Success,
New York
New Street Building (office building), Newark,
New Jersey
Australian House, New York
Murphy Houses, Bronx, New York

1960

Ponce de Leon Hotel, San Juan, Puerto Rico
Duck Key Yacht Club and Lanai, Florida
Golden Triangle International Hotel, Norfolk,
Virginia
Kipnis Causeway Motel, Tampa, Florida
Indianapolis Motel
International Inn, Washington, D.C.
Loew's Motor Inn, New York
Loew's Midtown Inn, New York
Hebrew Academy, Miami Beach
Terrace Towers Apartments, Belle Isle, Florida
Meridian Office Building, Miami Beach
Sterling Gardens Lodge, Tuxedo, New York
Lincoln Road (outdoor mall), Miami Beach
Sheraton Motor Inn, New York
Municipal Swimming Pool, Brooklyn, New York

1961

Crescent Park (housing development), East Orange, New Jersey
Skyline Motel, Washington, D.C.
Temple Beth Tfiloh, Baltimore
Arlington Office Building, Virginia
Cadman Plaza (housing development), Brooklyn, New York
Richmond Motel, Virginia
White Plains Motel, New York
Seacoast East (apartments), Miami Beach
Summit Hotel, New York

1962

Kings Bay Yacht Club, Miami
South Harrison Apartments, East Orange, New Jersey
Variety Children's Hospital, Miami
1800 G Street (office building), Washington, D.C.
Fairfield Towers, Brooklyn, New York
Concordia Gardens (apartments), San Juan, Puerto Rico
San Patricio Apartments, San Juan, Puerto Rico
Bay Towers (office building), Miami
Horizon House (apartments), San Juan, Puerto Rico
Professional Staff Apartments, Baltimore
Americana of New York Hotel, New York
Crystal House (apartments), Miami Beach

1963

Miramar Towers, San Juan, Puerto Rico
Lobby of Clyde Hall, Brooklyn, New York
Lobby of Ocean Terrace, Brooklyn, New York
Skylake Gardens (apartments), Miami
Grossinger's Hotel, Grossinger, New York
Trump Village Shopping Center, Brooklyn, New York

1965

El San Juan, San Juan, Puerto Rico
Metairie Avenue Apartments, New Orleans
Seacoast Towers East (apartments), Miami Beach
El Conquistador Hotel, Fajardo, Puerto Rico
North Meeting Room, Seacoast Towers, Miami Beach
Park Towers (apartments), New Orleans
Fairview Country Club, Greenwich, Connecticut
Temple Beth El, St. Petersburg, Florida

1966

Paradise Island Hotel, Bahamas
Hilton Hotel, Macon, Georgia
Jr. Chamber International Building, Miami Beach
Skylake Shopping Center, Miami
Fire Station, Miami Beach
Quality Courts Inc., Memphis, Tennessee

1967

Medical Office Building, Bay Harbor Islands, Florida
Belle Isle Apartments, Miami Beach
Portman Square Hotel, London
Oceanside Plaza (apartments), Miami Beach
Kensington Apartments, Jade Beach, Florida
Americana Hotel, San Juan, Puerto Rico
Mahoe Bay Hotel, St. Maarten's Isle, West Indies
Penn Wortman Apartments, Brooklyn, New York

1968

Parker Towers (apartments), Hallandale, Florida
Parker Plaza (apartments), Hallandale, Florida
Regency Tower Apartments, Miami Beach
Royal Coast Apartments, Pompano Beach, Florida
Arlen Beach Apartments, Miami Beach
Greater Miami Jewish Federation Office Building, Miami
Lauderdale Seasons Apartments, Fort Lauderdale, Florida
Great Neck Office Building, Great Neck, New York

1969

17 Battery Place (office building), New York
Surfside Royale Apartments, Surfside, Florida

1970

Second National Bank, North Miami
Jacksonville Skycenter (hotel/motel), Jacksonville, Florida

1971

555 Griffin Square (office building), Dallas
Rivergate Office Building, Miami
Villa Dorada Complex, Miami
Holiday Springs Complex (housing), Margate, Florida
Bonavista Hi-Rise, Miami
Blackstone Office Building, Jacksonville, Florida
Bonavida Hi-Rise, Miami
1122 Connecticut Avenue (office building), Washington, D.C.

1972

Arlen House East (apartments), Miami Beach
Coronado Condominiums, Miami
Office Building, New York Avenue at 13th Street, Washington, D.C.
Citizens Federal Savings and Loan Building, Miami
Oceans Two (apartments), Daytona Beach, Florida
Oceans Three, Five, Seven (apartments), Daytona Beach, Florida

1973

Bal Harbour 101 (apartments), Bal Harbour, Florida
Copa City Office Building, Miami Beach
Theatre of Performing Arts, Miami Beach
Flamenco (apartments), Miami
South Shore Community Center, Miami Beach
Trelawny Beach Hotel, New Falmouth, Jamaica

1974

Gusman Concert Hall, University of Miami

1975

TSS Carnivala cruise ship, Dodge Island, Florida
TSS Mardi Gras cruise ship, Dodge Island, Florida
Carnival Cruise Lines Terminal Building, Dodge Island, Florida
International Inn, Washington D.C.

1976

Ogun State Hotel, Abeokuta, Nigeria
Community College, Key West, Florida (with Carr Smith)

1977

Nueva Casa (apartments), Miami

1978

Grandview at Emerald Hills (apartments), Hollywood, Florida
Lausanne (apartments), Naples, Florida

Index

Note: "ML" stands for Morris Lapidus

Aalto, Alvar, 252
Aetna Marine, 135–37
Algiers Hotel (Miami Beach), *151–55*
Ambassador Hotel (Los Angeles), 225
Americana Hotel (Bal Harbour, Fla.), *191,* 192–97, *193, 212–15,* 235–38
Americana of New York, 99, 233–34, *242–43*
American colonial style, 71
American Institute of Architects, 135, 235–38
Anschon, Robert, 236, 237
Ansonia Building (N.Y.C.), 87
Ansonia shoe store (N.Y.C.), *109*
Arawak Hotel (Jamaica), 198, *202*
Archie (boyhood friend and sculptor), 46–48, 53–57, *164*
Architectural Forum, 91, 92, 128, 183, 231
Architectural League of New York, 135; "An Architecture of Joy" exhibit (1970), 11–13, 253–59, 263–64
Architectural Record, 183, 258
Arlen Company, 261
Armstrong's showroom (N.Y.C.), *108*
art deco, 63, 90, 296
Art in America, 258
Aruba Caribbean Hotel, 201–3, *216–21*
A.S. Beck shoe store (N.Y.C.), 142, *143,* 190

Bal Harbour (Fla.) mall, 203, 205
Ball, Mr., 69
Barcelona World's Fair, 63
Barton's (N.Y.C.), *112, 113*
Bass Museum of Art (Miami Beach), 287
Bauhaus, 64, 166
Bayliss, Mendel, 26
bean poles, 99, 108, 136, 145, *147*
Beaux Arts Institute, 135
Bedford-Stuyvesant, 9–11, 257, 265
Bender, Jack, 238–39
Bender, Morton, 238–39, 265, 275
Bendiner, Alfred, 237–38
Best & Company (N.Y.C.), 261
Biltmore Terrace Hotel (Miami Beach), 150
Birkhäuser Verlag, 291
Blake, Peter, 231
Blake Construction Co., 238
B & L Auto Lamp Co., 19
Block and Hess, 71–73
Boca Raton Hotel (Miami Beach), 225
Bond stores: Chicago, 138–40, *139;* Cincinnati, 140–42, *141;* N.Y.C., 138
Boring, Williams, 62, 64
Borsht Belt, 205
Bostonian shoe store (Chicago), *111*
Boys High School (N.Y.C.), 48
Breuer, Marcel, 166
Bronfman brothers, 115

Cadman Plaza (Brooklyn), 234
Caribbean cruise, 269–71
Carnival Cruise Line, 271
Century Strand Lighting Co., 253
Chambalin, Rene, 68
cheese holes, 99, 108, 113, 116, 136, 145
Chicago Tribune Building, 63
Chicopee (Mass.) hotel project, 228–29
Chinese hospital/hotel project, 285–86
Cohen, Arthur, 261, 262
Colony Theater (Miami), 286
color, ML's use of, 44, 97–98
Columbia University: Avery Library, 295–96; School of Architecture, 53, *58,* 59–65, 69, 295; Wallach Gallery, "Morris Lapidus — Mid Century Architect" exhibit (1993), 295
Concord (Catskills), 205
concrete, 234, 277–78
Coney Island, N.Y., *30,* 32–36, *34*
Convention Hall (Atlantic City), 65
Cook, John W., 239–40; *Conversations With Architects* (with Heinrich Klotz), 240, 295
Corbett, Harvey Wiley, 63
Cornell University, College of Hotel Administration, 251
Crystal House apartment building (Miami Beach), 221

Danbury (Conn.) hotel, *75, 76*
Daniel, Mann, Johnson and Mendenhall, 225
Daniel Tower Hotel (Tel Aviv), 284–85, 289, *290,* 291
Delano Hotel, 150
Dell Webb, 227
Diesel Construction Company, 234
Diplomat, The (London restaurant), 252–53
Distilled Spirits Institute Building (N.Y. World's Fair, 1939), *114,* 118–19, *120, 121*
Domus, 281–82
Doubleday book store (Detroit), *105*
Dudok, Willem, 64
Düttmann, Martina, 291–93, 297; *Morris Lapidus: Architect of the American Dream,* 291–93

eclecticism, 62
École des Beaux-Arts (Paris), 62
Eden Roc Hotel (Miami Beach), 85, *182,* 184–90, *185, 188–89,* 192, 194, *206–11*
Eisenman, Peter, 254–56
El Conquistador Hotel (Puerto Rico), 271–73, *272*
Ellis Island, N.Y., 19
Encyclopedia Britannica Yearbook, ML's entry in, 128
Eshbach, William W., 237

Ferriss, Hugh, 227
Firestone estate, 157, 158, *159*
Fisher, Carl and Jane, 203
Fontainebleau Hotel (Miami Beach), 9, 85, 99, *156,* 157–72, *159, 173–81, 183–84, 185,* 231, 235, 295, 296
Forsythe shoe store (N.Y.C.), *86*
Frankel, Evan, 79–81
Franzen, Ulrich, 256
French Provincial style, 164
Freundlich, August L., 99, 249

Gebrauchsgraphik, 96
Gesallpointiner, Helmuth, 281
Giral, Angela, 295–96
Gluckstein, Guy, 252
Goldberg, Bertram, 296
Gorlitz, Jules, 166–67, 170
Gothic style, 62
Grand Central Terminal (N.Y.C.), 65
Graves, Michael, 281
Great Depression, 90, 93, 95
Greenberg, Allan, 281
Greene brothers, 63
Gropius, Walter, 166
Grossinger's (Catskills), 205
"G Street Building" project (Washington, D.C.), 238–39
Gusman Center for the Performing Arts (Miami), 269
Gusman Concert Hall (University of Miami), 269, *270*

Hall, Edward, 236
Hamlin, A.D.F., 59–60, *61*
Harle, Abby, 137–40, 161, 205, 265–66
Harold (boyhood friend), 46, *47*
Harrison, Wallace, 64
Haus Rucker Co., 281
Heinz, H. J., Sr., 119
Heinz Company, 119–22
Held, John, Jr., 88
"Herbert's, the Home of Blue-White Diamonds" (N.Y.C.), 90–91
Hilton, Conrad, 233
Hiram Walker, 118
Hirons, Mr., 63
Hirsch, I. Seth, 49, 77
Hoffritz for Cutlery store (N.Y.C.), *107*
Holland, Mr., 65, 69
Hood, Raymond, 63
Horn, Rebecca, 281
Hornstein, Etta, 137
Hotel du Cap (France), *187, 189*
Hoving, Thomas, 9–10
Huxtable, Ada Louise, 258, 263

Ibeling, Hans, 292–93
Interior Design, 137
Interiors, 137
International Executive Service Corps, 266
International Generics, 277
International Inn on Thomas Circle (Washington, D.C.), *274, 275–76*
International Style, 166, 190, 197, 296
International Trade Center project (Fla.), *247*
Italian Renaissance style, 184

Jackie Gleason Theater, 269
Jaffee, Ben, 161, 170, *171*
Jamaica, 198–201
Jandl, H. Ward, 296
Jazz Age, 88
Jerusalem Broadcasting Station project, 282–83
Jews: Orthodox, 25–26, 54–56; in Russia, 15–17, 24; Sephardic, 276
Johansen, John M., 256–57
Johnson, Philip, 231, 281, 286, 295
Josephson, Mary, 258–59
Journal of the American Institute of Architects, 197, 237

Kennedy, Joseph, family, 189
Kirschschlager, Rudolph, 279–82
Kitchener, Lord, 276–77
Klotz, Heinrich, 240, 295
Knoxville, Tennessee, 93–94
Kornbluth, Leo, 205, 235
Kosciusko Street park (Brooklyn), *8, 9–11, 12, 257–58,* 265

LaGuardia Airport hotel project, 235
Lapidus, Alan, 163, 225, 239, 254, 261, 263–64, 266, 273, 287, 292, *294,* 296
Lapidus, Beatrice, *70,* 71, *72, 78,* 81–82, 84, *162, 288,* 293
Lapidus, Morris, *18, 47, 78, 162, 288, 294;* academic record, 48, 49; accident in youth, 41–44; acting aspirations, 45, 48, 49–53, 135; *Architecture: A Business and a Profession* (book), 239, 292; architecture philosophy, 60–65, 194, 239–40, 296; artwork of, *22, 249;* books and articles about, 197, 239, 246, 259, 291–93, 295; boyhood, 11–46; closing of Miami office, 286–87; Columbia University years, 59–65, 69; critics' views of, 183–84, 194–97, 231, 235–38, 253–59, 263–64, 291–92, 295–96; employment at architecture firms, 65–69, 71–84, 87–88, 90–96, 100–101, 115, 118, 122; exhibits of the work of, 11–13, 99, *248, 249,* 253–59, *255,* 263–64, 279–82, *280,* 292, 295; family's emigration from Russia to America, 17–19; father, *14,* 15–19, 21–25; first independent architecture practice, 122–28; first job at Bellevue Hospital, 48–49; first office announcement, *124;* first offices of, *125,* 128–33, *131, 132;* house in Flatbush, 85, *130;* immigrant experiences as youth, 11–13, 19–29; lecture cruises, 289, 290, 291; licensing exam, 88–89; *Man's Three Million Year Odyssey* (book), 291; mother, *14,* 15–19, 20–21, 25–29; *My World at Five* (painting), *22;* New York University years, 49–53; photographs of, *47, 162, 288;* projects never built, 226, *232,* 233, *260,* 261–65; psychosomatic illnesses of, 76–77; "A Quest for Emotion in Architecture" (article), 197; relatives, *38,* 44; retirement, 286–97; ship design and renovation work, 271; stage set work, 51–52, 53, 166; summer job at Camp Kiowa, 52; travels, 84, 94–95, 148–49, 186–89, 291; wedding and honeymoon of, 71, 84–85
Lapidus, Richard, 163, 269
Le Blanc, Sidney, *The Whitney Guide to 20th Century American Architecture,* 295
Le Corbusier, 64
Leibman, Harold, 205, 238–39
Lepofsky, Manny, 46, 198
Levien, Arthur, 261, 262
Lewitt, Sol, 281
Liberace, *191*
lighting, 99–100, *102, 109,* 148, 252–53
Lincoln Road project (Miami Beach), 203–5, *204, 222*
Lindbergh, Charles, 69
Linz University, Austria, "Forum Design" exhibit (1980), 13, 279–82, *280*
Little Harry, 144, 149, 160
Loew's Hotel (Monte Carlo), 250–51
Loewy, Raymond, 281
Louis XVI style, 68
Lower East Side, N.Y.C., 19–29, *22*
Luna Park (Coney Island), *34,* 35
Lynes, Russell, 231
Lyons Group, 252

Mangel apparel shop chain, 81–84, 94, 97, *106*
Marden, Ben, 95
Mardi Gras (ship), 271
Margolies, John, 253
Martin's store (Brooklyn), 123, *126, 127*
McCue, George, 236, 237
Mendelsohn, Erich, 63
Mendini, Alessandro, 281–82
Messina (Mass.) hotel project, 228
Miami Beach, 85
Miami Boom (1920's), 64
Mies van der Rohe, Ludwig, 63, 166, 197, 256
Mikey (boyhood friend), 39–41
Millstein, Gilbert, "Architect Deluxe of Miami Beach," 194–97
mirrors, 100, *102*
Mizner, Addison, 63, 66
modern style, 87–88
Moholy-Nagy, Sybil, 254
Moore, Charles, 258, 281

Morris Lapidus, Kornbluth, Harle and Leibman, Architects, 235
Morris Lapidus Associates, 266
Morse, Carl, *230,* 234
Moses, Robert, 148
moth complex, 99, *109,* 148
Mount Sinai Hospital (Miami Beach), 279
Mufson, Harry, 144–45, 160, 184
Mumford, Lewis, 234

Nash, John, 278
National Distillers, 118
National Park Service, 296
Nautilus Hotel, 150
Netherlands Architectural Society, exhibit of ML's work (1991), 292
New York Central Building (N.Y.C.), 65, 68, *68*
New York City Building Department, 73–74
New York Hilton (N.Y.C.), proposed, *232, 233*
New York Times, 263, 264
New York Times Magazine, 194–97
New York University, 49–53, 297
Niemeyer, Oscar, 149
Nigeria hotel project, 276–79
Norwegian Cruise Line, 271
Novak, Ben, 142, 144–45, 157–58, 160, 161–64, *165,* 166–69, 170–71, 184

O'Doherty, Brian, 258
Ogun State Hotel (Nigeria), 279
Olympic Airlines Building (N.Y.C.), 261, 262
Olympic Tower (N.Y.C.), proposed, *260,* 261–65
Onassis, Aristotle, 261, 262
ornamentation (ML's): New York Central Building, 68, *68;* United Order of True Sisters, 71; Vanderbilt mansion, *67*
O'Shay, John, 203

Palais Royale nightclub (N.Y.C.), 95–96
Palmer House Hotel (Chicago), 81, *82–83,* 296
Parisian Bootery (N.Y.C.), 91, *92*
Paris World's Fair (1925), 63
Pearce, Ronald, 65–66, 69
Piano, Renzo, 296
Pirelli Building (Milan, by Gio Ponti), 190
pogroms, 17, 26
Polshek, James Stewart, 269
Ponti, Gio, 190
Portmanteau Players, 51
Postman's glove and handbag store (N.Y.C.), *110*
"Preserving the Recent Past" conference (1994), 296–97
Progressive Architecture, 183
Prohibition, 115
Prudential Insurance Co., 227

Queen, Ellery, 197–98

Rainbow Shops designs, 137
Rainier, Prince, 250, 251
Rand, Ayn, *The Fountainhead*, 194
Regal Shoes (N.Y.C.), *104*
rendering, 60–61
Richardson, Henry Hobson, 62
Riklas, Meshulam, 262
Rock-A-Bye children's store (Brooklyn), 123
Rockefeller, Laurance, 233
Romanesque style, 62
Roosevelt, Franklin Delano, 93
Rosenblatt, Arthur, 253, 257–58
Ross-Frankel, 79–84, 87–88, 90–96, 100–101, 115, 118, 122
Roxy Theater (N.Y.C.), 96
Rubin, Barney, 138, 140–42
Russia, 15–17, 24

Saarinen, Eliel, 63, 252
Sanders, Morris, 118–22, 164
Sans Souci Hotel (Miami Beach), *134*, 142–48, *146*, *147*, 149, 158
Schenley, 118
Schine, David, 225–29
Schine, J. Meyer, 225–29
Schine, Richard, 225–29
Schine Center (Los Angeles), proposed, 226
Schine organization, 235
Schneider, Friederike, 292
Scully, Vincent, 239–40
Seacoast East apartment building (Miami Beach), *223*
Seagrams Company office (N.Y.C.), 115–18, *116–17*
Sheraton Motor Inn (N.Y.C.), 234–35, *244–45*
ship design, 135–37, 271
signaling searchlight design, 122–23
Singapore, 266
Singer Building (N.Y.C.), 31
Skidmore, Owings & Merrill, 138
Somerville, Randolph, 51–52
Spanish plateresque style, 66, *67*, 68
Spector, Charlie, 142, 144, 145, 190
Spence, Basil, 236, 237
Steinberg's restaurant (N.Y.C.), *102*
Stern, Robert A. M., 281
store design, 87–88, 90–91, 93–95, 96–101, 135, 137
Sucre, Señor, 249–51
Summit Hotel (N.Y.C.), 99, *224*, 229–31, *230*, *241*
Swank Showroom (N.Y.C.), *103*
Syracuse University, George Arents Research Library, 292

Taman, Leon, 276–79, 282–85, *290*, *291*
Temple Beth El (St. Petersburg, Fla.), *246*
Tennessee Valley Authority, 93
Theater Guild, 52
Theater Magazine, 52
Theater of Performing Arts (Miami Beach), 266–69
Theresa Pharmacy (N.Y.C.), 87–88
Tigerman, Stanley, 281
Tisch, Al, 190–94, *191*
Tisch, Bob, 190–94, *191*, 229, 230, 233–34, 251
Tisch, Larry, 190–94, *191*, 229, 230, 231, 233–34, 249–50, 251
traktier (Russian tea house), 21–23, 25
Trelawny Hotel (Jamaica), 266, *267*
Trocadero (London), 252
Trump, Donald, 205, 273
Trump, Fred, 35, 205
Trump Plaza (N.Y.C.), 273
Trump Village (Brooklyn), 35, 205
Tschumi, Bernard, 295
Tudor style, 115
Twentieth Century Limited (train), 94
249 East 49th Street (ML's office), 128–33, *131*, *132*

Uncle Harry (Elya), 31–37, 43
United Order of True Sisters, 71
University of Miami, Lowe Gallery, "Forty Years of Art and Architecture" exhibit (1967), 99, *248*, 249, *255*
Uris, Harold, 231–33
Uris, Percy, 231–33

Vallee, Rudy, 90–91
Vanderbilt, William K., residences, 66, *67*, 68–69
Variety Children's Hospital (Miami), 249
Venturi, Robert, 281
Victorian Gothic style, 62

Wadley and Smythe (N.Y.C.), 79
Wagner, Robert, *230*
Walker, Stewart, 51
Wallace, Mike, 231, 295
War Production Board (WPB), 122
Warren, Whitney, 65
Warren and Wetmore, 65–69
Washington Square College Players, 49, *50*, 52
Weiser, Arthur, 73–79
Wells, H. G., 97
Williams, Henry, 160–61
Wilson, Harold, *290*
woggles, 99, 108, 136, 145
Wolfe, Tom, 259
World War II, 122
Wright, Frank Lloyd, 63

Zeits, Fred, 123

Photography Credits

All photographs except those noted below courtesy of the archive of Morris Lapidus. Numbers refer to page numbers.